Building the East German Myth

Social History, Popular Culture, and Politics in Germany
Geoff Eley, Series Editor

A History of Foreign Labor in Germany, 1880–1980: Seasonal Workers/Forced Laborers/Guest Workers, Ulrich Herbert, translated by William Templer

Reshaping the German Right: Radical Nationalism and Political Change after Bismarck, Geoff Eley

Forbidden Laughter: Popular Humor and the Limits of Repression in Nineteenth-Century Prussia, Mary Lee Townsend

From Bundesrepublik *to* Deutschland: *German Politics after Unification,* Michael G. Huelshoff, Andrei S. Markovits, and Simon Reich, editors

The People Speak! Anti-Semitism and Emancipation in Nineteenth-Century Bavaria, James F. Harris

The Origins of the Authoritarian Welfare State in Prussia: Conservatives, Bureaucracy, and the Social Question, 1815–70, Hermann Beck

Technological Democracy: Bureaucracy and Citizenry in the German Energy Debate, Carol J. Hager

Society, Culture, and the State in Germany, 1870–1930, Geoff Eley, editor

Paradoxes of Peace: German Peace Movements since 1945, Alice Holmes Cooper

Jews, Germans, Memory: Reconstructions of Jewish Life in Germany, Y. Michal Bodemann, editor

Exclusive Revolutionaries: Liberal Politics, Social Experience, and National Identity in the Austrian Empire, 1848–1914, Pieter M. Judson

Feminine Frequencies: Gender, German Radio, and the Public Sphere, 1923–1945, Kate Lacey

How German Is She? Postwar West German Reconstruction and the Consuming Woman, Erica Carter

West Germany under Construction: Politics, Society, and Culture in the Adenauer Era, Robert G. Moeller, editor

A Greener Vision of Home: Cultural Politics and Environmental Reform in the German Heimatschutz *Movement, 1904–1918,* William H. Rollins

A User's Guide to German Cultural Studies, Scott Denham, Irene Kacandes, and Jonathan Petropoulos, editors

Catholicism, Political Culture, and the Countryside: A Social History of the Nazi Party in South Germany, Oded Heilbronner

Contested City: Municipal Politics and the Rise of Nazism in Altona, 1917–1937, Anthony McElligott

The Imperialist Imagination: German Colonialism and Its Legacy, Sara Friedrichsmeyer, Sara Lennox, and Susanne Zantop, editors

Framed Visions: Popular Culture, Americanization, and the Contemporary German and Austrian Imagination, Gerd Gemünden

Triumph of the Fatherland: German Unification and the Marginalization of Women, Brigitte Young

Mobility and Modernity: Migration in Germany 1820–1989, Steve Hochstadt

Building the East German Myth: Historical Mythology and Youth Propaganda in the German Democratic Republic, 1945–1989, Alan L. Nothnagle

The German Problem Transformed: Institutions, Politics, and Foreign Policy, 1945–1995, Thomas Banchoff

Building the East German Myth

Historical Mythology and Youth Propaganda
in the German Democratic Republic, 1945–1989

ALAN L. NOTHNAGLE

Ann Arbor

THE UNIVERSITY OF MICHIGAN PRESS

Copyright © by the University of Michigan 1999
All rights reserved
Published in the United States of America by
The University of Michigan Press
Manufactured in the United States of America
⊗ Printed on acid-free paper

2002 2001 2000 1999   4 3 2 1

A CIP catalog record for this book is available from the British Library.

Library of Congress Cataloging-in-Publication Data

Nothnagle, Alan L., 1962–
    Building the East German myth : historical mythology and youth
propaganda in the German Democratic Republic, 1945–1989 / Alan L.
Nothnagle.
        p.   cm. — (Social history, popular culture, and politics in
Germany)
    Includes bibliographical references (p.   ) and index.
    ISBN 0-472-10946-4 (acid-free paper)
    1. Youth—Germany (East)—Political activity.   2. Socialism and
youth—Germany (East)   3. Political socialization—Germany (East)
4. Mythology—Political aspects—Germany (East)   5. Patriotism—Germany
(East)   I. Title.   II. Series.
HQ799.2.P6   N68   1999
305.235'09431—ddc21   98-58051
                                                                           CIP

To My Mother and Father

Men make their own history, but they do not make it just as they please; they do not make it under circumstances chosen by themselves, but under circumstances directly encountered, given, and transmitted from the past. The tradition of all the dead generations weighs like a nightmare on the brain of the living. And just when they seem engaged in revolutionizing themselves and things, in creating something that has never yet existed, precisely in such periods of revolutionary crisis they anxiously conjure up the spirits of the past to their service and borrow from them names, battle cries, and costumes in order to present the new scene of world history in this time-honored disguise and this borrowed language.

—*Karl Marx*

We can (and must) begin to build Socialism, not with abstract material, or with human material specially prepared by us, but with the human material bequeathed to us by capitalism. True, that is no easy matter, but no other approach to this task is serious enough to warrant discussion.

—*V. I. Lenin*

What's Hecuba to him, or he to her,
That he should weep for her?

—*Hamlet* II.2

Contents

Acknowledgments

No study of this length can be completed without incurring a great many scholarly debts. The research was generously funded by the Deutscher Akademischer Austauschdienst and organized through the Berlin Humboldt-Universität. I would like to acknowledge the kind assistance of the archivists of the Stiftung Archiv der Parteien und Massenorganisationen der DDR im Bundesarchiv, the Jugendarchiv of the Institut für zeitgeschichtliche Jugendforschung in Berlin, and the Stadtarchiv in Leipzig. Thanks go to the staffs of the Berliner Staatsbibliothek/Preussischer Kulturbesitz, the library of the Otto-Suhr-Institut at the Free University of Berlin, the Gedenkbibliothek zu Ehren der Opfer des Stalinismus e.V., and to the staff of the Humboldt-Universitätsbibliothek.

My deepest personal thanks go to Georg and Wilma Iggers for years of patient advice and encouragement. Further thanks go to David Schoenbaum of the University of Iowa, as well as to David Gerber and William S. Allen of SUNY at Buffalo for comments and encouragement; and to Jürgen Kocka of the Free University. I am also indebted to the many former Young Pioneers and FDJ members who have shared their experiences with me over the years. All of the translations are my own, and the flaws and inaccuracies of this study are, it goes without saying, mine and mine alone.

Special thanks go to Helga Schultz for generously allowing me time to complete this book alongside my research and teaching duties at the Europa-Universität Viadrina in Frankfurt an der Oder.

The very best thanks of all go to my wife Almut, and to our children, Adrian and Johanna, who accompanied me to the fairy-tale films described in chapter 2. Although they were born into the world described in these pages, they will never have to experience it. Knowing this has made it all worthwhile.

Abbreviations Used in Notes

BZ	*Berliner Zeitung*
BzG	*Beiträge zur Geschichte der FDJ*
DA	*Deutschland-Archiv*
DGV	*Dokumente Gesetze Verordnungen* (supplement to *Junge Welt*)
JA IzJ	Jugendarchiv, Institut für zeitgeschichtliche Jugendforschung
JG	*Junge Generation*
JW	*Junge Welt*
ND	*Neues Deutschland*
NL	*Neues Leben*
SAPMO BArch	Stiftung Archiv der Parteien und Massenorganisationen der DDR im Bundesarchiv
StVv	Stadtarchiv Leipzig, Stadtverordneten-Versammlung
SzG	*Schriftenreihe zur Geschichte der FDJ*
ZfG	*Zeitschrift für Geschichtswissenschaft*

CHAPTER 1

Myth and Propaganda in East Germany

Pity the land that needs heroes.
—Bertolt Brecht

In the last years of his rule, East German leader Erich Honecker never tired of extolling the "undeniable realities" of the late twentieth century, above all the existence and permanence of the German Democratic Republic (GDR), "the first Socialist state on German soil." And by early 1989 most of the world had come to accept Honecker's "reality" as their own: while it enjoyed little affection in the noncommunist world, the GDR had long since lost its pariah status and was generally viewed as a stable socialist republic that was here to stay. By late 1989, however, all this had changed. Once its supposedly impregnable wall was breached, the GDR began losing thousands of its people a day, its leaders were toppled, and its citizens began openly demanding a radically new order and finally reunification with the Federal Republic.[1] How could the GDR collapse so quickly? And if the state was really so unstable, how could it have lasted as long as it did?

This book is about some of the ways the Socialist Unity Party of Germany (SED) retained the loyalties of its functionaries and other citizens for forty years and lost them in the forty-first. The structural parameters of the SED dictatorship are fairly well known: the forced merger of the Social Democratic Party (SPD) and the Communist Party (KPD) in 1946, the GDR's creation from the Soviet Zone of Occupation in 1949, the continued presence of half a million Soviet troops on GDR soil, the omnipresence of the *Stasi* secret police, press censorship, and finally the construction of the Berlin Wall in 1961. The benefits of

---

1. See Konrad Jarausch, *The Rush to German Unity* (Oxford, 1994).

GDR society (full employment, free medical care, low rents) are also widely understood. Rather than dwell on these essential but familiar factors, this book instead will concentrate on a critical but little-known dimension of GDR life, namely, how the SED established and perpetuated its power through the development of a unique GDR mythology.

Historical studies of the former GDR have flourished since the 1980s. The best overall surveys of East German history are probably Henry A. Turner's *Germany from Partition to Reunification*[2] and Hermann Weber's *Geschichte der DDR.*[3] The collapse of the GDR suddenly opened up the East German and (briefly) the Soviet archives and has made an entirely new perspective possible. Norman M. Naimark's *The Russians in Germany* uses previously unseen and now off-limits Soviet material to cast light on the previously unknown history of the Soviet Zone of Occupation,[4] and David Pike's *The Politics of Culture in Soviet Occupied Germany* provides a fascinating look into the early years of SED cultural policy.[5] Mary Fulbrook's *Anatomy of a Dictatorship* represents an early and particularly insightful attempt to analyze the inner workings of the SED regime on the basis of documentary evidence.[6] The most fascinating behind-the-scenes study of the GDR to date is Lutz Niethammer's *Die volkseigene Erfahrung,* which uses an exhaustive series of interviews to examine the life experiences and attitudes of East German industrial workers.[7] In an attempt to bridge the gap between government policy and day-to-day life Sigrid Meuschel has examined the GDR from the perspective of legitimacy and identity.[8] While a number of fairly conventional studies of traditions and political symbolism have appeared,[9] a few scholars have sought to "deconstruct" the rational facade of GDR society and examine

---

2. Henry Ashby Turner Jr., *Germany from Partition to Reunification* (New Haven, 1992).

3. Hermann Weber, *Geschichte der DDR,* 3d ed. (Munich, 1989).

4. Norman M. Naimark, *The Russians in Germany. A History of the Soviet Zone of Occupation, 1945–1949* (Cambridge, MA, 1996).

5. David Pike, *The Politics of Culture in Soviet-Occupied Germany, 1945–1949* (Stanford, 1992).

6. Mary Fulbrook, *Anatomy of a Dictatorship: Inside the GDR, 1945–89* (Oxford, 1995).

7. Lutz Niethammer et al., *Die volkseigene Erfahrung. Eine Archäologie des Lebens in der Industrieprovinz der DDR* (Berlin, 1991).

8. Sigrid Meuschel, *Legitimation und Parteiherrschaft in der DDR* (Frankfurt am Main, 1992).

9. Henry Krisch, *The German Democratic Republic. The Search for Identity* (Boulder, 1982); Maoz Azaryahn, *Vom Wilhelmplatz zum Thälmannplatz. Politische Symbolik im öffentlichen Leben der DDR* (Gerlingen, 1991). The most concise study on "the cultivation of tradition" is Peter J. Lapp, *Traditionspflege in der DDR* (West Berlin, 1988).

it from the perspective of myth.[10] So far, however, the use of myth has been largely reserved to the "antifascist" foundation myth of the GDR.[11] But as important as this particular myth was in the development of the GDR, it was only one among several. In this study I expand the notion of myth in order to lay bare the foundations of the GDR. The GDR I will examine here is not, however, the GDR of party congress reports and steel production statistics, but rather the GDR of emotion and popular memory—the "GDR myth." It is this constantly evolving GDR myth that remains with us now that the congress reports have been silenced and the production statistics filed away into oblivion.

What does the mythic approach offer that these other studies lack? As fine as some of these social and political histories of the GDR are, very few examine the question of passion and motivation. After all, leaving the coercions and benefits of GDR society aside for a moment, why should anyone have dedicated his or her life to the SED in the first place? Before the Berlin Wall was erected in 1961, why stay there at all when the Federal Republic offered an attractive alternative? There were many motives for this decision. Among those persons who became Communists before 1945, the SED later identified several paths to Marxism-Leninism, each based on personal experience. The most important by far was direct day-to-day experience or at least observation of the injustices of capitalism and "imperialism," such as the exploitation of industrial or rural labor, poverty, and above all the experience of the two world wars. Such experiences, combined with the utter disillusionment with capitalism that they brought with them, frequently led to the reading of the Marxist-Leninist classics, involvement with the labor movement and communist organizations, and finally membership in the Communist Party itself. A second path led through involvement in the Communist youth organization, with its action, excitement, and sense of mission. Intellectuals—appalled by war and injustice, and often living in exile—sometimes found their way to Marxism-Leninism through reading the classics of German literature and philosophy. The most dramatic path to communism led through the experience of the "antifascist resistance struggle," in which the anti-Nazi underground movement experienced comradeship in a life-or-death struggle against a regime that they viewed as the highest stage of capital-

---

10. Cf. Alan Nothnagle, "From Buchenwald to Bismarck: Historical Myth-Building in the German Democratic Republic, 1945–1989," *Central European History* 1 (1993): 91–113.

11. See, for example, Antonia Grunenberg, *Antifaschismus—Ein deutscher Mythos* (Reinbek, 1993); Lutz Niethammer, ed., *Der gesäuberte Anti-Faschismus* (Berlin 1994); see also the essays in Thomas Flierl, ed., *Mythos Antifaschismus. Ein Traditionskabinett wird kommentiert* (Berlin, 1992).

ism. Others were converted through a profound admiration of the Soviet Union, whether this admiration arose from a love of Russian and Soviet culture, a fascination with the achievements of Stalin's five-year plans, gratitude for good treatment at the hands of the Soviet Army during World War II, or a profound sense of shame at German behavior in the war. Finally, a comparative few—specifically German officers held captive in Soviet prisoner of war camps—were converted to Marxism-Leninism through German patriotism and the belief that communism offered the only hope for an honorable rebirth of the German fatherland.

According to SED propagandists, these paths to Marxism-Leninism, which overlapped in most cases, account for the conversion of most of the GDR's founding generation in a time when a public declaration of communist belief was not only unfashionable but also grounds for denunciation, persecution, imprisonment, and even death. But after 1945, and certainly after the GDR's founding in 1949, these motives no longer obtained. For one thing, by 1945 the majority of German Communist Party members had been liquidated by either the Nazis or the Soviets and needed to be replaced. Furthermore, the opportunism of those early years, as thousands of eastern Germans, many of them former Nazis, lined up to join the ruling SED in order to advance their careers, watered down the founding generation's sense of mission. More important, the younger generation, relied on by the party leadership to carry on their program, was rapidly being socialized under the radically different political and social conditions of the GDR itself and thus was only indirectly aware of the motives of their elders. This was the irony of the socialist system as practiced in the GDR: the closer the society moved toward realizing the socialist order, the less its citizens understood what socialism was really about and why it was worth fighting for. As successive five-year plans were "fulfilled and overfulfilled," capitalism became more and more of an abstraction—or, more typically, a tempting image on radio and television programs beamed in from the West. As Walter Ulbricht complained as late as 1969: "Individual practical-political experiences in the struggle against the class enemy and the immediate day-to-day confrontation with imperialism, which earlier were important elements in the development of class consciousness, are no longer present. The transmission of the historical experiences and lessons from the struggle of the working class against imperialism are thus necessarily all the more urgent."[12] Consequently, the bulk of GDR youth propaganda drummed in the lessons of the class struggle and the impending doom of the capitalist system. But this sort of

---

12. Cited in Hans-Dieter Schmidt, *Geschichtsunterricht in der DDR. Eine Einführung* (Stuttgart, 1979), 14–15.

propaganda always remained a half-measure, because the Party could not let the younger generation experience the shortcomings of capitalism as practiced in the Federal Republic and West Berlin without letting them experience the benefits as well. Therefore, in order to retain its identity as a socialist state and guarantee its future, the SED saw little choice but to perpetuate the lived experiences of youthful enthusiasm, high culture, anti-Fascism, admiration of the Soviet Union, and German patriotism in the form of a state-supporting mythology.

In this study I show how the SED systematically transmitted these myths to young East Germans in the Party's youth organizations between 1945 and 1989. My analysis of this myth-building concentrates on the Party's use of both historical events and traditional forms in youth indoc-trination programs, rhetoric, symbolism, ritual, and mass events. My own involvement with the GDR goes back many years and has been of both a professional and a private nature. My observations are based on annual visits to the GDR between 1983 and 1990, including a six-month stay in 1988 that I spent living in a two-room flat in Berlin-Prenzlauer Berg with my young East German wife and newborn twins, trying to arrange their emigration to the United States. After reunification, I followed up this "fieldwork" with several years of research in the libraries and archives of the former East Berlin. As an instructor at an eastern German university since 1994—in an office with a window facing the former "District Party School of the SED" in Frankfurt an der Oder—I have had a rare oppor-tunity to observe the lasting effects of GDR myth-building among stu-dents and colleagues at first hand.

But first it is necessary to explain what is meant by the nebulous term *myth.* The concept of myth has undergone a dramatic transformation in recent decades and should no longer be understood in its colloquial mean-ing of fiction, fairy tales, and outright lies. In the 1920s the anthropologist Bronislaw Malinowski did much to popularize the modern understanding of myth. To Malinowski, myth is "not merely a story told, but a reality lived. . . . It expresses, enhances, and codifies belief; it safeguards and enforces morality; it vouches for the efficacy of ritual and enforces practi-cal rules for the guidance of man. Myth is thus a vital ingredient of human civilization; it is not an idle tale, but a hard-worked active force."[13] The cultural anthropologist Mircea Eliade has a similar view of the truth con-

---

13. Bronislaw Malinowski, "Myth in Primitive Psychology," in *Magic, Science and Religion and Other Essays* (Glencoe, IL, 1948), 78–79. On the subject of modern mythologies, see Ernst Cassirer, *The Myth of the State* (New York, 1946); Burton Feldman and Robert D. Richardson, *The Rise of Modern Mythology, 1680–1860* (Bloomington, 1972); William H. MacNeill, "Mythistory, or Truth, Myth, History, and Historians," in *Mythistory and Other Essays* (Chicago, 1986), 3–22.

tained within myths and comes close to defining Honecker's notion of "reality": "The myth is considered a sacred story," Eliade writes in his *Aspects du mythe,* "but is nevertheless a 'true story' because it always refers to 'realities.' The cosmogonic myth is 'true' because the world is there to prove it; the myth of the origin of death is equally 'true' because man's mortality proves it, and so on."[14]

Since it exists in faith and emotion, myth resists exact definition, no less than "reality." A precisely defined myth is no longer a myth, and it goes without saying that one person's myth is another's fact. I will not try to square this circle, but a working definition of myth is essential. For the purposes of this study, historical myths are events, processes, or persons from an earlier time, which, typically estranged from their original meanings and contexts, transmit religious or ideological beliefs to a specified group in an easily comprehended, emotionally moving form. They are often based on personal experience, in which case they are, in Malinowski's words, quite literally "a reality lived." Stated simply, a myth is an abbreviated world-outlook, an ideology in miniature. Once the myth is generally understood, it can be reduced to symbolic form without losing any of its power: in religious imagery, an icon or totem pole; in political imagery, the swastika or the British crown jewels; in advertising, the world-renowned Marlboro Man. Political myths (which Clifford Geertz calls "master fictions")[15] always contain supernatural or at least suspension-of-disbelief elements. For example, it demands a leap of faith to believe that persons with "royal blood" are really better than the rest of us, or that the Great Socialist October Revolution was really the "turning point" in human history (even if the proponents of both theories have provided us with excellent reasons why each is true). Myths are most effective when unreflected. Very few myths can stand up to objective analysis.

Historical myths are both sincerely felt and manipulable. They perform five major functions.

1. They create and strengthen personal identity. Who am I? Where do I come from? Where am I going? Why do I do what I do? What purpose does my existence serve?

14. Mircea Eliade, *Aspects du mythe* (Paris, 1963), 17.

15. Sean Wilentz, ed., *Rites of Power: Symbolism, Ritual and Politics Since the Middle Ages* (Philadelphia, 1985), 15, 33. See also Geertz, *The Interpretation of Cultures: Selected Essays* (New York, 1973); George L. Mosse, *The Nationalization of the Masses: Political Symbolism and Mass Movements in Germany from the Napoleonic Wars through the Third Reich* (Ithaca, 1975); Eric Hobsbawm and Terence Ranger, eds., *The Invention of Tradition* (Cambridge, 1983); Benedict Anderson, *Imagined Communities: Reflections on the Origins and Spread of Nationalism,* rev. ed. (New York, 1991); Michael Kammen, *Mystic Chords of Memory: The Transformation of Tradition in American Culture* (New York, 1991).

2. They create and strengthen group identity. Who are we? Why are we together? Where are we going? Who are our lawful leaders, and where does their authority derive from? What distinguishes us from other groups?
3. They determine morality and societal norms. They help to define "necessary evils." They also provide valuable information. What is good and what is bad? What are the limits of our behavior? How far can we go in defending our group and its way of life? How do we identify and combat our enemies?
4. They offer an explanation of the creation of the community and demonstrate the interconnectedness of all things. They make possible the periodic re-creation of the community, whether in symbolic or "real" terms. They provide continuity and point the way to a common future.
5. They provide ready answers to the periodic blows of a complex and often unacceptable outside reality. They simplify and contextualize complex and unpleasant events. They justify such unsettling events as wars, natural catastrophes, oppression, and state-sponsored violence and reconcile them with the group's proclaimed values.

Is the cultivation of mythology unique to communist societies? Not at all. Mythology performs critical functions in nearly every state or institution. The Rütli oath of Wilhelm Tell fame has served Switzerland well for centuries. Both France and the United States have gained remarkable mileage from the distorted memory of their respective revolutions. Although the United States has been transformed enormously since its revolution, the "Spirit of '76" is still alive and waiting for its next enlistment in the political needs of the day. The Minuteman missile and President Ronald Reagan's depiction of the Nicaraguan Contra rebels as "moral equivalents of the Founding Fathers" in the 1980s are evidence of this phenomenon. The French *Résistance,* a classic example of politically expedient wishful thinking, served as the founding myth of the Fourth and Fifth Republics. In West Germany, mythology was essential in establishing a distinct identity and dispelling anti-German fears abroad. Hundreds of thousands of visitors to West Berlin were duly marched through the Reichstag exhibit on Germany's tenuous democratic tradition, to which the Federal Republic was laying claim. The conservative anti-Nazi resistance movement around Graf Stauffenberg provided the new state with considerable legitimacy, and early West German leaders (most notably the first federal president, Theodor Heuß) diligently mined the German classic writers for evidence of the continuity of German *Kultur.*

All of these state-supporting myths have been critically important in specific situations. They are especially important when trying to shore up the legitimacy of a new regime or social system. However, modern liberal democratic states, as opposed to communist societies, absolute monarchies, and other authoritarian systems, ultimately achieve legitimacy and stability in more tangible ways: through regular elections, at least a minimum of open exchange between the government and the governed, a bill of rights, an independent judiciary, an acceptable standard of living for the majority of the population, and through such confidence-inspiring features as liberal press laws and open borders. While the old Federal Republic's historical credentials may have been shaky, it did not have to rely on myth to retain its people's loyalty but relied instead on a social contract that was clear and openly arrived at. For example, if Stauffenberg had been revealed to be a fraud, this information would certainly have led to a minor scandal and some major scholarly conferences, but it hardly would have brought the government down, along with the entire social, economic, cultural, and intellectual system. Nor has civil society in Britain shown any signs of dissolution after imbibing daily reports of the monkeyshines of its formerly sacrosanct royal family. But in the whirlwind of 1989, similarly grave revelations did exactly that to the GDR.

But is it appropriate to apply the term *myth* to a "scientific socialist" society such as the GDR? The mythic and religious aspects of communism and of its ideology, Marxism-Leninism, are obvious and have been commented upon for decades.[16] In fact, communist states are especially dependent on myths, historical and otherwise: By toppling the existing order, any revolutionary movement simultaneously topples whatever legitimacy the old order might have had and is compelled to establish its own legitimacy quickly in order to stay in power. The difference is that once communist states, as utopian regimes, invoke their mythology they can never let it go. No utopian regime ever measures up to its millenarian goals, regardless of the quality of its propaganda, and hence it is always threatened by a worrisome lack of present. The social contract, essential for a stable civil society, can only be achieved within that utopian order, whose precise form and even desirability are not open to debate. Moreover, com-

---

16. As Eliade writes, "Marx's classless society and the resulting disappearance of historical tensions finds its most exact precedent in the myth of the Golden Age, which, following multiple traditions, characterizes the beginning of the end of History. Marx enriched this venerable myth through an entire Judeo-Christian messianic ideology: on the one side, the prophetic role and soteriological function which he accords the proletariat; on the other side, the final struggle between Good and Evil, which one can easily compare to the apocalyptic conflict between Christ and the Anti-Christ, followed by the definitive victory of the former." *Mythes, rêves et mystères* (Paris, 1957), 20–21.

munist regimes need to remind their subjects that paradise will be postponed for a while. Lenin believed that the communist era would begin soon after the victory of an imminent world revolution. Under Stalin, the new age was always a couple of five-year plans ahead. Under Khrushchev something approaching communism was scheduled to begin in 1970, or 1980 at the latest. Khrushchev's geriatric successors gave up detailed predictions, but periodically hinted that significant progress would be made on the road to communism "by the year 2000." In the meantime, mythology was needed to fill in the gaps between the regime's claims and its usually limited achievements. And just as much as these regimes needed the vision of a "happy future," they required a past in order to show how far they had come and how indispensable they really were.

Myths also served a critical didactic function. After all, Marxist-Leninist ideology, in its unadulterated, dogmatic form, has little appeal outside of the communist movement itself. "Vulgar Marxism" (promising peace, bread, justice, full employment, the Brotherhood of Man, etc.) has a much broader appeal, but is forced to compete with other ideologies promising pretty much the same thing but without the wait. (The West German "social market economy" promises nearly everything Marxism does and throws vacation trips to Majorca into the bargain.) Myths explain the differences by using language and symbols familiar to everyone, much the way missionaries have traditionally explained the benefits of Christianity by coopting pagan deities and seasonal festivals. This was the task faced by the Bolsheviks in 1917, when they were suddenly called upon to explain the relative benefits of "scientific socialism" to a vast population of illiterate and deeply religious peasants of different nationalities.

Myths prepared the citizens of the communist era for their future tasks. No one really knew what communism and the "socialist/communist personality" would be like once the new order had been achieved. Myths demonstrated the new ethical system on the basis of earlier patterns. Finally, myths in the Marxist-Leninist societies, as in all other societies, put people at their ease. It was to a large degree mythology that determined whether one perceived the GDR's relationship to the Soviet Union as "exploitation" or "friendship," and the GDR itself as a "totalitarian dictatorship" or simply "home."

Although all East Germans were exposed to the mythology in varying degrees, it was chiefly aimed at elite groups of various kinds. In this study I am mostly concerned with the GDR's ruling functionary and professional class. The GDR's ignominious collapse in 1989 has obscured the fact that the entire society at one time had been based on the principle of social mobility. If the Horatio Alger "rags to riches" myth remains powerful in the United States, in reality elevator operators who through hard work and honesty rise up to become corporate presidents are more the exception than the rule. By contrast, in the GDR and other socialist states rapid advancement from the shop floor to the halls of power was the rule.[17] Academics and other privileged members of society were generally required to present evidence of factory work or career training before being promoted. Among later generations the supposedly "proletarian" background of the children of functionaries is questionable, but in ideological terms the East Germans were a race of Horatio Algers or, in Marxist-Leninist language, citizens of a "workers' and peasants' state." This social mobility—which, young people were incessantly informed, was only possible and only sustainable under socialism—made the system extremely attractive to those willing to play the game. Socialism promised not only an idealistic future "victory" in the form of a classless society with privileges for all, but also immediate rewards for loyalists, namely the imminent prospect of exchanging one's place at the machine for a warm office or a professorial chair and so, in the words of a Free German Youth (FDJ) song, "building the future today." The myths of *Kultur,* antifascism, German–Soviet friendship, and the Socialist fatherland transmitted the goals, the heroes, the value system, and the self-justification of this new class to the younger generation. For young people on the way up, GDR mythology contained valuable information for an aggressive new class hoping to dispossess the old. Does this mean that loyal East Germans were mere opportunists? Not at all. Instead, I argue that the system's ingenious blending of self-interest and idealism explains the GDR's relative success until 1989.

As important as material privileges were in keeping functionaries content and eager for promotions, they were hardly sufficient motivation for the GDR's ruling elite to dedicate their lives to the socialist cause. Nor did they fully compensate East Germans for the many critical shortcomings and even dangers of GDR life. Instead, I propose an additional *immaterial* privilege, namely, the privilege of uncontradicted moral certainty. For this was one privilege that the West, with all its wealth and freedoms, simply could not offer. The loss of this moral dimension may represent the most painful loss of all for the former functionary class.

The term *myth-building* describes the process by which the SED and its subordinate institutions redefined events, institutions, persons, symbols, and forms from the past in order to mold a distinctive and politically expedient historical consciousness. The myths developed in the GDR

---

17. Cf. Lutz Niethammer, "Erfahrungen und Strukturen. Prolegomena zu einer Geschichte der Gesellschaft der DDR," in Hartmut Kaelble et al., *Sozialgeschichte der DDR* (Stuttgart, 1994), S. 104–5.

located the East German state in the past, present, and future of the common German experience. That is the essence of myth-making. But if a historical myth is to produce the desired effect, it obviously cannot simply be proclaimed at a Party congress, but instead must be broadcast to a wide audience. Dissemination through history books is also inadequate, since the appeal of standard historical writing is limited in even the most open of societies. Schools are an important medium, for, as one scholar of the cold war has written, "the only version of the past that most citizens will ever know is what they picked up in the textbooks of their childhood, fixed at one possibly impressionable moment."[18]

To achieve the goal of universality, therefore, this kind of myth cannot just be *made,* it must also be *built:* one stone on top of the other, through monuments, mass events, festivals, holidays, film, the press, and a variety of other media. Myth-building is about setting priorities and gaining control over the terms of public discourse. It means the calculated use of history. It is the deliberate and systematic transmission of a specific historical consciousness to a broad audience for the express purpose of securing political and institutional legitimacy. But although GDR myth-builders regularly used cynical methods in order to manipulate the public, they were not necessarily hypocrites themselves. Most were profoundly—and tragically—sincere in their intentions. For myth-building also meant the "cultivation of tradition," the fulfillment of a historic mandate.

In this study I distinguish between "intentional" and "functional" myth-building. Intentional myth-building refers to the use of myths for a new purpose. Such intentional myths have a *mobilizing* function. An example of such a mobilizing myth is the Thälmann cult, which was designed to create a new kind of human being. Functional myth-building, by contrast, uses preexisting myths to *stabilize* the Party's rule. An example of functional myth-building is the Honecker regime's use of high culture as a source of pride and identification with the GDR. Some myths have both functions. For example, in the myth of the "Socialist fatherland," the Party used German nationalist mythology as a source of legitimacy, but also used it to mobilize young people to join the army and pre-

18. Stephen J. Whitfield, *The Culture of the Cold War* (Baltimore, 1991), 56. On history instruction and historical propaganda in the schools, see Dieter Riesenberger, *Geschichte und Geschichtswissenschaft in der DDR* (Göttingen, 1973); Frank Reuter, *Geschichtsbewusstsein in der DDR. Programm und Aktion* (Cologne, 1973); Hans-Georg Wolf, *Zur Entwicklung des Geschichtsunterrichts in der DDR* (Paderborn, 1978); Hans-Dieter Schmid, *Geschichtsunterricht in der DDR. Eine Einführung* (Stuttgart, 1979); Karl Schmitt, *Politische Erziehung in der DDR* (Paderborn, 1980); Bodo von Borries, *Kindlich-jugendliche Geschichtsverarbeitung in West- und Ostdeutschland* (Pfaffenweiler, 1990).

pare for a potential World War III. To this must be added "positive" and "negative" myth-building. Positive myths sought to cultivate loyalty toward the GDR, its leaders, and Marxism-Leninism. Each positive myth, however, had its negative counterpart. Hence love of the Soviet Union entailed hatred of American imperialism. Loyalty to the "antifascist" GDR meant rejection of the "fascist" Federal Republic.

While the SED invested heavily in adult propaganda, it always subscribed to the idea that "who has youth has the future." Most SED propaganda was aimed at young people, who practically from the moment of birth were to be molded into "new human beings." The chief agents of youth socialization were the Young Pioneers and the so-called Free German Youth or FDJ. Adult events, such as the elaborate cultural ceremonies of the Ulbricht era, were usually accompanied by special youth events, and Young Pioneer or FDJ delegations were nearly always on hand to represent the "bond of the generations" at adult events. Of course, not all young people, even future elites, believed in the mythology described in this study. For hundreds of thousands of young East Germans the myths propagated by the Party and its youth organizations were simply a dull formality, a necessary evil they had to endure in order to finish school and get a good job. For these nominal members youth organization life was restricted to putting on a colored neckerchief or a blue shirt on special days, wearing a "Blue Sputnik" badge, attending the twice-monthly rallies in the school courtyard, and listening to the occasional Lenin lecture at a *Heimabend.* As adults, many of them made an art of ignoring Party propaganda entirely. Thousands of loyal non-Party members, often far removed from any kind of public responsibility, flew the GDR flag on holidays and sent birthday cards to Ulbricht and Honecker, while SED members were often the most cynical of dissenters, even if they kept it to themselves. But whether one "believed" in the myths or not, they were inescapable. All East Germans were exposed to the propaganda described in this study and were forced to come to terms with it.

Throughout this study we will see numerous parallels to the cold war ideology of the Federal Republic and other noncommunist societies. Does this mean that the SED's mythology was the equivalent of standard Western demagoguery? Not really. The structural and ideological differences are simply too great to make such generalizations. In fact, without some understanding of these differences GDR mythology itself is hardly comprehensible. So before plunging into the enchanted world of GDR mythology it is necessary to pause and examine some of the parameters within which it functioned.

The East German Youth Movement and
Its Propaganda Apparatus

In contrast to the Federal Republic, the GDR maintained a broad and vastly influential centralized youth movement.[19] The Young Pioneers for school children and above all the FDJ for older pupils and young adults played a critical socializing function in the GDR. In its early years the FDJ sought to win over young people for its activities and for socialism itself by recalling such traditions as the largely middle-class youth movements, Baden-Powell's Boy Scouts, the Socialist Workers Youth (SAJ) of the interwar SPD, and the KPD's Communist Youth Organization (KJVD). As FDJ cofounder Edith Baumann put it in 1947, "Let us combine the political open-mindedness and youthful combat-readiness, which has survived from the *Burschenschaften* to the Communist Youth organization, with the nature-loving life of the *Wandervogel* groups, and the Christian tolerance of the confessional organizations, into a unified, free youth organization encompassing all of German youth."[20] The FDJ maintained a certain continuity by retaining the blue shirt of the SAJ, the hiking and singing traditions of the *Wandervogel* and other youth groups, the spectacular "Pentecost Meetings" of the *Bündische Jugend* and the workers' movement, the *Heimabende* or club meetings of the *Bündische Jugend,* and an idealistic vocabulary reminiscent of youth movements everywhere. But this was largely window dressing. The East German youth movement was built upon the ruins of the Hitler Youth. The Young Pioneers and the FDJ were formed in 1946 on the model of the Soviet Lenin Pioneers and the Komsomol. After some early difficulties attracting members in the late 1940s and early 1950s, they eventually encompassed around 80 percent of the young population. In Marxist-Leninist terminology, the FDJ was the "transmission belt" between the Party and the younger generation, the "combat reserve" and "cadre forge" of the SED. As such it produced virtually the entire second- and third-generation elite of the GDR, including such prominent leaders as Erich Honecker, Hermann Axen, Heinz Kessler, Egon Krenz, Margot Feist-Honecker, and Hans Modrow, all of whom began their Party careers as Young Pioneer or FDJ functionaries. The myth-building and youth propaganda of the FDJ were also the myth-building and youth propaganda of the short-lived West German FDJ and

---

19. See Helga Gotschlich, ed., *Aber nicht im Gleichschritt. Zur Entstehung der FDJ* (Berlin 1997); Gotschlich, ed., *"Links und links und Schritt gehalten . . ." Die FDJ: Konzepte–Abläufe–Grenzen* (Berlin 1994); Ulrich Mählert, *Die Freie Deutsche Jugend 1945–1949* (Berlin 1995).

20. Edith Baumann, *Geschichte der deutschen Jugendbewegung* (Berlin, 1947), 32.

later of the various West German Communist youth organizations and other leftist movements under SED supervision. During the Ulbricht era, much of the GDR's youth propaganda was aimed directly at West German young people, although with uncertain results.

The most important means of propaganda in the GDR was always the press, in this case the weekly FDJ functionary's journal *Junge Generation* and the daily newspaper *Junge Welt.* Founded in 1947, *Junge Welt* amounted to a youthful version of the SED central organ, *Neues Deutschland.* It is difficult for an outsider to appreciate the importance of *Neues Deutschland* and *Junge Welt,* considering the uniform dullness of GDR newspapers. The political pages of the FDJ newspapers were intended primarily for agitators, and less for ordinary members. In 1952 the journal *Der junge Agitator* provided propagandists a list of helpful hints for using *Junge Welt* in their daily work. The fictional agitator, "Manfred W.," spends at least an hour each day studying the newspaper. In fact, it is his first task of the day. First he goes through the entire newspaper and then divides it up. "He reads the important articles immediately and makes notes in a book, which he then uses in his day's work. In the conferences he has with his colleagues during the course of the day, he right away gives them the necessary directions for their work." In the evening he reads other articles that are not directly relevant to his own agitation, but that are useful for his own knowledge. "He also has acquired folders into which he has daily fastened the most important articles according to their content. If, for example, he has to write a speech on the details of the war policy of the Adenauer government, then he only needs to reach for the corresponding folder and then he has all the documentation he needs."[21] The success of newspaper propaganda ultimately rested on the agitator's skill in interpreting it to his own immediate audience.

But the newspaper's possibilities were limited, and the FDJ made heavy use of other media in cooperation with other state institutions. These book publications and other media productions were then discussed at length at FDJ meetings and *Heimabende.* From the late 1940s on, the FDJ had close links to the DEFA film corporation and cooperated in the production of many propagandistic films aimed at young audiences. Radio and later television were especially important as instruments for the transmission of information and propaganda. But, far more important than the propaganda apparatus itself, the mass organization dominated nearly all youth life in the GDR. Sporting events, rock concerts, excursions, and school functions were all organized by the FDJ. Even those

---

21. "Die 'Junge Welt'—ein unentbehrliches Hilfsmittel für unsere Arbeit," *Der junge Agitator* 1 (1952): 27.

young people who rejected the organization on principle were forced to come to terms with its members, its functionaries, its institutions, its rhetoric, and its myths.

Marxism-Leninism and *"Parteilichkeit"*

The ideological basis for all SED and FDJ events was Marxism-Leninism. For the SED, Marxism-Leninism was a "scientific world-outlook." It "is the theoretical foundation for the practical activity of the Communist and labor parties." Furthermore, "it makes possible the scientifically founded leadership of the proletarian class struggle and Socialist and Communist construction and thus serves as a theoretical guide for the practical-revolutionary transformation of the world."[22] Marxism-Leninism originated from three intellectual currents. The first is the concept of dialectical and historical materialism, which originated in the writings of Hegel and Feuerbach and was later developed by Marx, Engels, and Lenin. This mechanism provided a theory of the relationship between consciousness and matter. Building upon the theory of evolution, it offered a materialist explanation of progress from the lower to the higher. It helped determine the role of the individual in society and within the natural universe itself. By rejecting the existence of all divine and supernatural forces, it postulated the scientific knowability and hence the infinite malleability of all reality. The theory also provided a model of history and society. Stated simply, it saw human history as a continuous series of class struggles, in which the resolution of class antitheses in the form of the synthesis of the revolution provided the driving force.[23]

The second current was that of political economy, which derived from the English economists Smith and Ricardo and their theory of surplus value. Political economy proved the existence of capitalist exploitation and so provided the basis for the theory of the special mission of the working class to create a classless society without exploitation.[24] Finally, the tradition of utopian socialism as propagated by Robert Owen, Saint-Simon, and Fourier gave rise to the concept of "scientific socialism," which replaced dreams of a just society with a "scientific" analysis and a strategy for victory.[25]

With the victory of the Bolshevik Revolution in Russia, Marxism

---

22. "Marxismus-Leninismus," in *Kleines politisches Wörterbuch,* 7th ed. (East Berlin, 1988), 602.

23. Autorenkollektiv, *Dialektischer und historischer Materialismus. Lehrbuch für das marxistisch-leninistische Grundlagenstudium* (East Berlin, 1987), 18–19, 46.

24. *Dialektischer und historischer Materialismus,* 18–19, 25.

25. *Dialektischer und historischer Materialismus,* 19, 26.

became the official ideology of the new Soviet Union. During the dictator-ship of Joseph Stalin, Soviet ideologues codified Marxism-Leninism in its present form and transformed it into an instrument of political and ideo-logical control. As Soviet influence expanded throughout eastern Europe after World War II, Marxism-Leninism accompanied it and quickly gained ascendancy. If Marxism-Leninism proved to be an effective ideol-ogy in the Soviet bloc, in practice its inadequacy as a diagnostic tool criti-cally undermined the parties and states it ostensibly supported. As the for-mer SED functionary Wolfgang Leonhardt realized several years after his own rigorous Marxist-Leninist training in the Soviet Union and his escape from the Soviet Zone of Occupation (SBZ) in 1949, "it is a characteristic trait of Stalinism to strip dialectical materialism of its actual meaning . . . [which is] to explain the processes within the society and to draw certain conclusions from them, and instead degrade it to a point where they use it to justify political decisions or resolutions after the fact."[26]

The version of Marxism-Leninism promoted in the GDR was an especially orthodox one allowing virtually no divergence from Soviet prac-tices. It justified all SED policies and was an incontrovertible authority on all aspects of life in the GDR. It was less an ideology than a religion. Its influence extended not just to the public sphere (politics, economics, edu-cation, etc.) but in theory also to the most intimate spheres of private life-styles and morality. For example, the editors of a popular East German marriage manual felt compelled to precede an otherwise pedestrian list of tips for a fulfilling sex life with a Marx epigram—"the relationship between man and woman is the foundation of human society." Every course of instruction offered (at elementary and high schools, vocational schools, and universities, let alone the FDJ and Party academies) was taught from the Marxist-Leninist viewpoint and entailed a thick dose of pure Marxist-Leninist ideology. Indoctrination played a vastly greater role in the GDR than it had under National Socialism. As one historian of the Third Reich writes, "The image of millions of little Hitler Youths diligently and enthusiastically studying or learning by heart Hitler's *Mein Kampf* is one derived from fiction and not from reality. . . . Such so-called ideologi-cal tenets as nationalism and the belief in the moral and physical superior-ity of one's own country and a latent and overt racialism among young-sters were not specifically National Socialist but could have been found in any moderate right-wing party before 1933."[27] By the same token, such ideological tenets as peace, gender equality, solidarity, and so forth can be found in any moderate left-wing party. The SED was understandably wor-

---

26. Wolfgang Leonhardt, *Die Revolution entläßt ihre Kinder* (Berlin, 1990), 318.
27. H. W. Koch, *The Hitler Youth: Origins and Development, 1922–1945* (New York, 1975), 131–32.

ried about losing its monopoly on these principles, and hence its legitimacy in the GDR. The schools and the youth organizations were the Party's first line of defense against such "poisons" as "Trotskyism," "revisionism," "Social Democratism," "Titoism," "objectivism," "cosmopolitanism," "cultural barbarism," and so forth. In practice, Marxism-Leninism in the GDR squeezed all of human existence into the categories of ideology, production, and class struggle. To the orthodox, any thought or action, any poem, play, novel, history book, or painting that was not supportive of these principles or that could not be used to propagate them was at best irrelevant, or, more likely, "formalistic" or reactionary. Marxism-Leninism was "scientifically founded, openly *parteilich,* and a guide for practical-revolutionary action. It expresses in scientific form the historical task of the working class: . . . to establish Socialism and Communism, i.e., the classless society."[28]

Marxism-Leninism maintained supremacy through the principle of *Parteilichkeit. Parteilichkeit* means "partisanship," or, more accurately, "taking sides." Outsiders regularly confuse *Parteilichkeit,* also referred to under the Marxist-Leninist term *political correctness,* with cynicism. In fact, cynicism in the usual sense of the word was surprisingly rare in the GDR. According to the SED, "*Parteilichkeit* is . . . a theoretical-methodological principle; it demands that one approach all questions of societal life from the standpoint of the interests of the working class, its struggle for peace, societal progress, and the establishment of Socialism and Communism."[29] Since the SED was the "party of the working class," *Parteilichkeit* literally meant the strict subordination of all political, intellectual, and cultural activity to the Party's directives. Stated simply, "the Party is always right," a slogan understandable to everyone and thus repeated endlessly by the SED propaganda machine. This principle is summed up in the official SED anthem, written by the Party poet Louis Fürnberg.[30]

The Party, the Party, the Party is always right,
And, comrades, it will stay that way.
For who fights for what's right is always right,
Against lies and exploitation.

To an outsider it appears astonishing that the SED could in all seriousness proclaim such a crude and self-serving slogan as "the Party is

---

28. *Kleines Politisches Wörterbuch,* 2d ed. (East Berlin, 1973), 655–66.

29. "Parteilichkeit," in *Kleines politisches Wörterbuch,* 738.

30. Louis Fürnberg, "Die Partei hat immer recht," in Michael Glaser, ed., *Auferstanden,* Deutsche Schallplatten GmbH, 0 03 040, 1990.

always right," or that it could "prove" such assertions as the inevitability of the victory of socialism by using Ulbricht and Honecker speeches—or even back issues of *Neues Deutschland*—as "evidence." This mystery is explained by the principle of *Parteilichkeit*. Loyal SED members believed that the glorious end justified the admittedly messy means, the end being the "ideal" of "the establishment of Socialism and Communism." The SED unabashedly claimed a monopoly not only on political and economic power, but also on human ideals and reality itself. Moreover, since the ideals were always projected into an inescapable "happy future," the GDR's obvious shortcomings and contradictions in the here and now were ultimately irrelevant. They were by-products of change, and thus— seen from a dialectical standpoint—evidence of progress.

The East German dissident Robert Havemann, who broke with the SED after learning the facts of Stalin's rule in the Soviet Union, later explained his *Parteilichkeit* as follows.[31]

> Today the mental state in which I found myself back then seems downright ridiculous to me. But back then it was nothing of the sort. In fact, for a good Communist it was a matter of course. We had a hard, decades long struggle behind us. At one stage of this struggle, which was a life and death struggle, I had taken part in the anti-Fascist German resistance struggle. My best friends had fallen in this struggle. The collapse of the hated Hitler regime was a great victory for our cause. It was achieved under the leadership of Stalin . . .

The principle of *Parteilichkeit* was thus not only a cynical method of ideological control, but derived from the mythic aspects of Marxist ideology itself. As Leszek Kolakowski has written in his analysis of Lukács's thought,[32]

> Marxism is not a theory which simply states something about the world and as such is acceptable to everyone, regardless of whether one shares the values of the political movement of Marxism; Marxism is an understanding of the world which develops only within this movement, only in political commitment. For precisely this reason a Marxism understood in this way resists rational argumentation: an outsider cannot effectively criticize it because an outsider cannot fundamentally understand it.

---

31. Robert Havemann, "Warum ich Stalinist war und Antistalinist wurde, 7. Mai 1965," in Hermann Weber, ed., *DDR. Dokumente zur Geschichte der Deutschen Demokratischen Republik, 1945–1985,* 3d ed. (Munich, 1987), 281–82.

32. Kolakowski, 325–26.

The GDR was, of course, a Party dictatorship, and it is easy to believe that GDR *Parteilichkeit* in thought and action was caused by ignorance, fear, censorship, and so on. These factors clearly facilitated *Parteilichkeit* by suppressing many awkward facts at the source. Nevertheless, a great deal of information was available to those who were interested. The mechanism was largely voluntary and responded to the individual communist's or sympathizer's need to sort out irreconcilable facts and to stifle unbearable realities. In fact, the system continues to function among German Communists today, if on a smaller scale. This is demonstrated by a typical letter to the editor of *Neues Deutschland* (once the "central organ" of the SED, now the newspaper of the reform-communist "Party of Democratic Socialism") in 1993 in response to the newspaper's publication of the names of several hundred German Communist émigrés massacred by the Soviet NKVD secret police in the 1930s.[33]

> I have absolutely nothing against coming to terms with the past and publishing documents which until now have been stored away in archives. But even here one question has to stand in the center: *Who benefits?* With the publication of its documentation "Shot by the NKVD," *Neues Deutschland* . . . has done those a favor who from the very beginning—i.e., from 1917 on—were and will remain mortal enemies of the defunct Soviet Union. And what will be the result? All that will be left of the former Soviet Union will be a "criminal state" even worse than Hitler-Germany was. (emphasis added)

So much for "coming to terms with the past"! This is *Parteilichkeit* in its purest form.

The SED demanded a foundation of absolute *Parteilichkeit* both inside and outside its ranks in order to maintain its power. However, since not all East Germans and not even all Party members were as orthodox as the Party wished, it had to devote much of its energy to establishing this orthodoxy in the first place. "Training for Socialist *Parteilichkeit* in thought and action, for the enabling of all toilers to answer correctly the questions of our time from the standpoint of the working class and to champion societal progress, is a principal task of the ideological work of the Marxist-Leninist Party," ideologists proclaimed.[34] *Parteilichkeit* was thus both the starting point and the goal of GDR historiography, language, propaganda, and myth-building in general.

---

33. Horst Lohse, "Wem nützt es?", Letter, ND, 22 June 1993.
34. "Parteilichkeit," 739.

Historiography

GDR historiography has been the object of intense research in recent years.[35] Since this study is not directly concerned with the relative merits or shortcomings of individual historical works and their authors (or, as was usually the case in the GDR, "author collectives"), it will not seek to prolong the discussion. Nevertheless, since historiography provided the historical basis for GDR myth-building, a brief examination of some of the issues is essential.

To the SED, historiography's function was clear.[36]

> Marxist-Leninist historiography is an instrument of the Socialist society for the working out of a scientific *Geschichtsbild* [historical conception] as an essential element of Socialist ideology, which is formed in its entirety by Marxism-Leninism. It must thus be regarded in its practical-political and theoretical-ideological unity with the struggle of the working class and Marxism-Leninism.

From this self-understanding, it is clear that the Marxist-Leninist historians of the GDR were principally involved in the business of providing the SED and its momentary policies with historical legitimacy. This ranged from clear-cut historical propaganda to the general task of rewriting history from the perspective of the working class, that is, from the perspective of the SED. In this way, the Marxist-Leninist functionary class became the subject of world history itself. While this type of work made up the bulk of GDR historical writing, there is no denying that some historians did in fact produce readable works of historical research, especially during the limited ideological opening that began in the mid-1970s. This observation applies above all to innocuous tomes on medieval and early modern history, areas relatively untouched by politics and ideology.[37] But this fact is in no way surprising for it confirms the second principal function of GDR historiography, namely, that of representation abroad. The

---

35. Among the better studies are Günter Heydemann, *Geschichtswissenschaft im geteilten Deutschland* (Frankfurt am Main, 1980); Andreas Dorpalen, *German History in Marxist Perspective: The East German Approach* (Detroit, 1988); Alexander Fischer and Günter Heydemann, eds., *Geschichtswissenschaft in der DDR*, 2 vols. (Berlin, 1990); and Jan Herman Brinks, *Die DDR-Geschichtswissenschaft auf dem Weg zur deutschen Einheit* (Frankfurt am Main, 1992). For a comprehensive overview, see Ulrich Neuhäusser-Wesspy, "Die SED und die deutsche Geschichte," in Ilse Spittmann, ed., *Die SED in Geschichte und Gegenwart* (Cologne, 1987), 98–111.

36. Herausgeberkollektiv, *Einführung in das Studium der Geschichte*, 4th ed. (East Berlin, 1986), 19.

37. See, for example, Georg Iggers, ed., *Marxist Historiography in Transformation. New Orientations in Recent East German History* (New York, 1991).

SED was desperate for international recognition, and its normally flat and parochial historiography had no hope of prevailing at international historians' conferences. Thus a cautious opening in the area of scholarly writing aimed at Western historians did not mean a devaluation of Marxism-Leninism, but instead good public relations.

Given how important historiography was, GDR historians were especially bound to the *Parteilichkeit* principle. In Marxist-Leninist theory, the historian could only be "objective," that is, perform his job, by embracing Marxist-Leninist ideology and emphasizing the historical role of the working class. According to Lenin's classic formulation, "The more *parteilich* scholarship is, the truer and more objective it becomes; the harder and more decisively we maintain the subjective standpoint of the proletariat, the truer and more objective our position will be."[38] Using the closed logic of Marxism-Leninism, *Parteilichkeit* thus meant that the historians recognized the leading role of the SED as the "party of the working class" and subordinated their research and their writing to its policies of the moment.[39]

In practice, *Parteilichkeit* in historiography meant that "in each phase of research, teaching, and propaganda the unity of politics and scholarship must be guaranteed at all times. This unity does not develop automatically but instead must be brought about deliberately. It begins with the laying down of priorities, the development of the research conception, and continues through the methodology, [all the way] to the consideration of the researchers' responsibility for the presentation, transmission, and reception with the greatest mass effectiveness."[40] These guidelines were laid out in five-year plans for history that were worked out by a special ideological commission under Politburo control.

It is easy to exaggerate the amount of political control this really meant. As a former chief ideologist of the historical profession has pointed out in his colleagues' defense, direct political interference in most historical research was not nearly as severe as outsiders imagine. Exceptions to this were politically sensitive projects touching on matters of ideology and Party history, that is, anything touching on real political issues. In these cases control was extremely strict. Otherwise, orders from above were usually of a general nature and political supervision during the phase *between* the assignment of a project and its eventual censorship by an ideological commission was moderate.[41] This point is intriguing—not because of what

---

38. Quoted in I. Fetscher, *Von Marx zur Sowjetideologie* (17/1972), 84.
39. Heydemann, 212.
40. *Einführung in das Studium der Geschichte,* 34.
41. Walter Schmidt, "Geschichte zwischen Professionalität und Politik. Zu zentralen Leitungsstrukturen und -mechanismen in der Geschichtswissenschaft der DDR," in *Zeitschrift für Geschichtswissenschaft* (11/92), p. 1025.

our ideologist intended to suggest about the potential quality of GDR historical writing, but because of how it refutes the concept of "Stalinism." In practice, the SED scarcely needed direct interference. Its historians, as dues-paying SED members and firm believers in the ideals of socialism, were already *parteilich;* otherwise, they never would have been allowed to become historians in the first place, let alone climb the academic ladder. One must also keep in mind the narrow horizons of a profession trained under strict Marxist-Leninist control and shielded from outside influences. Were the historians to abandon their *Parteilichkeit,* the result could have been (and in extremely rare cases was) a ruined career and expulsion from the Party. More significantly, the lucky few with travel privileges were entirely dependent upon the good will of the Party to keep them.

The goal of the Marxist-Leninist "historical conception" (*Geschichtsbild*) worked out by the historians was the socialist "historical consciousness." *Mythology* would be a more accurate term. The *Kleines politisches Wörterbuch* defines historical consciousness as[42]

> part of the social and individual consciousness in which knowledge and experiences of the historical development of the society and the resulting lessons for the future are expressed. Historical consciousness, and the corresponding conception of history, both of which always possess class character, develop through an extremely complex process. . . . The decisive operative factors are the respective dominant political and ideological conceptions as well as the general (history of the people, of the country, etc.) and personal (background, education, experiences, etc.) traditions of the widest variety. Historical consciousness and the conception of history both contain and create concrete historical valuations which, not least as a result of their extraordinarily powerful emotional effectiveness, are of the greatest importance for the ideological-political attitudes and the resulting actions of human beings. Socialist historical consciousness is based upon the scientific world-outlook of the working class, Marxism-Leninism; the historical conception acquired by historical scholarship forms its core.

In the development of this consciousness, the Marxist-Leninist historian understood himself primarily as a propagandist of a *parteilich* conception of history.[43]

---

42. "Geschichtsbewusstsein," in *Kleines politisches Wörterbuch,* 7th ed. (East Berlin, 1988), 319.

43. "Geschichtsbewusstsein," 319

Socialist historical consciousness and the Marxist-Leninist conception of history make a significant contribution to the molding of socialist personalities, especially in the formation of socialist fundamental convictions, in which scientific knowledge and life experience combine and translate into conscious action.

The extraordinarily difficult job of turning these ideas into reality fell primarily to history teachers in the GDR's authoritarian school system (and at a different level, as we will see in the following chapters, to the GDR's youth organizations).[44] The history teacher's "principal task lies in the transmission of the historical conception of the working class and in the education of the pupils for the purposes of the Communist world view and morality. . . . As a *propagandist of Marxism-Leninism* he provides a multifaceted societal activity, through which he actively contributes with his subject to the worldwide class confrontation between Socialism and Imperialism" (emphasis in original).[45] Unlike the party elite, who could afford to devote themselves to loftier issues of world peace and international solidarity, and unlike ordinary citizens, who could at least try to ignore the ideology altogether and get on with their own lives, history and other teachers were on the front lines of the class struggle. They had to propagate and defend the SED's version of reality through a combination of personal charisma, imagination, threats, and dialectical reasoning. Both their own careers and the GDR as a whole depended upon their success in the classroom. Yet their room for maneuver was extremely limited.

Just like Marxist-Leninist ideology itself, history—especially that intended for historical propaganda in the schools and mass organizations—could admit no errors and allow for no doubt concerning the correctness and wisdom of GDR and Soviet policies. "Objectivity" existed only in the Marxist-Leninist term *objectivism,* which meant *Unparteilich-keit* or "taking sides with reaction."[46] According to a directive issued in 1951, a teacher of contemporary history must never

---

44. See Dieter Riesenberger, *Geschichte und Geschichtsunterricht in der DDR* (Göttingen, 1973); Frank Reuter, *Geschichtsbewußtsein in der DDR. Programm und Aktion* (Cologne, 1973); Hans-Georg Wolf, *Zur Entwicklung des Geschichtsunterrichts in der DDR* (Paderborn, 1978); Hans-Dieter Schmid, *Geschichtsunterricht in der DDR. Eine Einführung* (Stuttgart, 1979); Karl Schmitt, *Politische Erziehung in der DDR* (Paderborn, 1980); Bodo von Borries, *Kindlich jugendliche Geschichtsverarbeitung in West- und Ostdeutschland 1990* (Pfaffenweiler, 1990); Körber-Stiftung, eds., *Offenes Geschichtslernen in einer geschlossenen Gesellschaft? Historische Bildung in der DDR* (Berlin 1995).

45. *Einführung in das Studium,* 568–69.

46. Fritz Scheffler, notes on "Objektivismus im Geschichtsunterricht," (1951) SAPMO BArch IV 2/904/92, Bl. 8.

ask his pupils "*Is* the German Democratic Republic a decisive factor in the struggle for peace?"[47]

> This question contains uncertainty. It gives the pupils the possibility of orienting themselves toward "both sides"; that is an example of objectivism.
>   The concrete question must be: "Why is the German Democratic Republic a decisive factor in the struggle for peace?"
>   Now the pupil has the possibility of bringing in evidence on the basis of fact.

In the rarest instances the instructor could allow at best for the existence of long since corrected "excesses." But to ensure the necessary *Parteilichkeit,* popular history systematically reduced complex and potentially controversial events to symbolic events phrased in a special language that permitted only limited discussion and no contradiction. As the West German political scientist Odilo Gudorf writes,[48]

> If, for example, the expression "struggle for the anti-Fascist democratic upheaval" is used [to describe] the Stalinist pre-history of the GDR's foundation, it contains the expression of an ideologically "known" development of history following established laws. Historiography thus does not need to provide a precise definition of [this] revolutionary formula . . . through an exact presentation of the practices by which the SED and the Soviet Military Administration enforced their objectives without legitimacy among the population. It would be considered to be historically irrelevant.

Details could also be subversive. When historians actually attempted detailed popular depictions of complex and controversial events—fully in accord with the *Parteilichkeit* principle—their work could be held up for years by bureaucratic interference and outright censorship by party functionaries. One example of this phenomenon is the monumental *Geschichte der Freien Deutschen Jugend* (History of the Free German Youth), which became the standard history of the youth organization.[49] This book was unusual among institutional histories of its kind for its heavy use of documentary materials and especially photographs to provide a (relatively speaking) realistic depiction of the FDJ. Of course, the book was con-

---

47. Ibid., Bl. 7.
48. Odilo Gudorf, *Sprache als Politik. Untersuchung zur öffentlichen Sprache und Kommunikationsstruktur in der DDR* (Cologne, 1981), 132.
49. Autorenkollektiv, *Geschichte der Freien Deutschen Jugend* (East Berlin, 1982).

ceived from the start as blatant historical propaganda and the historians among its "author collective" were genuinely interested in strengthening the organization by making its history more believable to young people. However, its reliance on detail put the Party's own historical simplifications into question. Furthermore, by providing the "masses" with actual names and faces, it added unwanted contours to the carefully constructed personality cults surrounding Erich Honecker and his associates, who were presented not only as mythic figures but also as real human beings. The book consequently underwent years of revision, and the final product, while still valuable as a reference source, is virtually unreadable. Although a more credible presentation might perhaps have improved the image of socialism, it could only have damaged the Party. Originally intended to appear at the time of the GDR's thirtieth anniversary in 1979, the *Geschichte der FDJ* was withheld from publication for three more years until after the appearance of Erich Honecker's memoirs, which had ideological preeminence.[50]

This distrust of detail contributed to the consistently flat treatment given to socialist heroes. As Andreas Dorpalen wrote, "Marxist historical accounts do have heroes, but the heroes are mouthpieces rather than profiled individuals. Even as the subjects of biographies, outstanding personalities rarely are brought to life, but are depicted primarily in terms of their social functions. The ultimate hero is always the exploited but struggling masses, and above all the industrial working class."[51] This phenomenon represents the application of *Parteilichkeit* to all historical figures, both "progressive" and "reactionary." A true revolutionary both in past times and in the present can only think and act in the interests of "the working class and its Marxist-Leninist Party," and a reactionary can likewise serve only the cause of Capital and Imperialism. Of course, Marxist-Leninist historiography made it possible to dissect controversial historical figures and isolate their "progressive" and "reactionary" aspects. But these aspects were always societal in nature. The examination of personal and especially psychological factors was irrelevant and counterproductive since it challenged the unquestionable authority of the *Parteilichkeit* principle. We will see this factor in action later on in the SED's depiction of such communist heroes as Ernst Thälmann and Artur Becker, and even of such noncommunist "progressive" figures as Goethe and Bach.

Some propagandists understood this problem and fought against it. As one youth propaganda expert wrote, "outstanding personalities are role models because they acquired the ability to prove themselves in

---

50. Interview with Karlheinz Jahnke, Rostock, 1 December 1992.
51. Dorpalen, 43.

difficult situations, to master conflicts, to learn from mistakes, to take to heart the advice and critical remarks of friends and comrades. In a word: role models must not be presented without fault and blemish, without problems and difficulties; for one should be able to identify oneself with role models."[52]

But such attempts were ultimately futile. After all, would Artur Becker, the communist martyr of the Spanish civil war, have thought it worthwhile dying for the decrepit Honecker regime of the 1980s? It was best not even to think about it. This was the dilemma of historical myth-building. *Parteilichkeit* demanded the stifling of details and imagination. Bureaucratic routine was rewarded while sincere devotion to the socialist cause remained suspect. A genuinely interesting historical account could lead to new and potentially embarrassing questions. Myth-building had to be tendentious and dull to protect the SED's tenuous hold on power. Nevertheless, if it was to be believable and create the required historical consciousness, it had to be emotional and make concessions to human individuality and complexity. Thus myth-building regularly choked on its own contradictions. While the Marxist-Leninist conception of history provided the SED with the legitimacy it needed in order to govern, these contradictions also planted the seed for the regime's destruction in 1989.

"The Awful German Language," GDR-style

Perhaps the most striking feature of GDR mythology is the appalling rhetorical style of its purveyors. Since this rhetoric did not derive from simple poor style but rather from the inner workings of the SED itself, it is worthwhile to take a closer look at this aspect of GDR myth-building.

According to one disillusioned former SED member, the former GDR can be reduced to three component parts: the Wall, the Soviets, and the *Stasi* Secret Police. While this view is cynical, it accurately points to the three pillars of the SED's power. Nevertheless, it neglects a fourth, equally essential dimension: language. No study of the GDR is complete without an examination of its peculiar adaptation of what Mark Twain once called "the awful German language." A distinctive history, a distinctive ideology, and propaganda are not enough to create a different society. It was, after all, language that set the GDR apart from the Federal Republic and created its identity. GDR myth-building was based upon language. In fact, it is only a slight exaggeration to claim that the GDR itself was largely a linguistic construction. Everyone used the language at one time or

52. Rolf Döhring, "Studien zur Rolle des marxistisch-leninistischen Weltbildes für die sozialistische Bewusstseinsbildung Jugendlicher" (Diss., Institut für Gesellschaftswissenschaften beim ZK der SED, Berlin, n.d. [mid-1970s]), 85.

another, and thus everyone literally paid lip service to the ideology and the regime it supported.

Mythology, as Roland Barthes once pointed out, is a form of language, and language itself is at the core of any mythic system.[53] In the GDR, as in any other society, language at some point gave expression to myths, which in turn transformed the language, which in turn further developed the myths, and so on. The German philosopher Ernst Cassirer described this endless cycle in his book *Language and Myth.*[54]

> If myth be really . . . nothing but the darkening shadow which language throws upon thought, it is mystifying indeed that this shadow should appear ever as in an aura of its own light, should evolve a positive vitality and activity of its own, which tends to eclipse what we commonly call the immediate reality of *things,* so that even the wealth of empirical, sensuous experience pales before it. As Wilhelm von Humboldt has said in connection with the language problem: "Man lives with his objects chiefly—in fact, since his feeling and acting depends on his perceptions, one may say exclusively—as language presents them to him. By the same process whereby he spins language out of his own being, he ensnares himself in it; and each language draws a magic circle round the people to which it belongs, a circle from which there is no escape save by stepping out of it into another."

The SED spun much of its language out of its own being during its long reign in the GDR. But even more important influences were the rhetoric of Marx, Engels, and Lenin, the omnipresent Soviet example, the lingering memory of the rhetoric of the Third Reich, as well as the peculiarities of "the awful German language" itself.

The use of melodrama and heightened moralism in public rhetoric are two of the many techniques that the SED carried over from the Third Reich. The Dresden philologist Victor Klemperer observed this phenomenon shortly after the war. "For example," he writes in his book *LTI* ("Lingua Tertii Imperii," or "the language of the Third Reich"), "how many times since May 1945 have I heard talk—in radio speeches, at impassioned anti-Fascist rallies—of 'character' attributes, or about the 'militant' nature of democracy! Those are all expressions from the center—the Third Reich would say 'from the middle of being'—of the LTI."[55]

But intentional borrowings from the Nazis were fairly rare, for this

53. Roland Barthes, *Mythologies* (Paris, 1957), 91.
54. Ernst Cassirer, *Language and Myth* (New York, 1946), 9.
55. Victor Klemperer, *LTI. Lingua Tertii Imperii. Die Sprache des Dritten Reiches* (Leipzig, 1975), 20

rhetorical style was rooted in Marxist-Leninist ideology itself. GDR rhetoric greatly surpassed Third Reich rhetoric in its incessant high-mindedness, its dedication to good-doing. After all, the Nazis sought to do good only to Germany and the "Aryan race," or destroy themselves (and the rest of Europe) in the attempt. Communism itself was incessantly defined, in the Soviet author Nikolai Ostrovsky's words, as "the most glorious thing in the world—the struggle for the liberation of humanity."[56] Socialism was the sum of all that was good and generous in human history, and only an ignoramus, a madman, or a criminal could claim otherwise. Such a lofty goal meant that SED leaders and functionaries expended considerable energy in trying to persuade East Germans and the rest of the world that their policies were not merely expedient—since other policies might be more expedient—but were at all times devoted to "the liberation of humanity." The flip side of all this goodness was of course the isolation cell of the *Stasi* prison or the border guard's bullet, but even these were for a good cause: "watchfulness" in the first case, "peace" in the second. GDR functionaries hardly ever viewed their interference in other people's private affairs as oppression, but always had the best interests of "our young people" or "our toilers" at heart.[57] The inevitable result of this high-mindedness was a distinctively moralistic and priggish rhetorical style, which after 1949 at the very latest colored nearly all public discourse in the GDR.[58]

---

56. On Ostrovsky's importance in the FDJ's propaganda work, see chapter 4.

57. Typical of this phenomenon is the following letter from a former *Stasi* officer to the editors of *Neues Deutschland* on the touchy question of *Stasi* informers: "The mass of former MfS (Ministry for State Security) officers recruited persons for the MfS out of conviction in order to eliminate flaws and abuses in the society through their help. These informal employees/societal employees served mostly, but not exclusively, as informers. They were assigned (to spy on) persons on the basis of their personal ability to eliminate the abuses, and their personal influence." The officer concludes: "As far as I personally am concerned, my main guilt lies in the fact that I supervised and indirectly personally wronged persons who likewise wanted nothing else than to eliminate abuses." By this he means the informers, not those being informed on. Uwe Meissner, Letter, ND 18 May 1993. I experienced this attitude myself while trying to get my wife and children out of the GDR in 1988. What I saw as pure chicanery from the GDR bureaucracy, the various officials assured me was all in my wife's best interests. Once in the United States after six months of waiting, the same officials saw to it that we were provided with a free subscription to *Neue Heimat,* the GDR's colorfully illustrated monthly overseas propaganda magazine.

58. This obsession with goodness was by no means limited to the GDR and the cold war era as a whole. As Paul Fussell writes about Allied literature and rhetoric during World War II, "If each member of the Allies was engaged on God's work, there arose from time to time uncertainty about one's entire moral worthiness for the task. Are we virtuous enough? This became the anxious question implied in many wartime attempts to understand what was going on. One had to be aware of an obligation not just to buy war bonds and stamps but to be consciously a virtuous person at all times." Paul Fussell, *Wartime: Understanding and Behavior in the Second World War* (New York, 1989), 167–68.

The language of the GDR, even more than the language of the Third Reich, was characterized by an inflation of superlatives. Everything relating to the Soviet Union was *ausserordentlich* (extraordinary), the Red Army was always *ruhmreich* (glorious), the Revolution always *siegreich* (victorious), every contribution was *massgeblich* (decisive), every certainty *unerschütterlich* (unshakeable). This practice did not merely reflect fanaticism or wishful thinking, but was part of a deliberate strategy to stifle discussion. By the same token, the GDR was always *unsere sozialistische DDR* (our socialist GDR) and Wilhelm Pieck always *unser beliebter Präsident* (our beloved president). The word *our* implied intimacy, and the words *socialist* and *beloved* suggested a self-evident unity of pretension and reality.

The *Parteilichkeit* of official GDR language is obvious from its avoidance of indirect discourse and the subjunctive (e.g., "Lenin said that the working class would . . ."). Both linguistic techniques, especially when combined in standard German usage, suggest a distancing on the part of the speaker from the subject matter being described. This manner of speech was potentially subversive, since it allowed for the individual interpretation of nondebatable issues. This explains the SED's heavy use of endless direct quotations by Lenin, Stalin, Honecker, and other figures where a simple paraphrase would otherwise have sufficed (e.g., "Lenin said: 'The working class will . . . !' ").[59]

At the same time, the SED made heavy use of the passive voice in its specifically heavy-handed, impersonal German form. The result was a style that was at once bureaucratic, technocratic, and priggish. For example, in an encyclopedia article detailing the prevalence of criminality in capitalist society, the author pointed out that under socialism "there is being developed a new relationship of the individual to society which rests on a fundamental harmony of interests and which is increasingly being expressed in relationships of comradely co-operation, mutual respect, help, and responsibility."[60] This technique got the ideological message across but nothing else. The reader or listener could either accept this assertion *in toto* or reject it *in toto,* thereby taking sides with either the cause of socialism or "reaction." Since no details were offered, no discussion could take place.

The language of the GDR was also affected by Soviet influences, although much less than the language of the FRG was affected by Anglicisms. These were most obvious in the GDR's direct adoption and Germanization of such Soviet terms as *Intelligenz* (intelligentsia), *Kulturhaus*

---

59. Cf. Karl Friedrich Boree, "Die Sprachentartung in der Sowjetzone," *SBZ-Archiv* 3 (1953): 24.

60. "Kriminalität," in *Kleines politisches Wörterbuch,* 545.

(house of culture), and *Volkskorrespondent* (people's correspondent, meaning a Marxist-Leninist journalist). More important was the subtle redefinition and encoding that familiar words underwent under SED rule. These words cannot easily be translated, since their meaning exists only within Marxist-Leninist ideology. For example, *democratic* (as in the expressions "German *Democratic* Republic," "*democratic* centralism," or "the *Democratic* Sector"—an early euphemism for East Berlin) can only be translated as "dictatorial," since "democracy" in the Marxist-Leninist view could only be realized under the "dictatorship of the proletariat." In practical terms, "true democracy" (as opposed to bourgeois "formal democracy," meaning "capitalism") could only exist under SED leadership.[61]

Likewise, the term *free* (as in "*Free* German Youth" or "*Free* German Trade Union Federation") meant "Marxist-Leninist." In ideological terms, freedom had no abstract existence but was instead the "relationship of man to objective laws," and was thus a "specifically societal category." In Friedrich Engels's standard definition, freedom was "the recognition of necessity." It developed through the subordination of the individual to natural and societal laws. To an SED ideologist, Western-style freedom meant "chaos," and "free elections" meant "freedom to vote for reactionaries and fascists." Thus freedom could only be achieved after "the consolidation of the political power of the working class and its alliance with the class of cooperative peasants and all other working people."[62]

Progressive specifically meant "communist," since the communist movement under the leadership of the Soviet Union embodied all societal and scientific progress and would inevitably achieve victory, while the anachronistic imperialist order was destined to die out.

The use of these terms in this way might sound cynical, but is really *parteilich.* The intentions behind this usage were the very best. Until socialism had been perfected, the words were a weapon in the class struggle. Thus a term like *German Democratic Republic* was not derision. It was a daily lesson in Marxist-Leninist ideology.

Official rhetoric in the GDR was also characterized by the heavy use of euphemisms to deflect attention from unpleasant facts by using words and phrases implying harmlessness and normality. This process is best illustrated by the most memorable symbol of SED rule, the Berlin Wall. Its official titles were the melodramatic "*Antifaschistischer Schutzwall*" (Antifascist defensive wall) or the euphemistic "*Staatsgrenze der DDR*" (State border of the GDR). The construction of the Wall in 1961 was

---

61. "Demokratie," in *Kleines politisches Wörterbuch,* 7th ed. (East Berlin, 1988), 179.
62. "Freiheit," in *Kleines politisches Wörterbuch,* 291–93.

officially described as the *"Sicherung der Staatsgrenze der DDR zu Westberlin"* (securing of the state border of the GDR to West Berlin). Since every state secures its borders in one way or another (a point the SED made at every opportunity), the term expressed the normality and international recognition the regime longed for. However, a leap over the Berlin Wall or the fortified inner German border was not prosaically called *Flucht* (escape), but *Republikflucht* (Republic desertion, by analogy with the military term *Fahnenflucht,* or desertion). By consequence, a successful practitioner of this crime was not a *Flüchtling* (refugee), but a *Republikflüchtiger* (Republic deserter). It was the use of such ideologically colored euphemisms, combined with a bureaucratic terminology, which made both the Wall and its victims possible in a "humanistic" society.

However, an outside observer would be wrong to imagine that language was nothing more than a one-sided instrument of SED oppression. Language is always a two-way medium, even in dictatorships, and the advantages of such a culture of dishonesty to those clever enough to exploit it are obvious (and the GDR schools and mass organizations were marvelous teachers of dissemblance). The SED did not want trouble from the population and so made compliance fairly simple. A skillful practitioner of this language could easily cover up his own indifference, sloth, or even subversion by spouting back well-measured doses of hollow SED rhetoric. In his novel *The Wall Jumper,* the West German author Peter Schneider illustrates this phenomenon in the apocryphal tale of a young East Berlin worker who gets himself into serious political trouble with the police. In order to get himself out of it again, he simply showers his persecutors with pompous and melodramatic prosocialist and pro-Soviet propaganda slogans. "From then on I had peace and quiet! Scout's honor! What were they supposed to do? Why, they aren't allowed to doubt!"[63]

The two-sidedness of the GDR language had critical implications for myth-building. Since myth-building was based mostly upon language, it ensured that the myth-building itself worked both ways. A typical example of this process was the ritual Young Pioneer responsive slogan *"Seid bereit!"*—*"Immer bereit!"* (Be prepared!—Ever prepared!). The Young Pioneer group leader's incantation of *Seid bereit!* expressed the SED's claim upon youth's unswerving cooperation in its struggle for socialism and communism. But when the Young Pioneers themselves (who had no say in the matter) invariably responded with a rousing *Immer bereit!,* they in turn built up the SED's myth of its own infallibility. It is thus incorrect to describe the culture spawned by the GDR language merely as one of fear or dishonesty. It is more accurate to call it a culture of mutual deception.

---

63. Peter Schneider, *Der Mauerspringer* (Darmstadt, 1985), 100.

Socialist Collectivism and Mass Events

It is a commonplace that communist and other modern societies depend on the masses for self-representation and legitimacy. Religious movements have always relied on the suggestive power of mass rituals and processions. The use of mass events as an instrument of mass politics dates back at least as far as the French Revolution and was perfected in the Soviet Union and by the KPD of the Weimar era. The Nazis in turn adopted the mass event in grand style, most notably in their spectacular Nuremberg rallies. But the concept of the masses transcends mere decoration. Just as the GDR only really existed in its own special language, its citizens only really experienced socialism in its mass events. As described by Elias Canetti in his classic study of the masses and power, the infectious fascination of the "rhythmic mass" derives from its constant desire to grow even larger, the feeling of equality it creates within its boundaries, its great density, and its movement toward a goal. "It is in movement and is moving toward something. The direction, which is common to all members, strengthens the feeling of equality. A goal, which lies outside of each individual and which comes together for all, drives the private, unequal goals, which would be the death of the mass, underground. For its maintenance the direction is essential. The fear of dissolution, which is always active inside of it, makes it possible to steer it toward a variety of goals. The mass exists as long as it has an unattained goal."[64] This is the very essence of the Marxist-Leninist ideal of socialism.

In daily life in the GDR, mass society was represented by the "collective." If the concept of council (or "Soviet") democracy was rejected from the beginning in favor of the dictatorship of the SED, GDR society was nevertheless strictly coordinated in a network of overlapping collectives: work collectives, research collectives, author collectives, youth collectives, peasant collectives, Party collectives, and so on. The collectives helped facilitate work, socialization, surveillance, and indoctrination.[65] The idea of the collective was derived from Marxist-Leninist ideology and from the "cradle to grave" workers' culture of the Weimar era, but also reflected the cult-like, conspiratorial ideal of the SED and Communist Parties everywhere, whose members always address each other in the informal *du* form and are trained to think always in terms of *we* and never *I*. Collectivism was not merely an organizational form but pervaded all of East German society, where individual rights consistently yielded to collective rights, and individual truths to the collective truths of GDR mythology. It was in

---

64. Elias Canetti, *Masse und Macht* (Frankfurt am Main, 1980), 26–27.
65. Lydia Lange, "Kollektiv, wo bist du hin?" *Die Zeit,* 5 November 1993.

collectives of various sorts that most of the myth-building took place. FDJ clubhouses and "Socialist Circles," in which FDJ members studied for the "good knowledge" test, were just such collectives. The myth-building slogans and speeches documented in this study lose most of their impact when read silently to oneself. They were not really designed for private study. Even if they had been, most FDJ members did not read the political and propagandistic sections of *Junge Welt* of their own accord. But they were forced to read and discuss them in meetings of their collectives. And when presented by a skillful and thoroughly *parteilich* youth agitator, with a straight face and a firm voice, even the driest anecdote from the most recent Party congress could come alive.

But as important as indoctrination in the collectives was, it was in the SED's periodic mass events that actual myth-building took place. Communist mass events were normally conceived as the climax of nationwide propaganda campaigns or "socialist competitions" of various kinds. They were characterized by seas of hundreds of red and blue flags, banners, slogans, giant portraits of political figures, torches, agitprop floats, giant peace doves, surface-to-air missiles, and so forth. These events created the atmosphere of a permanent state of emergency. At a mass event, otherwise dull or unpersuasive material became exciting, persuasive, and enthralling—at least for the duration of the event. The sight of thousands of blue-uniformed FDJ members marching, rhythmically clapping their hands over their heads, and shouting the praises of the government could be thrilling, even if one had not particularly cared for the government until that moment. Mass demonstrations sometimes counted seven hundred thousand participants and more. Parades past the reviewing stand in East Berlin could last up to eight hours. The great peace demonstration on the East Berlin *Marx-Engels-Platz* during the Third World Youth Festival in 1951 counted one and a half million participants.[66] Among such masses of singing, chanting human beings everything seemed possible. Dissent became unthinkable. The fascination of such elaborate, colorful events in an otherwise colorless GDR was extremely powerful, especially among young people. It was a wonderful privilege to know for certain that you and thousands of others just like you were *right*.[67]

As exciting as these events often were for ordinary citizens, the ritualized adulation of the masses had an intoxicating effect on the GDR's leaders and gave them a dizzying sense of omnipotence for which there is no other plausible explanation. The events created the illusion of unity

---

66. *Geschichte der Freien Deutschen Jugend. Chronik,* 2d ed. (East Berlin, 1978), 84.

67. For several evocative descriptions of the atmosphere of GDR mass events, see Ralph Giordano, *Die Partei hat immer Recht. Ein Erlebnisbericht über den Stalinismus auf deutschem Boden* (Cologne, 1961).

between the Party and the masses. Doubts evaporated at the sight of thousands of smiling, waving young people. Mass events were the opiate of the Party. The imposition of mass propaganda had the same effect on propagandists, whose job it was to make the illusion work. As one FDJ functionary wrote approvingly in his dissertation, "Only by means of the ideological work of the mass organizations under the leadership of the united workers' party was it possible to gain influence over the thinking of millions of heads. Only in this way could the theory grab hold of the masses and become a material force."[68]

Organizational life in the GDR was characterized by incessant furious activity and ever-larger mass events. In the Honecker era the events seem to have lost some of their ideological bite, and many former East Germans describe them as mammoth social events where people met their friends and often fell in love. The events had a Mardi Gras atmosphere. Mass youth events invariably included exciting sporting events, and there were usually parties and dancing offered afterward. The SED successfully transformed mass events into a part of the GDR's mass culture, in which the ideological content of the events was largely taken for granted. In this form they served a critical socializing function. One of the most interesting phenomena one can observe in the former GDR is the way former Party members, FDJ secretaries, and so on actually measure past time: not by years, but by youth festivals, FDJ parliaments, and other such mass events, much the way certain traditional societies keep track of time by noting floods and lunar eclipses.

The SED and its mass organizations generally gave themselves high marks in their internal reports on the results of their mass campaigns and mass events. While these reports undoubtedly reflect a great deal of book-cooking (which was a matter of self-preservation, since unsatisfactory propaganda was invariably blamed on its organizers, never on its ideological content), they are probably largely accurate. SED and FDJ functionaries were all the more downcast about the apathy of their charges between events, and that is why each new mass event had to be more opulent than the last.

The Limits of Ideological Control

This examination of the parameters of myth-building raises the inevitable question of how seriously SED members and East Germans as a whole actually took these Marxist-Leninist thought structures and the language

---

68. Jürgen Pfeiffer, "Die Schulungsarbeit der FDJ von den Anfängen der antifaschistisch-demokratischen Jugendarbeit 1945 bis zum III. Parlament der FDJ 1949" (Diss., Rostock, 1975), 16.

in which they were expressed. How successful was this myth-building program in the GDR? Unfortunately, it is almost impossible to check the success or failure of the Party's public image with any kind of statistical accuracy. The SED was always leery of public opinion polls. While the Politburo on Ulbricht's urging created a public opinion institute in 1965 and conducted scores of polls on various issues, the Honecker regime showed little interest in the personal views of its subjects. In 1979 the institute was closed and its archive duly shredded.[69] The few reports that survive reveal a general passive acceptance of the SED dictatorship and the ideals of socialism. In fact, there is virtually no evidence at all of widespread opposition to the SED before the start of the GDR's long decline in the early 1980s. Moreover, the polls themselves shed little light on the themes examined here, and even if they did the methodological problems of these opinion polls put their results into serious question. For example, when poll takers in 1967 asked Berlin factory workers, "In your opinion, to what social order does the future in all of Germany belong?" 74.8 percent answered "socialism," and only 5.4 percent answered "capitalism."[70] Such a result says nothing about how it was attained and what "socialism" and "capitalism" actually meant to Berlin factory workers. The same problem applies to the reports of the Leipzig Institute for Youth Research, established in the mid-1970s. Nevertheless, some studies have brought interesting results. For example, in 1967 a West German scholar studied four hundred thousand East German students between 1952 and 1963, of whom fifteen thousand escaped to the West. The scholar determined that 5 percent of the students who remained were committed socialist activists, 10 percent were careerists, 15 percent were opponents, and 70 percent had arranged themselves with the system.[71] Careful studies carried out by the Institute for Youth Research during the 1970s and early 1980s show similar results: until the mid-1980s approximately 80 percent of young people surveyed strongly identified themselves with the GDR and its proclaimed ideals. This acceptance changed beginning around 1985, when Gorbachev's reforms began and the conservative GDR fell into its terminal crisis.[72] However, one of the Leipzig reports, dealing with young people's views of Fascism in the late 1980s, is presented in depth in chapter 3. If FDJ officials had forgotten why they were not expected to disclose their members' "objective" attitudes, they were reminded on 9 October 1989,

---

69. Heinz Niemann, *Meinungsforschung in der DDR. Die geheimen Berichte des Instituts für Meinungsforschung an das Politbüro der SED* (Cologne, 1993), 16–21.

70. Niemann, 148.

71. Ernst Richert, *Sozialistische Universität* (West Berlin, 1967), 247–48.

72. Peter Förster, "Weltanschaulich-politisches Bewusstsein," in Walter Friedrich and Hartmut Griese, eds., *Jugend und Jugendforschung in der DDR* (Opladen, 1991), 135–50.

when a delegation made up of the leaders of both youth groups presented Honecker with a devastating report on young people's attitudes toward the SED. "This is the first time in the history of the GDR," Honecker snapped, "that the FDJ leadership has joined together to attack the policies of the Party and its Central Committee!"[73] Honecker went on to order the firing of several leading functionaries.

Except for scattered survey data and occasional internal reports, it is nearly impossible to gather objective evidence on the success or failure of such a subjective phenomenon as a state-supporting mythology. Instead, I will concentrate almost entirely on the SED's attempt to develop a distinct mythology in the GDR.

But if objective evidence is lacking, what can we say about this phenomenon? Seen from today, the SED's myth-building program was an obvious failure. As the events of 1989 and 1990 demonstrated, the myths described here never came close to making the GDR into, as it were, "a machine that would run of itself." But one could also say the same of the East German economy, which was once counted among the ten most advanced in the world. Like the planned economy, East German myth-building was conceived within a narrow set of parameters. The GDR was by definition a dictatorship, held together by the supreme control of the Party and its mass organizations, strict police and *Stasi* control, kept in place by the Berlin Wall and the fortified inner German border, and backed up by a half million Soviet troops stationed on its soil. The events of 1989 were not supposed to happen, and until they did the myths served the Party fairly well. While never a success by Western standards, the GDR had the highest standard of living among all the socialist states. The GDR, whose leadership craved acceptance, gradually gained wide international recognition as seen by the numerous state visits, medals, and honorary doctorates that Erich Honecker presented to an incredulous home television public toward the end of his career.

In any case, the Party's control of the non-*parteilich* was by no means total. The ready availability of Western radio and later television broadcasts throughout most of the GDR instantly neutralized the regime's pretensions for those who cared to tune in and take seriously what they heard and saw. The presence of state-run foreign currency shops filled with Western goods and accessible only to people with Western connections represented a state-sanctioned contradiction of the Party's permanently optimistic economic forecasts and destroyed the Party's promise of equality. A bad experience, such as a politically motivated demotion or the arrest of a

---

73. Cited in Gerd-Rüdiger Stephan, "'Wir brauchen Perestroika und Glasnost für die DDR.' Zur Reflexion des Zustands der Gesellschaft durch die Leipziger Jugendforschung 1987–1989," in DA, vol. 28, no. 7 (July 1995): 721–33.

friend, could shatter the illusion in an instant. For a sizable minority of East Germans, letters and visits by Western friends and family members, religious beliefs and church affiliation, the quiet weekends spent in the suburban allotment garden, and withdrawal into private "niches" and friendship circles all helped preserve an independent spirit.

Unfortunately, it is impossible to ascertain what percentage of East Germans consciously believed what they were taught, to the extent that they gave the matter any serious thought at all. It is likely that a small percentage believed everything they were told and that an equally small percentage believed nothing. A sizable majority of East Germans and many foreign visitors consciously believed in certain aspects of the ideology and accepted others without thinking. Since the system of "really existing Socialism" in the GDR placed greater weight on compliance than on conviction, this represents a triumphant victory of Marxist-Leninist indoctrination. After all, compliance is by nature *parteilich*. Individualistic socialist idealism in a time of changing party lines is fundamentally subversive, and the SED did not need any more Wolfgang Leonhardts or Robert Havemanns.

A future historian might be forgiven for imagining that the SED's overwhelming propaganda apparatus, with its endless spree of parades and pamphlets, red banners and empty rhetoric, *was* the GDR. Of course, this would be a distortion. For all but the most ideologically blindered, the mythology—along with economic and social policy—was a means to an end, namely the creation of an ideal classless society. The mythology was the lubricant that kept the gravely maladjusted wheels of the SED dictatorship from squeaking too loudly. But all machines need lubricant, and myth-building is a crucial and largely unexplored aspect of GDR history. It would be worth looking at for this reason alone. Surely anyone dealing with either German history or the new united Germany should be aware of East German mythology, which formed so much of the texture of GDR life. Former members of the FDJ may enjoy reliving their youth in these pages. But this study was not born out of an antiquarian interest in old FDJ events. After all, the speeches delivered at Thälmann ceremonies and Goethe retrospectives were extremely forgettable and are long since forgotten. But the mindset they engendered lives on for millions of eastern Germans, as well as for many foreign observers. Most of the people who were exposed to the GDR socialization process described here are still with us today, as school teachers, civil servants, journalists, officers, mayors, and national political leaders, and many see little need to question their upbringing. Many outsiders take this mindset to be a nostalgia for the Ulbricht-Honecker era, although in reality very few eastern Germans really wish to return to those days. Instead, the legacy of myth-building is a distinctive outlook on life, an unmistakably East German use of language, a vast constellation of shattered dreams and hurt feelings, a widespread distrust of "Western" values, a general inability to look critically at the recent past and at one's own role in it, a unique setting of priorities molded by forty years of life in a socialist society and unremitting assaults by the SED's myth-building machine. For better or worse, the new united Germany now lives with this legacy.

In the introduction to his book *Wartime,* a study of American and British culture during World War II, Paul Fussell writes: "The damage the war visited upon bodies and buildings, planes and tanks and ships, is obvious. Less obvious is the damage it did to intellect, discrimination, honesty, individuality, complexity, ambiguity, and irony, not to mention privacy and wit."[74] This observation applies also to the cold war, whose damage list for all the nations participating in it—East and West—would have to be extended to include "a sense of proportion." Physical evidence of the East German experience is vanishing every day, but this hidden damage will linger long after the GDR's decayed cities have been rebuilt and its antiquated factories have been either torn down or retooled. These "other losses" are, in the end, the subject of this study.

---

74. Paul Fussell, *Wartime: Understanding and Behavior in the Second World War* (New York, 1989), ix.

CHAPTER 2

In Goethe's Footsteps:
The Myth of *Kultur*

It is essential to develop German youth into honest, upright human beings who are worthy of a people which has brought forth such men as Goethe, Schiller, Heine, Marx, Engels, Beethoven, Thomas and Heinrich Mann, Johannes R. Becher, and others.

—*KPD proclamation, 1945*[1]

Defend the great German Kulturerbe *against the disgrace of American cultural and moral degeneracy!*

—*FDJ slogan, 1950*[2]

The image that most non-*parteilich* Westerners took home after visiting the GDR was one of guard dogs and barbed wire, goose-stepping soldiers, Soviet military convoys rumbling over potholed roads, and bookstores clogged with shelf after shelf of Marxist-Leninist primers printed on bad paper. But—was there not also another GDR? A highly literate land, offering inexpensive literary editions that people actually read, with more than eighty orchestras offering subsidized tickets and playing to full houses? A land without violent films, without MTV, and without video-cassette recorders? A land dedicated to the cultivation of every aspect of the German cultural heritage? In short, was not the GDR, despite everything else one could say about it, nevertheless a country where Goethe still mattered?

This was indeed one face of the GDR, but it would be mistaken to assume that this image was merely a happy by-product of "really existing

---

1. "Erlass der SMA, die Bildung antifaschistischer Jugendkomitees zu erlauben," *Deutsche Volkszeitung,* 1 August 1945.

2. "Losungen zum Deutschland-Treffen der Jugend, 12.4.50.," SAPMO BArch NL 36/727.

Socialism." It would also be misguided to attribute the SED's intense recy-
cling of past culture entirely to the grayness of contemporary life in the
GDR, to a lack of new ideas, or to the stifling effects of pervasive government censorship. Instead, the GDR's myth of *Kultur* was carefully built up
between 1945 and 1989. *Kultur* was the founding myth of the GDR. Even
if it was later overtaken by the myths of antifascism, German–Soviet
friendship, and the Socialist fatherland, it remained at the core of GDR
identity—internal and external—until the very end.

It may seem odd to speak of German high culture as a myth, as if it
did not exist. German high culture does exist. However, this study is not
concerned with the relative merits of German high culture vis-à-vis, say,
French or Italian high culture. As always, it is concerned with the expedi-
ence, not the absolute reality, of a given myth. Hence the myth of culture
in its uniquely German form: *Kultur*. *Kultur, Kulturerbe* (cultural legacy),
and *Kulturgut* (cultural asset) are key words of what Harold D. Lasswell
has called the "language of power."[3] They have long served the same function in German society as the concepts of "rights," "freedom," "democracy," and "equality" in the public discourse of the United States. Hardly
anyone denies that the latter concepts exist, or at least should exist, even if
there will never be complete agreement on what they actually mean. But
their use is inflationary. In day-to-day use they are more often propagated
than they are practiced, and serve mainly to foster group identity. They are
used most often by persons who combine the least understanding of cultural issues with the greatest need of them for the sake of political legitimacy: "We have freedom (or *Kultur*, or anything else) but you never will
unless you start listening to us." Marxist-Leninists certainly have no
monopoly on this sort of cant. During the cold war, the greatest preachers
of (in Brecht's phrase) *"Freiheit und democracy"* abroad might indeed have
memorized the first line of Lincoln's Gettysburg address, but could at the
same time ignore the plight of the poor in their own country. With *Kultur,*
the SED could systematically elevate bad taste to a state art form and pursue the sovietization of all aspects of life, all the while singing the praises of
Heine and Handel. Neither group was aware of any contradiction.

The myth of *Kultur* reached its apogee with the German cultural pes-
simists of the early twentieth century, but existed long before and is still
with us today.[4] It basically asserts that Goethe, Schiller, Bach, Beethoven,
and associates are in fact *representative* of Germany, rather than, as one
might think, absolutely *exceptional*. *Kultur* is profound. *Kultur* is authen-

3. Cf. Harold D. Lasswell et al., eds., *The Language of Politics* (New York, 1949), 13.
4. See George L. Mosse, *The Crisis of German Ideology. Intellectual Origins of the Third Reich* (New York, 1964), 6–7; Mosse, "Culture, Civilization and German Antisemitism," *Germans and Jews* (Detroit, 1987), 34–60.

tic. *Kultur* is organic. It is firmly rooted in the German soul and in German soil, as opposed to the superficial *Zivilisation* of the Western world. In its crudest but most prevalent form, *Kultur* is a badge of distinction that every German can wear after mastering a few names and concepts. Unlike such controversial distinctions as ethnic background, social class, or party affiliation, the possession and public display of *Kultur* elevates the individual to a universally admired elite group, and it does this without giving him a bad conscience. It makes him, if not superior, at least equal to members of the cultural elites of other nations. More important, *Kultur* is power. Whoever commands *Kultur* also commands respect. *Kultur* is the key to academic recognition. Traditionally, no one seeking power and respectability in Germany could do so without paying due homage to the myth of *Kultur*.

In the Federal Republic of Germany (FRG), *Kultur* set West Germans apart from the rest of the world, especially from Americans (who, one still occasionally hears, by definition "have no culture"), and made them feel culturally superior despite whatever else they lacked. For the first decade or so of the FRG's existence, its leaders regularly emphasized their state's roots in the German classical heritage. Of course, it might appear that the Germans' lapse into the barbarism of National Socialism might nullify many of the claims of *Kultur*. Yet by virtue of its tremendous profundity and absolute uniqueness, German *Kultur* has also served as a kind of alibi for Hitler (who was, after all, an Austrian). The unspoken motto of cultured West Germans has always been: "Yes, we may have had Hitler once, but we will always have Bach, Beethoven, Goethe, Schiller, etc." The Swiss author Max Frisch recognized this alibi function in 1949. "It is not surprising, but it is horrifying," Frisch wrote, "how many letters from Germany represent this very intellectual type; whenever the German question is discussed they constantly mention Goethe, Hölderlin, Beethoven, Mozart and all the others which Germany has brought forth, and it almost always takes place to the same effect: genius as alibi. Fundamentally it is the harmless-revolting concept that a people has culture if it has symphonies, and in the same circle belongs of course that lofty concept of the artist, who, free of all contemporaneity [*Zeitgenossenschaft*] lives entirely in the spheres of pure intellect, so that in other matters he can freely be a rascal, for example as a citizen, and as a member of human society generally. He is simply a priest of the Eternal, which will surely outlast its daily betrayal."[5] Today, many western German critics regularly denounce the American television miniseries *Holocaust, Schindler's List,* and subsequent

---

5. Max Frisch, "Kultur als Alibi," in *Gesammelte Werke in zeitlicher Folge,* Hans Mayer, ed., vol. II (Frankfurt am Main, 1986), 341.

films on this topic as "American *Kitsch*," and as such beneath their dignity—as if the categories of *Kultur* and *Kitsch* were more relevant to the
subject matter than more troubling concepts such as "collective guilt" and
"collective shame," let alone "collective responsibility."

If *Kultur* served as a stabilizing myth in the Federal Republic, it was
the central stabilizing and mobilizing myth of the SBZ and of the GDR
during the "Antifascist Democratic Upheaval" and the "Construction of
Socialism." There it had a slightly different meaning: "*You* have Hitler,
but *we* have Bach, Beethoven, Goethe, Schiller, etc." And since the SED
classified its state as "internationalist," the GDR was the heir to the best of
world culture as well.

What follows is hardly intended to be history of GDR cultural policy,
which would go far beyond the parameters of this study.[6] Instead, we shall
examine what the Party and youth organizations did with and to the *Kultur* myth. This myth-building strategy was a paradox: it combined the
clichés of Spenglerian cultural pessimism and bourgeois self-representation with all the excesses of Marxist-Leninist *Parteilichkeit* and language
as described in chapter 1. It combined the highest idealism with the most
cynical political manipulation. It is doubly tragic: in the way it betrayed
the dreams of the émigré generation and in its disastrous effects on the cultural and intellectual life of the GDR.

The myth of *Kultur* was directed toward the educated classes and
intellectuals. Through the invocation of *Kultur* and the clothing of political statements in cultural metaphors and symbols, intellectuals were to
learn to identify themselves with the SED and its policies. The myth's
youthful version had the purpose of winning over the children of these
groups and preparing working class youth for their new social status as
privileged functionaries of the SED. The preferred symbols of the *Kultur*
myth were the concert of the "polyphonic community" and the drama of
national liberation. Compared with later, headier myths, the myth of *Kultur* was poor in ceremony and symbolism. This was because the proclamation of and the participation in *Kultur* were already symbol and ceremony
in themselves.

The Cultural Policy of the KPD, 1935–45

An uncharitable observer might conclude the GDR's cultural-political
myth-building derived from the SED's own parochial understanding of
Kultur and its members' inferiority complex toward the educated classes

---

6. For a solid introduction to the basic issues behind GDR cultural policy, see David
Pike, *The Politics of Culture in Soviet-Occupied Germany, 1945–1949* (Stanford, 1992), and
David Bathrick, *The Powers of Speech: The Politics of Culture in the GDR* (Lincoln, 1995).

and the West in general. These factors were certainly important, and Leszek Kolakowski's terming of the late-Stalinist culture of the Soviet Union as a "culture of parvenus" certainly applies to the GDR. According to Kolakowski, the Stalinist functionaries felt a deep inferiority complex toward the West and the old intelligentsia and were obsessed by the need to "show off" with a facade of bourgeois and aristocratic culture.[7] The new rulers of eastern Germany (such as Ulbricht, Pieck, Grotewohl, and Honecker) were likewise characterized by a proletarian background, poor education, long years of bitter political struggle and illegality, a hatred of traditional privileges, and blind devotion to the Socialist Unity Party and the Soviet Union, to which they owed everything. Like their Soviet counterparts, they never intended to abolish the principle of privilege itself but rather to create a new system of privileges patterned after the only model they knew: aristocratic and bourgeois culture. This parvenu quality applies especially to the fresh cadres groomed at the Party and FDJ academies, who were drawn primarily from the working and peasant classes and suddenly thrust into positions of great authority as plant directors, district Party secretaries, university professors, and so on. All of this is expressed with a revealing bluntness in Louis Fürnberg's SED anthem, "The Party is Always Right": "She gave us everything . . . and what we are, we are because of Her!" It certainly helped a functionary's public image and self-confidence to deliver speeches on Goethe and Schiller, or just to be photographed attending a Bach concert. This representational function underlay the GDR's entire forty-four year construction of the *Kultur* myth. However, this motive was only one among many.

The myth of *Kultur* began long before the socialist movement. Ever since Madame de Staël first referred to Germany as the *Land der Dichter und Denker* (land of poets and philosophers) in the early nineteenth century, the concept of *Kultur* has been inextricably tied to that of the *Bildungsbürgertum* (educated middle classes). As Konrad Jarausch has written, "In principle egalitarian . . . , the educated class formed, in practice, a stratum that sought to perpetuate itself by turning its cultivation [*Bildung*] into a guarded possession, ostensibly based on merit. . . . A curious blend of individualism, idealism, and neohumanism, *Bildung* postulated 'improvement of our inner selves' as the path toward true humanity and focused on cultural rather than political progress."[8] The bourgeoisie had long since taken over aristocratic culture and celebrated it in their ostentatious art museums and opera houses. The cult of *Kultur* began as an

---

7. Leszek Kolakowski, *Die Hauptströmungen des Marxismus,* vol. 3 (Munich, 1989), 162–63.

8. Konrad H. Jarausch, *Students, Society, and Politics in Imperial Germany: The Rise of Academic Illiberalism* (Princeton, NJ, 1982), 8–9.

expression of bourgeois civic culture and, in the authoritarian Wilhelmine period, gradually degenerated into a surrogate civic culture. In 1914, Thomas Mann and other middle-class intellectuals, desperately searching for a new role for themselves, actually argued that World War I was really all about the struggle of *Kultur* against *Zivilisation,* and boasted that German soldiers had marched off to battle with copies of Goethe's *Faust* and Nietzsche's *Zarathustra* tucked into their knapsacks.

Such elitist notions as these should have been easy targets for a revolutionary. But nineteenth-century socialist intellectuals such as Marx and Engels were, after all, *Bildungsbürger* themselves and as such products of bourgeois society and bourgeois *Kultur.* Their dream of a communist society amounted to one where proletarians would be able to spend their plentiful leisure time enjoying the Goethe poems and Mozart operas that lay close to their own hearts. Thus the overturning of bourgeois society never included the destruction of bourgeois *Kultur.* On the contrary, its adoption by the workers was to be a critical feature of the revolutionary renewal of mankind and would give them almost magical powers. Exactly what the workers would do with these powers once they had them always remained vague. As Clara Zetkin wrote in 1911, "every rising class finds its artistic models in the apex of the earlier development. The Renaissance drew on the art of Greece and Rome, German classical art drew on antiquity and the Renaissance. . . . Socialism is the logical extension and transformation of cosmopolitan liberalism. . . . The art of Socialism—so to speak—will be an extension of the grand, classical, bourgeois art."[9]

Lenin viewed high culture the same way. At the Third All Russian Congress of the Komsomol in 1920, Lenin proclaimed:[10]

> Proletarian culture must be the logical development of the store of knowledge mankind has accumulated under the yoke of capitalist, landowner, and bureaucratic society. All these roads have been leading, and will continue to lead up to proletarian culture, in the same way as political economy, as reshaped by Marx, has shown us what human society must arrive at, shown us the passage to the class struggle, to the beginning of the proletarian revolution.
>
>   . . . You can become a Communist only when you enrich your mind with a knowledge of all the treasures created by mankind.

---

9. Clara Zetkin, *Kunst und Proletariat* (Stuttgart, 1911), 14; cited in Vernon L. Lidtke, *The Alternative Culture: Socialist Labor in Imperial Germany* (New York, 1985), 197.

10. V. I. Lenin, "The Tasks of the Youth Leagues" (1920), in *Collected Works,* vol. 31 (Moscow, 1966), 287.

This backward orientation did not preclude innovation. For Lenin, and later Stalin and the Marxist-Leninist aestheticians they inspired, communism did not represent a radical break with past culture, but rather its culmination. In a class society, culture was a class phenomenon and was thus always in the hands of the ruling class, "while the toilers usually have control over that portion which is essential for the historical-concrete reproduction demands of their labor power. Under Imperialism this contrast is carried to extremes."[11] In the course of the "Socialist cultural revolution" the tables would be turned and a new and superior classless culture would be developed by the classless society. This culture would then transform mankind. It was therefore only a very small step to proclaim the works of Marx, Engels, Lenin, and Stalin to be the most "progressive" and therefore highest achievements of German and Russian culture—indeed, "classics" of world philosophy. With such illustrious offspring, Goethe and Pushkin become less important for what they themselves wrote than for their early progressive contributions to Marxist-Leninist theory. It was an even smaller step to view the very notion of "culture" as a mere instrument—indeed, a weapon—of Marxist-Leninist politics.

In the 1920s and the 1930s these theories were still in the making and were overshadowed by more pressing concerns in the Soviet Union and in Germany. Many communist idealists of the Weimar era dreamed of one day opening *Kultur* up to the masses. But throughout this period the KPD itself had little use for bourgeois *Kultur* and in effect abandoned this propaganda tool to the Nazis, who exploited it in grand style, even going so far as to set up orchestras in concentration camps. Parvenu Nazi leaders also used cultural figures as political icons and German status symbols while (especially in the case of writers) largely ignoring their actual works, which they viewed as a liability. In the school textbooks of the Third Reich, one scholar has found, "Goethe was not a mere 'gift of heaven' to the Germans but a 'magnificent proof of the quality of the collective German folk, that precisely this Goethe had come about.'"[12]

The Communists learned quickly. At the "Brussels Conference" of 1935 the KPD adopted the "popular front" resolutions of the Seventh World Congress of the Comintern and adapted them for the German situation. The KPD consequently changed its strategy and called upon its remaining members in Germany as well as all "progressive forces" "to rescue the cultural and spiritual treasure of the German people, its language,

---

11. "Kultur," *Kleines politisches Wörterbuch,* 7th ed. (East Berlin, 1988), 548–49.
12. Gilmer W. Blackburn, *Education in the Third Reich. Race and History in Nazi Textbooks* (Albany, 1985), 58.

its literature, its art and science from the Fascist barbarians and to struggle for the higher development of [these] *Kulturgüter.*"[13] Given the KPD's desperate situation in the mid-1930s, this appeal expressed little more than wishful thinking. Nevertheless, some local antifascist youth groups began using classical literature to neutralize Nazi indoctrination. In Leipzig, for example, the local underground KJVD organization passed around not only books by Marx and Engels, but also satirical poems by Heinrich Heine in order to make fun of the Nazi regime.[14]

Much of the KPD's and later SED's cultural policy also developed from actual experiences in the Third Reich. Humanist ideals and the vision of "the other, the better Germany" that would be restored after Hitler's fall sustained many intellectuals in exile.[15] In this regard, the Communists' myth of *Kultur* was not merely, in Malinowski's words, "a story told" but very much "an experience lived."[16] In a letter written from his Nazi prison cell in 1936, Ernst Thälmann urged his daughter Irna to "read the works of our great poets Goethe, Schiller, Lessing, and our Fritz Reuter" in order to keep her spirits up.[17] And in a book entitled *Goethe in Dachau,* which was disseminated by the FDJ during the Goethe celebration of 1949, a young Dutch Communist described in diary form how the concentration camp inmates—Communists and noncommunists—kept up their courage and their dream of a future humanistic Germany through regular discussions of Goethe and other classic authors. "As long as *it* is still there, as Goethe says, nothing is lost; I still have something to hold on to, I can still stand with both feet firmly on the ground and can look with confidence into the future. There is no reason to despair. . . . Goethe is right again and I thank him for it."[18] As Anna Seghers, herself an émigrée, wrote in her introduction to the German edition, "The entire weight of the account lies in the fact that every discussion, ever page of reading, every line of the book was painfully wrenched from death."

KPD ideologists in Soviet exile, however, viewed *Kultur* as a therapeutic device. Just reading the classics, they believed, could serve as an antidote to Nazi propaganda and improve morale. The Bern Conference

---

13. "Der neue Weg zum gemeinsamen Kampf aller Werktätigen. Für den Sturz der Hitlerdiktatur," in *Revolutionäre Parteiprogramme* (East Berlin, 1967), 149.

14. Alfred Nothnagel, "Meine Erfahrungen aus dem antifaschistischen Widerstandskampf in Leipzig in den Jahren 1938 bis 1945," *Schriftenreihe zur Geschichte der FDJ* 7 (1966): 156–58.

15. George L. Mosse, "The Heritage of Socialist Humanism," in *Masses and Man: Nationalist and Fascist Perceptions of Reality* (Detroit, 1987), 141–56.

16. Rost, 9.

17. "Aus einem Brief Ernst Thälmanns an seine Tochter Irna," in Karl Heinz Jahnke, ed., *Ernst Thälmann—Freund und Vorbild* (East Berlin, 1974), 56.

18. Nico Rost, *Goethe in Dachau* (East Berlin, 1948), 13. See review in JG 5 (1949): 231.

of the KPD, held in early 1939, recommended that antifascist parents "patiently and systematically" attempt to imbue "their children—through the use of the great intellectual works of the German past—with the spirit of the ideals of progress, freedom, justice, and humanism." This time the Party included Marx, Engels, and Lenin among its list of inspirational "classics."[19]

At a KPD functionaries' meeting in Moscow in February 1945, the poet and future cultural minister Johannes R. Becher gave a programmatic lecture in which he outlined the Party's postwar cultural strategy. The key to the realization of the Party's goals, Becher explained, was a system of broad alliances joining "progressive circles" of all social strata under the leadership of the working class. Cultural policy would support these alliances "in connection with the liberal traditions of our people, under the critical evaluation of our classical inheritance and above all on the basis of and in the creative application of Marxism." Furthermore, cultural policy would join forces "with the liberal traditions and progressive forces of all peoples and above all the evaluation of scientific discoveries and the cultural achievements of the Soviet Union." In Becher's words, only such an intellectual alliance policy made it possible "to exterminate Nazi ideology and to lay the foundations for the creation of a new free and democratic ideology, of a spiritual rebirth of Germany."[20]

A year later, in his primer *Education for Freedom,* Becher summed up the principles of this "antifascist/democratic consciousness," which he saw rooted in German classical *Kultur:* the belief in the equality of human beings and peoples, the concept of war as a "societal phenomenon," the recognition of objective laws in nature and society and the progress of human society, the concept of the leading role of the working class in history and society, and the ideals of democracy and social cooperation.[21]

Just as important as the KPD's own plans were the ideas of the Soviet cultural officers who accompanied the Red Army to the Soviet sector. Many of these functionaries, such as the Soviet commander Tulpanov, idealized German high culture and saw their stay in the SBZ as an opportunity to put these ideals into action.[22] Thus many Marxist notions of *Kultur* survived the Third Reich and, after going through a further transformation during a quarter century of Stalinist cultural policy, returned in triumph to the SBZ in 1945.

---

19. "Berner Konferenz der KPD," *Revolutionäre Parteiprogramme,* 176, 189.
20. Johannes R. Becher, "Zur Frage der politisch-moralischen Vernichtung des Faschismus," in *Gesammelte Werke,* vol. 16 (East Berlin and Weimar, 1978), 406.
21. Johannes R. Becher, *Erziehung zur Freiheit* (East Berlin, 1946), 100–101.
22. Cf. Manfred Jäger, *Kultur und Politik in der DDR* (Cologne, 1982), 15.

Kultur as Antidote, 1945–49

As soon as the antifascist youth committees were formed in the summer of 1945, KPD and other "antifascist" activists went to work teaching young people about German *Kultur*. Walter Ulbricht emphasized the therapeutic aspects of *Kultur* at a meeting of KPD functionaries in June. After a crash course in denazification, he told them, "we must start to make them acquainted with German literature, with Heine, Goethe, Schiller, etc. Don't begin with Marx and Engels! They won't understand it. We must first get the ideology of Nazism out of their heads, and it has to become clear to them that National Socialism has nothing to do with Socialism."[23] Even though the KPD did in a sense have a monopoly on power in the SBZ through its special relationship with the Soviet Military Administration in Germany (SMAD), it had no power in the other zones. The future of Germany had not been settled yet. Indeed, nothing at all had been settled beyond the fate of the Third Reich.

In the course of the land reform of the summer of 1945, the KPD enlisted Goethe's verse from *Faust II:* "Aye! such a throng I fain would see, / Stand on free soil among a people free," as a slogan to help sell its campaign to dispossess the landed Junker class.[24] But in the cities the Communists proceeded extremely slowly, their work hindered by the exhaustion and apathy of the young people, the warm summer weather, and an obsession with dancing and other entertainments. As a status report from a Berlin youth committee admitted, "We are forced to realize again and again that we have to begin with very simple things in order to elicit any interest at all. Unfortunately, the more shallow and superficial something is, the more enthusiastic the youths get. We can only win a very few for serious and difficult presentations and discussions."[25] Nevertheless, the movement soon showed success. Among the many theatrical productions of the youth committees in 1945 and 1946 were Lessing's *Nathan der Weise,* Goethe's *Iphigenie auf Tauris,* and many others.[26] The SBZ youth press also did its part. The very first issue of the youth magazine *Neues Leben* (published by Erich Honecker and edited by Paul Verner) in the autumn of 1945 included an article on Heinrich Heine along with a

23. Walter Ulbricht, "Protokoll einer Beratung mit Parteileitern der KPD der Provinz Brandenburg in Berlin, 27. Juni 1947," *Aus der Geschichte der deutschen Arbeiterbewegung,* vol. 2, 1st supp. vol. (East Berlin, 1965), 234.

24. Wolfgang Leonhard, *Die Revolution entlässt ihre Kinder* (Cologne, 1990).

25. "Bezirksverwaltung Neukölln, Amt für Volksbildung, Jugendausschuss/Kultur: Leistungsbericht-Kultur für die Zeit vom 1.-15.7.45," SAPMO-BArch NL 36/726, Bl. 29.

26. Günter Schwade, "Die Kulturarbeit der FDJ und ihre Rolle bei der ideologischen Erziehung der Jugend in der Zeit der antifaschistischen Umwälzung von 1945/46 bis 1949" (Diss. Wilhelm-Pieck-Universität Rostock, 1979), 32–33.

selection of his poems. The article is remarkable only for the fact that it fails to mention Heine's Jewish background as a reason for the abuse he suffered during his own life and later in the Nazi period.[27] Subsequent issues carried straightforward articles on Beethoven, Ferdinand Freiligrath, and Georg Büchner, along with Russian classic authors such as Tolstoy, Chekhov, and others. By this time *Neues Leben* was already "the magazine of the FDJ." The ostensible purpose of this campaign was to reintroduce young people to these figures and to correct the distortions the Nazis had created around them. Youth concerts also played an important role in this process. The founding ceremony of the FDJ was symbolically opened with a performance of Beethoven's "Egmont Overture." This piece had also been played by the camp orchestra following the liberation of the Buchenwald concentration camp.[28]

If the SED postponed the full-scale Marxist-Leninist indoctrination of eastern German youth until 1951, it did not do so for lack of will but rather from the uncertainty of the German question in the immediate postwar years. Such a massive effort is only possible under a dictatorship. In the late 1940s the FDJ was still hoping to "win over" all of German youth, not just young workers, and thus needed more gentle methods of persuasion. That is why FDJ leaders carefully avoided mentioning Marx and Engels, even when they were actually talking about them. In his keynote speech at the Brandenburg Parliament, Otto Grotewohl slighted Marx and instead called upon the FDJ "to see to it that German youth" once again surrounded itself "with its good spirits." Among these classical spirits Grotewohl named Beethoven, Mozart, Goethe, Hölderlin, Albrecht Dürer, and Immanuel Kant. However, he went on to mention the popular science writer and monist Ernst Haeckel, the mechanic Rudolph Diesel, the physician Robert Koch, and last of all Friedrich Engels.[29] In November 1946 Erich Honecker delivered a programmatic speech to a group of mostly "bourgeois" young people on "German youth in the spiritual struggle of our time." Although he clearly defined "freedom" as "the recognition of necessity," he did not give credit to Engels, but instead traced this notion to Goethe.[30]

For much the same reason, the new training programs for FDJ functionaries also avoided direct ideological indoctrination, while the Party schools were already conducting crash courses in Marxism-Leninism. The

27. P. Hildebrandt, "Heine," NL vol. 1, no. 1 (1945): 7–9.

28. *Geschichte der FDJ,* 99; Autorenkollektiv, *Buchenwald. Mahnung und Verpflichtung. Dokumente und Berichte* (East Berlin, 1961), 590.

29. *I. Parlament der FDJ,* 18–19.

30. "Die Jugend im geistigen Ringen unserer Zeit," speech delivered by Erich Honecker, 28 November 1946, IzJ JA A2102, Bl. 18.

Central Youth School in the former Goebbels villa on the Bogensee lake (later the *Jugendhochschule Wilhelm Pieck*) did not offer courses on Marxism-Leninism as such in its first semesters. Instead, it offered a broad array of courses taught from a Marxist-Leninist point of view. Some of the topics covered in the history lectures were "economic conditions in the development of human society," "imperialism and its peculiarities in Germany," "German predatory imperialism in its fascist characteristic features," "state organization and the constitution of the Soviet Union," and so forth.[31] These were new and exciting topics for a disillusioned generation trained in Nazi schools. The same basic pattern was true for the regional FDJ functionary schools. As Jürgen Pfeiffer, the thoroughly *parteilich* scholar of FDJ indoctrination in its early years, writes concerning the related *Landesschule Conrad Blenkle* in 1947,[32]

> Although the instructional material was imbued with Marxism-Leninism, which was intentionally not expressed outwardly in the course titles in order to make them easier to approach, the regional school was not a miniature version of the Party school. It was a school of the FDJ where the priority was placed on the education of young anti-Fascists and democrats in the spirit of the working class. In the few weeks of learning and collective experience at an FDJ school no young Socialists could have been or should have been developed. But with many a complete break with the resilient Fascist thought material could be brought about and a turn toward the ideology of the working class could be accomplished through a first acquaintance with it.

The myth of *Kultur* was an important part of this "antifascist/democratic" education. An order for furnishings at the FDJ school on the Bogensee consequently included "large portraits of Goethe, Schiller, Marx, Engels, Beethoven, Heine, Hölderlin, Georg Büchner [and] Ernst Thälmann."[33]

The FDJ's "Meissen Parliament" or convention of 1947 devoted particular attention to the organization's cultural policy. In the various proclamations issued from the Parliament, the FDJ shifted its emphasis

---

31. "Lehrplan für die zentrale Jugendschule der FDJ im Waldhof am Bogensee. 1. Lehrgang vom 22. Mai bis 6. Juli 1946," SAPMO BArch IV 2/16/100, Bl. 180–95.

32. Jürgen Pfeiffer, "Die Schulungsarbeit der FDJ von den Anfängen der antifaschistisch-demokratischen Jugendarbeit 1945 bis zum III. Parlament der FDJ 1949" (Diss. Rostock, 1975), 106–7.

33. List of furnishings for the Central Youth School, SAPMO BArch IV 2/16/100, Bl. 75.

away from the broad "antifascist" orientation of the former youth committees and instead moved toward the building of socialism and consequently direct (if still cautious) indoctrination. In an "Appeal to the Creators of *Kultur* of Germany," the FDJ called upon artists of all kinds to "lead us to the old sources of *Kultur,* that we may draw from them; lay the cornerstone for a new literature, especially youth literature, in the service of life, freedom, and progress. . . . Give us stage plays and amateur theatricals. Create songs which encourage us to live and to work. Support young, creative people, so that they may one day become mature enough to develop cultural life on their own in a united, democratic Germany, whose citizens are respected by the world."[34]

By this time, many former members of the Weimar intelligentsia had returned from exile and settled in the Soviet zone, which they viewed as the beginning of that elusive "other Germany." Most of them allowed themselves to be coopted by the SED to help build this new Germany on the Party's terms. At an FDJ-sponsored writers' conference in October 1948, the *Zentralrat* formally requested SBZ authors to write for the youth organization, a request that many of the writers eagerly accepted. Over the next several years the FDJ formally commissioned the SBZ's and later the GDR's best (meaning, by this time, the most *parteilich*) writers to create inspiring novels, stories, plays, and songs for the youth organization and its cultural-political struggle. While these works oriented themselves on the *Kulturerbe,* they dealt with such immediate themes as industrial work, "the happy life," antifascism, and defending the fruits of socialist labor from imperialist saboteurs. Among the writers who offered their services in this way were Friedrich Wolf, Johannes R. Becher, Gustav von Wangenheim, Bodo Uhse, Hedda Zinner, Bertolt Brecht (through his *Aufbaulied der FDJ* and other classics), Anna Seghers, and many others.[35] In early 1949 the SED put its cultural policy into the service of its first two-year plan, and the Party's Department of Propaganda, *Kultur,* and Education issued detailed guidelines to SBZ writers urging them to place the plan and German workers at the center of their creative work. They were to go into the factories, talk to the workers, and read their works there.[36] A typ-

---

34. "Appell an die Kulturschaffenden Deutschlands," ibid., 27.

35. Cf. "Gesprächsprotokoll, Genossin Sonja Schneider, 23.12.1975," in Schwade, "Die Kulturarbeit der FDJ," app. 23, 4–5.

36. In justifying these demands the SED stated that "the complete societal reorganization of rural conditions (land reform, the concerns of new farmers), the school reform—its implementation on one side, the resistance to it on the other—the essential demands of the half year plan in the economy, and the great central demands of the two year plan must give the writer a new content and new forms for his work in the clear ideological understanding of our path." "Richtlinien: Schriftsteller und Zweijahresplan (PKE), 1949," SAPMO BArch IV 2/906/69, Bl. 140.

ical example of this was the proletarian poet "Kuba" (Kurt Bartel), best remembered for his melodramatic agitprop poem *"Der Plan."*

These works were published in the FDJ's own newspapers and magazines for immediate use within the local organization. They are characterized by a crude propagandistic style. A typical example of this sort of literature was the short play "Rats in the Village" by Bruno Pfeiffer, which described acts of sabotage committed by a West German agent in a collective farm at harvest time. As suggested by the title, the agent and his like are consistently identified with vermin throughout the play. After his capture, the remorseful agent actually admits that he is, in fact, a rat. As in most agitprop plays of this type, specific instructions were included to elicit the appropriate response from the young audience. For example, "The leading role of the party, embodied by Party secretary Schmidt, must be put into proper perspective through the few words [that he speaks]."[37]

In order to foster *Parteilichkeit* among young people and to achieve the loyalty of the intellectuals and the educated classes, the SED set about coordinating all aspects of cultural activity. In November 1946 the *Zentralrat* organized a *Kulturausschuss* (cultural committee), which took charge of all cultural activities within the organization. Under the chairmanship of Horst Brasch, whom we met earlier as the organizer of the *"Freie deutsche Jugend"* in Great Britain during the war, the *Kulturausschuss* was broken down into six areas: radio, theater and amateur theatricals, film, literature, music and song, and finally painting and pictorial art.[38] Since the FDJ channeled nearly all of its propaganda through its cultural policy in its early years, the *Kulturausschuss* became perhaps the single most powerful instrument of SED and FDJ ideological control over East German youth. The *Kulturausschuss* took over the FDJ's previous haphazard organization of song festivals, dances, youth libraries, discussion circles, *Heimabend* materials, and so on. In its resolution on "the transferral of the folk art groups and popular educational associations into the existing democratic mass organizations" of November 1948, the Party specified that "the Goethe Society shall be incorporated both centrally and locally into the *Kulturbund* for the Democratic Renewal of Germany." Furthermore, "all other similar associations, such as literary, artistic and philosophical societies shall exist only on a local basis within the *Kulturbund* and shall be considered to be study groups of the local chapters of the *Kulturbund.*"[39]

---

37. "Ratten im Dorf. Ein Laienspiel in fünf Bildern," in *Heim und Klub* 1 (1952): 36.
38. "Satzung des Kulturausschusses beim ZR der FDJ," IzJ A 463.
39. "Beschluss des Zentralsekretariats der Sozialistischen Einheitspartei Deutschlands, Überführung der Volkskunstgruppen und Volksbildenden Vereine in die bestehenden demokratischen Massenorganisationen (Entwurf)," SAPMO BArch IV 2/16/1, Bl. 161.

Thus by 1949 cultural life was firmly in the hands of the SED, the *Kulturbund,* and the FDJ. This applied to both *Kultur* and agitational material. Although individual artistic freedom was never entirely stamped out, henceforth no large-scale cultural activities could take place without the SED's approval and control. Now that *Kultur* was what the Party said it was, the SED and the FDJ could begin the wholesale construction of a positive, mobilizing myth of *Kultur* directed at all Germans, East and West.

American "*Kulturbarbarei*" and "Formalism"

The founding of the two German states occurred at the high point of the cold war. The Federal Republic was developing a close alliance with the United States and Britain, and was working to build up its own "social market economy" through the Marshall Plan and anchor it in the new European Economic Community centered around France and the Benelux countries. As such it represented a severe challenge to Soviet foreign policy goals and the SED's reunification plans. The FRG's Western orientation, combined with its emerging *"Wirtschaftswunder,"* proved increasingly attractive to East Germans, especially younger ones, who in the early 1950s were fleeing from the East at a rate of up to 200,000 a year.[40] West German politicians, led by the Christian Democratic Chancellor Konrad Adenauer, reached into the treasure chest of German heroes and proclaimed themselves to be defenders of "Christian-Occidental *Kultur*" against the "heathen hordes" of the Bolshevik east. Adenauer even went so far as to let himself be dubbed a Knight of the Teutonic Order in 1958. Rhetoric of this kind had a long tradition in Germany and had been used most recently to justify the German invasion of the Soviet Union in 1941.[41]

The SED turned the tables on the Federal Republic by substituting the FRG's warmed-over Nazi anti-Soviet propaganda with what on the surface appeared to be its own warmed-over Nazi anti-"Anglo-American" propaganda. The SED used this rhetoric in its campaigns for German reunification under socialism, against the FRG's proclaimed "community of values" with the United States, and for "friendship" with the Soviet Union against the FRG's signing of the "General War Treaty" (the European Defense Community), and above all its entry into NATO.

The SED expressed its anti-Western course in the symbolic language

---

40. Hermann Weber, *DDR. Grundriss der Geschichte, 1945–1990* (Hannover, 1991), 289–96.

41. Jost Hermand, *Kultur im Wiederaufbau. Die Bundesrepublik Deutschland 1945–1965* (Munich, 1986), 234–44.

of *Kultur,* which by the end of the "Antifascist Democratic Upheaval" had fulfilled its antidote function. The positive myth of *Kultur* was accompanied by its inverse, the GDR version of "the barbarians at the gate." The SED regularly compared the political and cultural situation in western Germany circa 1950 with that of Germany as a whole in the thoroughly barbaric Thirty Years' War. The FDJ's "Manifesto to German Youth," proclaimed by the "Congress of Young Peace Fighters" to young people in the East and the West in May 1950, stated:[42]

> The fragmentation of the West German population into dozens of parties and hundreds of youth organizations, [as it is] promoted by the Anglo-American and French interventionists, makes it hard for the German man between the Rhine and Elbe to represent the genuine interests of the German people. The youth of West Germany is to be poisoned by the *Kulturbarbarei* [cultural barbarism] of the so-called "American way of life." They are, through American trash and smut [*Schund und Schmutz*], to forget their own misery and the misery of the German people.

The key term in the above document is *Kulturbarbarei,* an expression usually linked to the United States (but occasionally to Britain and the American "lackeys" in the Federal Republic) and intended to lure educated Germans back to the true *Kultur* being promoted by the SED itself. Beginning in 1949, the campaign combined an incongruously bourgeois understanding of *Kultur* with conventional anti-Americanism and a manipulation of German war resentment. In the SBZ, most of this popular resentment was really aimed at the Red Army, which did much of the damage, raped thousands of eastern German women, detached Germany's eastern provinces, driving some ten million Germans from their homes forever, and after the war continued the wholesale dismantling of eastern German factories and railroad tracks despite solemn promises to stop. The myth of *Kultur* solved this nagging public relations problem by painting the *Amis* (the German epithet for Americans) and the imperialist West in general as fundamentally destructive—indeed, the very embodiment of *Unkultur*—and the Soviet Union, by contrast, as benign: the defender and restorer of *Kultur.* Beginning in 1949, for example, those ubiquitous plaques with the four words *"Zerstört durch anglo-amerikanische Bomber"* (Destroyed by Anglo-American bombers) began appearing on war ruins throughout the East. The destruction inflicted by the "Anglo-

---

42. "Manifest an die deutsche Jugend," *Dokumente und Beschlüsse der FDJ,* vol. 2 (East Berlin, 1951), 35.

Americans" was not only unprovoked, SED propaganda suggested, but also did double duty for the equally severe devastation wrought by Soviet artillery in Berlin and other eastern cities. Thus young East Germans learned the following typical explanation for the destruction of their capital: "On 3 February 1945 at 12:30 the air raid sirens wail in Berlin. Bombers hurl their death-bringing cargo onto apartment houses, onto women and children. Valuable German *Kultur* monuments crumble to ruin. The air pirates rage for over three hours. On the wings of the death birds the American emblem glints sneeringly." They were taught that, in fact, the "Anglo-Americans" were partially responsible for the war itself through guilt by association. While nominal members of the "Anti-Hitler Coalition," they were not genuine antifascists. In fact, since their leaders, the "finance hyenas" and "Wall Street sharks," were capitalists, they were akin to the German "Fascists" who started the war and who were reestablishing themselves in the western zones under Konrad Adenauer.[43] The cold war, and especially the Korean War, were a direct continuation of the imperialist World War II against peace-loving people: "Under the same emblem, in the employ of the same criminals from beyond the Atlantic, the same gruesome murder is today taking place in Korea. And under the American star-spangled banner *Ami*-bombs are once again—today only in practice—tearing up West German soil, jack hammers are gouging detonation chambers into German bridges, the American locusts in West Germany are raping women and girls."[44]

The notion of *Kulturbarbarei* also took care of another problem. Alongside their internal archenemies (Socialists, Communists, and Jews), the two main external targets of the old German Right and, later, the Nazis had been "*Amerikanismus*" ("an 'obsession with economics' and instinctual 'oppression' linked to mass production and consumption")[45] and "Bolshevism," which amounted to the destruction of all human values. By the Soviet occupation at the latest, anti-Bolshevism had become a mass phenomenon throughout Germany. American *Kulturbarbarei* expressed both fears, and so it provided a foil for Soviet Communism, which the SED presented as the protector and the very embodiment of world *Kultur.* The SED and FDJ celebrated the Soviets' return in 1955 of a collection of Dresden paintings (among the thousands of works of art stolen by the Red Army in World War II) as an example of the profound cultivation of the Soviet people, a cultivation impossible under imperial-

---

43. For a discussion of the Marxist-Leninist understanding of the term *fascism* see chapter 5.

44. Edmar Hunger, "Nie wieder Ami-Bomben auf Berlin," JW 1 February 1952.

45. Jeffrey Herf, *Reactionary Modernism: Technology, Culture, and Politics in Weimar and the Third Reich* (Cambridge, 1984), 163.

ism. "We only need recall the art treasures which American swindlers on a grand scale secretly smuggled to the USA and sold off, depravedly tearing apart entire collections."[46]

The FDJ itself first justified its anti-American stance in cultural terms. Unlike the militant *Junge Welt,* which had been publishing straightforward anti-imperialist, anti-Truman, anti–Marshall Plan articles from the very beginning, the FDJ magazine *Neues Leben* had presented a neutral view of American culture and society, offering occasional articles on such benign topics as Mark Twain, the great American cities, and even "the American college girl." Even though the magazine printed an article in 1947 denouncing jazz as *kulturfeindlich* (inimical to *Kultur*), the following issue allowed jazz fans space to express their own views. But by early 1948 the magazine reflected the SED's harder line in several bitter articles on American race relations and the Marshall Plan. Then, during the Berlin Blockade, the December 1948 issue contained a leading article denouncing American claims of being "the defender of Western civilization." Alongside a full-page photo of ragged one-legged boys leaning on their crutches among the ruins of Cologne, the author wrote, "[The Americans] don't give a damn about the *Kultur* of Europe, that is proved by their bomber squadrons which smashed our cathedrals to rubble and set our museums afire. Europe means just as little to the current power-wielders in the USA as a 'dead dog'; the venerable old *Kultur* monuments interest them just as much as a negro god from Zambesi or a Buddha statue from Nakhon-Thon fills them with awe." In fact, as this article and many others suggested, the Americans did not actually engage in combat during the war. Instead, the United States' sole contribution to the war was the deliberate destruction of *Kultur.* "The *Amis* with their bombs and their pressed-trouser soldiers did not finish off Hitler-Germany, it was the 'destroyers of the West' who did it, the same ones who today are restoring the Zwinger, one of the wonders of Western *Kultur*—which *Ami* bombs smashed to bits. It was the Russians with their guns and their blood."[47] Thus began the SED's and the FDJ's long campaign against "American *Kulturbarbarei.*"

Much of this rhetoric stemmed from passive myth-building, namely the Party's exploitation of the old cliché of Americans as boors and Germans as "poets and philosophers" in order to discredit the United States and shore up its own legitimacy. This explains why in his speeches Wilhelm Pieck (who began his career as a cabinet-maker from Guben on the Neisse) habitually referred to Harry Truman as a "haberdasher" and "backwoodsman from Missouri." The campaign also represented active

46. "Die Dresdener Meister," JW 7 April 1955.
47. Hein Burchert, "Mister Dollar wird seinen Krieg nicht bekommen," NL 2 (1949): 2–3.

myth-building in the ideological and cultural revolution taking place within the GDR itself. The FDJ was particularly worried about American *Schundliteratur* (trash literature), which referred to the American comic books and detective stories that were flooding the West German market. It was made responsible for the rising crime rate of both the West and the GDR and for breeding militarism. In effect, the term referred to contemporary American literature as a whole, since the FDJ rarely conceded the existence of any middle ground between the "progressive" (i.e., communist) writer Howard Fast and the likes of Mickey Spillane. Young people of the 1950s and beyond were to learn about youthful idealism from committed SED authors like Anna Seghers and Hermann Kant, not from J. D. Salinger. They were to learn about the moral implications of modern war from Bruno Apitz's antifascist epic *Naked Among Wolves,* not from Joseph Heller's *Catch-22.* According to *Junge Generation,* "the reading of *Schundliteratur* is comparable to swallowing poison, which harms the spirit and the soul, and . . . such behavior is irreconcilable with the principles of a progressive young person." What's more, "this 'literature' is a weapon of the imperialists, it is a poison with the help of which our German youth is to be exterminated."

The anti-*Kulturbarbarei* campaign was most vigorous in the area of popular music and was eerily reminiscent of the equally vigorous campaign against American *"Niggermusik"* in the Hitler Youth just a few years earlier. Like the FDJ, the Hitler Youth had felt threatened by young people in its own ranks who got together and danced to contraband swing records. The FDJ campaign was aimed primarily at the West Berlin "poison station" RIAS (Radio in the American Sector), whose combination of boogie-woogie and critical reporting on conditions in the GDR was declared to be "the war drum of the American war arsonists. Its goal is to contaminate German youth spiritually and morally in order to lead them to the death for the American masters."[48] Caricatures in the youth press actually showed radios vomiting forth snakes and lizards. The campaign probably had little effect on nonorganized East German youths, who continued listening to RIAS and other Western stations in secret, but many FDJ members took notice.

It is only natural that the Party and the FDJ blamed the 1953 workers' uprising partly on the evil influence of *Kulturbarbarei.* Soon after the uprising was crushed by Soviet tanks, the Soviet High Commisssioner in East Berlin urged the Party to begin the mass production of the *Volks-*

48. Gerhart Eisler, "Der Ami-Rias—der Todfeind der deutschen Jugend," JG 9 (1952): 4. For a concise and thoroughly entertaining overview of U.S. cultural policy in the American occupation zone, see Ralph Willett, *The Americanization of Germany, 1945–1949* (London, 1989).

empfänger, a cheap radio of the Nazi era designed to receive only a small range of preselected stations that would not include RIAS. This plan was halted only by a shortage of the necessary radio tubes in the GDR.[49]

But as so often in the history of GDR myth-building, the campaign was carried out with such enthusiasm that it soon became a liability. By the early 1950s the very concept of a good time had begun to be subsumed under the category of American *Kulturbarbarei* to the point that many came to see social dancing itself as "not consistent with the dignity of an FDJ member."[50] Indeed, the campaign contributed to the development of a generation of dedicated FDJ functionaries and young SED leaders whose musical horizons ranged from Beethoven's "Egmont Overture" to "The Song of Stalin" and "We Love the Happy Life." The result was bored young people and empty clubhouses. Over the next several years the Central Council exerted considerable energy persuading its functionaries that even though rock 'n' roll was "poison," they could still dance the foxtrot and be progressive.

As one SED propaganda pamphlet pointed out in 1960, the *Kulturbarbarei* campaign was not racially inspired, or even directed against all *"Amis,"* but was instead directed against the "especially reactionary, antihumanistic, and antinational policy of the ruling circles of the U.S.A." Thus the Party did concede the merits of such "progressive" cultural figures as Paul Robeson, Theodore Dreiser, or Michael Gold—the SED's earlier favorite author, Howard Fast, having abandoned the Communist Party in 1956.[51] Thus it is tempting to dismiss the SED's identification of America and Americans with decadence, degeneracy, war, poison, and death itself as mere expedient propaganda designed to identify scapegoats for the GDR's domestic troubles and the constant drain of young refugees to the West. But the daily presentation of Americans and their "lackeys" as vermin and pestilence points to a genuine hysteria within the SED and other communist parties. During the Korean War the SED's gravely misnamed "Office for Information" propagated allegations that the U.S. Air Force was dropping potato beetles over GDR fields with the intention of destroying both the GDR and the entire Eastern European potato crop. The Nazis had circulated the same story during World War II.[52] This story

---

49. Armin Mitter and Stefan Wolle, *Untergang auf Raten. Unbekannte Kapitel der DDR-Geschichte* (Munich, 1993), 151–52.

50. "Leeres Jugendheim—"weil das Tanzen sich nicht mit der Würde eines FDJlers vereinbart," JG 4 (1952): 9.

51. Autorenkollektiv, *Gift in bunten Heften. Ein Münchner Zeitungskiosk als Spiegel des westdeutschen Kulturverfalls* (East Berlin, 1960), 197–98.

52. Ilse Spittmann and Gisela Helwig, eds., *DDR-Lesebuch. Stalinisierung 1949–1955* (Cologne, 1991), 127; *Halt! Ami-Käfer. Dokumentation zum Kartoffelkäferabwurf* (East Berlin, 1950); Dieter Vorsteher, ed., *Deutschland im Kalten Krieg 1945 bis 1963. Eine Ausstellung des Deutschen Historischen Museums* (Berlin, 1992), 92–93.

was followed some time later by likewise unconfirmed charges that the Air Force was dropping plague-carrying fleas, flies, spiders, rats, mice, shellfish, and feathers onto Korean villages. This campaign, which was broadcast worldwide by the North Korean government and the international communist movement, was not only meant to draw attention away from Korea's own grievous sanitation problems during the war. In fact, it is directly related to the anti-U.S. cultural campaign in its proponents' genuine belief that Americans really were vermin poised to infect wholesome world youth. As *Junge Welt* put it: "The entire world is justly beginning to say: Wherever an American appears there lurks not far away the Black Death or cholera or typhus or another epidemic fabricated in the U.S.A. And if yesterday people in every country where the Americans have set foot have said: *Ami* go home! they will soon be saying: Plague-*Ami* go home!"[53]

Articles like this—featuring General Matthew B. "Plague-Ridgway," the American commander in Korea—appeared in the GDR press nearly every day in 1952, invariably alongside articles praising the cultural and social triumphs of the Soviet Union. In a chilling poster released by the Office for Information in 1952 three giant fleas come crawling, one in the foreground with a fang-mouthed Truman head and two more with the heads of Adenauer and Churchill behind. The caption reads: "PLAGUE FLEAS. KOREA IS A WARNING! Fight for peace against those who seek to destroy mankind."[54]

The anti-Semitic style of this campaign suggests that the SED was merely continuing the propaganda war of the Nazis. But even if some SED propagandists had indeed gained experience in this sort of thing during their earlier careers in Goebbels's Propaganda Ministry, this impression is misleading. In fact, as Sam Keen has shown, the depiction of one's enemies as barbarians, vermin, pestilence, and death is typical of all propaganda everywhere.[55] More important was the direct influence of Soviet propaganda, which was itself strongly anti-Semitic ("anti-Zionist") during this period. Far from being just an anti-American, anti-Western campaign, the *Kulturbarbarei* slogan formed part of the Soviet Union's campaign against the "poisons" of "formalism," "cosmopolitanism," and "objectivism," which were the most dangerous elements of American *Kulturbar-*

---

53. "Pest-Ami go home!" JW 27 March 1952. For a concise account of the germ warfare propaganda campaign, see John Halliday and Bruce Cummings, *Korea: The Unknown War* (London, 1988), 182–86.

54. "The Image of America as the Enemy in the Former GDR," *Deutsches Historisches Museum Magazin* 7 (1993): 32.

55. Sam Keen, *Faces of the Enemy: Reflections of the Hostile Imagination* (San Francisco, 1986), 43–48, 60–66.

barei.[56] Formalism roughly corresponded to what the National Socialists had called "degenerate art." The campaign was aimed against all aspects of modern culture, from abstract painting to architecture, theater, literature, and music. The works of German abstract artists (such as the *Blauer Reiter* circle in turn-of-the-century Munich) were declared off-limits, as were the sculptures of Ernst Barlach and the ideas of the *Bauhaus* designers. The antiformalist campaign eventually caught up with some of the old Weimar intelligentsia residing in the GDR. Even the thoroughly compliant Bertolt Brecht was publicly accused of exhibiting formalistic traits. "Formalism means the decay and destruction of art itself. The formalists deny that the decisive meaning lies in the content, in the idea, in the thought of the work. . . . Wherever the question of form gains independent meaning, art loses its humanistic and democratic character."[57] "Realism," by contrast, reflected reality as it was or as it soon would become after the perfection of socialism. Socialist realism usually depicted steel workers at rest, or collective farmers driving tractors. Practically speaking, a work of art or literature was "realistic" if it could be used for the purposes of Marxist-Leninist propaganda.

The campaigns against formalism and *Kulturbarbarei* did not only arise from old-fogeyness and prejudice. Beyond the question of taste, abstract art and Anglo-American pop culture not only made allowances for the less idealistic aspects of human existence but actually drew attention to them. The irony and moral ambiguity they described were a genuine threat to the Marxist-Leninist image of a militant class-conscious youth, and hence to the *Parteilichkeit* principle. *Kulturbarbarei* really was poison to the SED's legitimacy and to socialism itself. So, faced with the threat of losing their precious younger generation to the likes of Fats Domino, the Party went on the offensive.

Kultur as a Weapon

The instrumentalization of *Kultur* proceeded quickly. In 1950, commenting on the cultural program of the vast *Deutschlandtreffen* (a great meeting of German youth, East and West, under the auspices of the FDJ, which was repeated at regular intervals even after the construction of the Berlin Wall in 1961) in the spring of that year, an FDJ functionary wrote that toiling youth had "proven that, together with the progressive intellectuals, it has made the development and cultivation of our new, democratic *Kultur*

---

56. Stefan Heymann, "Kampf gegen die Kulturbarbarei des amerikanischen Imperialismus," *Neuer Weg* 14 (1950): 24–25.

57. "Der Kampf gegen den Formalismus in Kunst und Literatur, für eine fortschrittliche deutsche Kultur," in *Dokumente der SED,* vol. 3, 434.

its concern, that it is the appointed heir to our national *Kulturgüter* [cultural assets]. This is a further step toward the breaking of the educational monopoly [of the bourgeoisie]." Through their performance of "new songs, new dances, new games" telling "of the beautiful new life, of the untiring struggle for a better future," along with old folk songs rendered from a *parteilich* point of view, "our friends demonstrated that they are not prepared to let our *Kulturgüter,* our national treasures, be destroyed by boogie-woogie strategists." This "breakthrough" proved that "our *Kultur* work no longer functions alongside our organizational work, but has become an instrument, a sharp weapon in the struggle against American imperialism and its *Kulturbarbarei.*"[58]

We have already seen how this "weapon" was used inside the GDR to attract young people and what remained of the educated classes to the SED. But equally important was the impression this policy made on foreign visitors, above all West German young people and adults. In the early 1950s the German question still appeared to be open, despite the creation of two German states and the slow beginnings of an "economic wonder" in the West, and the SED had committed itself to achieving a peace treaty that would reunite the country. In this united German state, the SED would have to "win over" West Germans the way it had the East Germans. In the meantime, the SED sincerely believed that it could offset the loss of hundreds of thousands of skilled workers through "Republic desertion" to the FRG by persuading West German skilled workers and specialists to move to the GDR.[59] Cultivation of the *Kulturerbe* appeared to be a promising means of fulfilling both goals. In a Central Committee meeting in 1951, Education Minister Paul Wandel described a visit by a group of West German physicists in Halle and Leipzig.[60]

> They all agreed that their deepest positive impression in our Republic was seeing how we cultivate our *Nationalkultur.* They ran their fingers over the theater posters in Leipzig and Halle and observed that *Minna von Barnhelm, Maria Stuart, Der Freischütz, The Magic Flute,* and many other plays were on the program. These are people whose importance no one can deny and who embody certain typical characteristics of the German bourgeoisie, who spoke openly against the American influence and were most impressed by our Party line—the cultivation of our great *Nationalkultur.*

---

58. Sonja Klinz, "Der Durchbruch in der Kulturarbeit," JG 5/6 (1950): 272.

59. Mitter and Wolle, 35–36.

60. Quoted in Horst Haase et al., eds., *SED und kulturelles Erbe. Orientierungen, Errungenschaften, Probleme* (East Berlin, 1986), 135.

These factors—the winning of GDR intellectuals for socialism, the need to recruit West German specialists and intellectuals, the framework of Marxist-Leninist ideology and socialist realism, the exigencies of Soviet and GDR foreign policy, and finally the demands of SED politics—combined to form a profoundly conservative, almost iconographic understanding of the classical inheritance. It was this interpretation of the classical *Erbe* that the SED presented to the East German people and the world.

But proclamations and theater programs were not enough. In order to build up the myth, the Communists needed to mobilize public participation in the classical *Erbe.* To be sure, many residents of the Zone attended theaters and concerts, but interest was not high enough to justify the myth of a land of poets and philosophers. The city of Weimar caused the SED particular concern. In the summer of 1945 a photograph had circulated through newspapers around the world showing Soviet soldiers carefully removing the stone walls that the Nazis had built around the Goethe–Schiller monument to protect it from Allied bombing attacks. From that moment on the photograph formed the symbolic basis for the myth of *Kultur* in the Soviet Zone of Occupation. But only a few meters behind the monument, the famous National Theater, one of Germany's most renowned theaters and the birthplace of the Weimar Republic in 1919, was not filling its seats in 1949. Furthermore, the patrons were mostly local and high-brow. Such an audience hardly befitted the national cultural shrine of a workers' and peasants' society. In early 1949 the SED Department of Propaganda, *Kultur,* and Education got in touch with the Thuringian provincial administration and sought ways to attract a broader public to the National Theater without lowering its standards to appeal to a less cultured audience. The department suggested that the best means of doing this was through heavy public subsidies to both the theater itself and to regional bus lines to transport workers there directly from the factory gate. "On the other hand, of course, there must take place a real mobilization of the public through the party and other mass organizations. Here a great deal is in a sad state and I believe that extraordinary measures have to be taken."[61]

These "extraordinary measures" took shape beginning in 1949 in a series of *Gedenkjahre* (commemorative years) devoted to the classical *Erbe.* Events of this sort are celebrated everywhere and have a long tradition in Germany, where the educated classes traditionally celebrated patriotic *Kultur* festivals in order to show off their cultivation to the aristocracy

---

61. Letter, "Abtlg. PKE an das Land Thüringen, der Minister des Innern Werner Eggerath, 4 January, 1949," SAPMO BArch IV 2/906/69, Bl. 78.

and the lower classes. It was only logical that the SED would decide to continue this tradition from its own perspective. But what made these mass cultural events so extraordinary in the Zone was the immense expenditures the SED lavished on them at a time when most East Germans lived in desperate poverty and were paying massive reparations to the Soviet Union. In fact, these events were not intended as entertainment. Each combined the SED's overall building of the myth of *Kultur* with specific political needs reflecting the GDR's position in the cold war. They were intended for the entire German people—East and West—and were a propaganda message to the entire world. But as always, they were mostly aimed at eastern and western youth.

The first full-scale *Gedenkjahr* was the "National Goethe Celebration" of 1949, which today is remembered mostly for Thomas Mann's attendance and his recitation of the same speech text in Frankfurt am Main and in Weimar on 25 July and 1 August respectively.[62] Goethe celebrations took place in the western zones too, although they were conducted by the traditional elites who emphasized gleaning vague humanist inspirations from his spirit and works.[63] The SED was positively obsessed with Goethe in the 1940s and 1950s. Its veneration for the poet went so far that in 1951 the Berlin city planning commission actually considered the creation of a national Goethe shrine in the "*Neue Wache*" on the Unter den Linden boulevard in East Berlin—an intriguing prospect, considering that structure's later use as a memorial for the "victims of Fascism and militarism," complete with a goose-stepping honor guard.[64] The idea for the "Goethe Celebration of the German Nation" originated in the Politburo and was organized through the Party's cultural commission, the mass organizations, and the regional SED organizations. The Party needed the celebration to shore up its wobbly legitimacy among the population, to underscore its demands for a peace treaty, and in its agitation for the two-year plan.

Thus the Party celebrated Goethe as an enemy of nationalism and chauvinism, yet at the same time as the embodiment, "in a fragmented and

---

62. Wilhelm Bleek, "The Competition over German History between the Two German States," *Tel Aviver Jahrbuch für deutsche Geschichte* 19 (1990): 209–10. For a thorough discussion of the mechanics of the Goethe Year and contemporary communist interpretations of Goethe, see Jens Wehner, *Kulturpolitik und Volksfront: ein Beitrag zur Geschichte der Sowjetischen Besatzungszone Deutschlands 1945–1949* (Frankfurt am Main, 1992), 889–913.

63. See Hermann Glaser, *Kulturgeschichte der Bundesrepublik Deutschland. Zwischen Kapitulation und Währungsreform. 1945–1948* (Munich, 1985), 318–22.

64. Birgit Spies, "Aus einem unabgeschlossenen Kapitel," in Daniela Büchten and Anja Frey, eds., *Im Irrgarten der deutschen Geschichte. Die Neue Wache 1818–1993* (Berlin, 1993), 40.

torn Germany, of *German unity* in the spiritual and linguistic spheres."[65] It also needed to justify its claims that the SED (and not the SPD or any other party) was the real "party of the working class" and as such the potential leader not only of the Soviet sector, but of all of Germany. Amid the tremendous melodrama of the proclamations one can discern what was probably a genuine belief in the therapeutic powers of *Kultur:* "The German working class is called upon to take the cultivation of our cultural *Erbe* into its hands and to defend it against all falsifications and distortions, to increase the assets and treasures of our *Kultur,* and to build a new, united, democratic Germany."[66] Goethe was also useful as a spiritual grandfather of Marxism-Leninism. "Goethe was inspired by the conviction that progress is the law of human development. That is why he labored his entire life to fathom the developmental laws of nature and society."[67] Furthermore, "Goethe towered over the greatest of his contemporaries through the knowledge that his work was not the isolated accomplishment of an individual, but a product of a collective character."[68] But it was equally important as an expression of the highly nationalist Soviet cultural policy and internal Soviet conflicts, especially the campaigns against formalism and cosmopolitanism. "It is therefore a conscious fraud and a falsification of Goethean humanism to 'justify' cosmopolitan propaganda for a Europe pact and a Pan-Europe in the service of American monopoly capitalism with references to Goethe's *Weltbürgertum* [cosmopolitanism]."[69]

Given the tremendous importance of the event, it was clear to the SED that its celebration could not be left to literature professors and teachers alone, but that it required "a profound commitment from our great societal organizations and our [local] administrations."[70] Therefore the young FDJ chairman Erich Honecker suggested that the organization sponsor a youth-oriented Goethe celebration in Weimar to take place several months before the official ceremonies in August, and during which Minister President Otto Grotewohl would deliver an address to German youth. Since the event coincided with "World Youth Day," an event honoring the World League of Democratic Youth, the Goethe celebration put

65. "Manifest zur Goethe-Feier der deutschen Nation," *Dokumente der SED,* vol. 2, 333.

66. Ibid., 334.

67. "Unsere Aufgaben im Goethe-Jahr," *Dokumente der SED,* vol. II, 230.

68. "Manifest," 333.

69. "Unsere Aufgaben," 231.

70. "Plan zum Goethe-Jahr, vom Landesausschuss Sachsen für das Goethe-Jahr, 11.3.1949," SAPMO BArch IV ZPA IV 2/906/69, Bl. 78.

an international emphasis on the festivities and invited numerous young people from the western zones and other countries.[71]

Erich Honecker introduced the *Goethe-Feier* on 21 March with a short speech in which he redefined Goethe for German youth. "The progressive, peace-loving people all over the world," Honecker proclaimed, "honor in Goethe not only the inspired master of German classical literature, but at the same time also the brave champion of a militant humanism, for a just and enlightened social order, for the dignity and development of mankind, and *the incorporation of the individual into the community*" (emphasis added). Honecker then thanked the Soviet people and "its glorious and invincible army," in which "the works of Goethe have since the great October Revolution found a home." He also thanked Soviet youth and the Komsomol ("the excellent connoisseurs of Goethe") whose sacrifices had freed "the German people from its destroyers" and who had consequently "rescued the *Kultur* of humanity from soldiers' boots and the gas ovens of Auschwitz and Maidanek. . . . In the struggle to win German youth for the ideals of democracy and peace, for the opening of the best German and foreign cultural assets, the Free German Youth is aware of the great importance of the knowledge of Goethe's works. We bow our heads before his greatness of mind and endeavor to emulate his example."[72] The first day of the celebration concluded with a presentation of Goethe's *Tasso* in the Weimar National Theater.

The next day FDJ members were invited to attend a program of readings from and commentaries on the young Goethe's works together with SBZ literary personalities. That afternoon in the *Weimar-Halle,* Hans Mayer of the University of Leipzig delivered a speech on Goethe's meaning in German literature, after which Otto Grotewohl delivered his keynote speech "Hammer or Anvil." In this speech, Grotewohl stood beside a bust of the poet and appealed to young Germans to follow in Goethe's footsteps and build a new humanistic society. In order to give them a new personal relationship to the poet, he concentrated on the young Goethe of the *Sturm und Drang* generation of the late eighteenth century. "See, dear young friends, here lies your task: to complete the great work which that youth began two hundred years ago. . . . You can become the ray of hope of a new spring if you are prepared to raise higher the banner of humanity, which slipped from the hands of the past,

---

71. "Entwurf, Beteiligung der FDJ an der Ausgestaltung der Feierlichkeiten im Rahmen des Goethe-Jahres 1949," JA IzJ A 10.478.

72. Erich Honecker, "Begrüssungsansprache zur Goethefeier der Jugend in Weimar," 21 March 1949, JA IzJ A 336, 1–2, 4.

if you are prepared to wash off the stains with which ruthless hands have defiled it."[73]

For Grotewohl, Goethe was most important as a messenger of freedom.[74]

> But freedom, according to Friedrich Engels, means the recognition of necessity! Action, human action does not mean recklessly letting fly and unscrupulously pursuing one's own drives and inclinations, as the prophets of individualism proclaim. To act as a human being means: grow beyond your self by growing into human society. Action means: become a useful member of human society, . . . only with human beings do you become a human being.

Grotewohl made clear, however, which human society Goethe was aiming at. "What is the point of prattling on about the freedom of the personality when at the same time one makes all kinds of preparations to exterminate mankind in the most diabolical manner?" Capitalist society, "degenerated into bestiality," had thrown the Goethean tradition overboard in favor of property. "What it defends is not *Kultur* but property. That is nothing other than the path from humanity to bestiality. . . . Today, those who want to defend *Kultur,* those who want to defend the living world of Lessing and Goethe, Heine and Thomas Mann, must stand on the other side of the barricade. The rule of inhumanity, the rule of the threat of the atomic bomb must be broken if humanity is to triumph. Mankind is fed up with being an anvil, it must finally become a hammer."[75]

The published text of the speech, which contained several unabridged Goethe poems and ballads, is over eighty pages long, and by the time it was over many of the FDJ members may have wondered who was really the hammer and who the anvil in the *Weimar-Halle* that day. In any event, the speech fell short of Grotewohl's expectations. As the literary scholar Hans Mayer recalls in his memoirs, the youthful audience was polite but the speaker's labored Goethe interpretations did not ring true. Nevertheless, the 1949 speech was vastly superior to what Mayer calls "the boring and bored poet and artist speeches which later became part of the rigid ritual of the GDR."[76] Even the *Junge Welt* correspondent on the scene did

---

73. Otto Grotewohl, *Amboss oder Hammer: Rede an die deutsche Jugend auf der Goethefeier der Freien Deutschen Jugend am 22. März 1949 in der Weimar-Halle* (East Berlin, 1949), 26–27.

74. Ibid., 32–33.

75. Ibid., 42–46.

76. Hans Mayer, *Der Turm von Babel. Erinnerung an eine Deutsche Demokratische Republik* (Frankfurt am Main, 1991), 60.

not deny that the festival's success was mixed at best (this was still possible in early 1949), that "unfortunately very many friends did not understand the meaning of [the *Tasso* production] and were repelled by its difficulty," and that some young people thought the entire event was "not appropriate for youth."[77] The event certainly failed in giving young people a relationship to Goethe in any way comparable to the life-and-death variety described in *Goethe in Dachau.* Nevertheless it helped establish Honecker (a roofer from Neunkirchen/Saar) and Grotewohl (a printer from Braunschweig) not just as political but also as enlightened cultural figures ("splendid connoisseurs of Goethe," in Honecker's words) for the next forty years.

The festival's conclusion was probably much more effective. The FDJ followed up Grotewohl's speech with a torchlight parade from the *Weimar-Halle* through the streets and parks of the town. Along the way memorial ceremonies were performed at such stations as the Herder monument, Goethe's *Gartenhaus,* Goethe's city house on the Frauenplan, and at the *Schillerhaus.*[78] The march concluded with a solemn ceremony at the Goethe–Schiller monument in front of the Weimar National Theater, where the FDJ members laid their torches onto the paving stones. As a journalist described the ceremony,[79]

> It was a very impressive image as the flames, fanned by the rising night wind, blazed skyward. A glow like summer-lightning lit up the two figures of the great poets. "Only he deserves freedom and life who must daily conquer them." These last words of the dying Faust, recited by a young Weimar actor, sounded like a battle cry. The World Youth Song formed the solemn conclusion of the rally.

The FDJ continued its Goethe programs throughout 1949. In the late spring it cosponsored a student conference on Goethe in which "progressive" students from the West were invited to participate. Among the topics discussed at the Leipzig conference were "Goethe's realism," "The meaning of Goethe for the formation of the national consciousness," "The falsification of Goethe's work and personality by the Fascists and the present-day Reaction," and "Goethe's meaning for today's democratic youth." The resolutions the progressive students passed in preparation for the conference were initiated by the SED's Office of Party Indoctrination, *Kultur,* and Education (PKE) in Berlin. They included an appeal to artists and writers "to develop today the great tradition of Goethe in a lively

---

77. "Goethefeier der Jugend in Weimar," JW 30 March 1949.

78. "Veranstaltungsplan—Goethe-Feiern der Jugend," SAPMO BArch IV 2/906/70, Bl. 113.

79. "Goethefeier der Jugend in Weimar."

way," and a resolution "for the maintenance of the cultural unity of Germany and thus the overall unity of Germany."[80]

Most important of all were the *Heimabende,* which reached a much wider audience than the events themselves. The FDJ's own publishing house, *Neues Leben,* issued a youth book entitled *Goethe. Vermächtnis und Aufruf* (Legacy and appeal). Written by the Party author Johannes Resch, who had previously taught workers about Goethe's progressive thought for some thirty years at an academy in Remscheid, it contained much the same sort of thing only spread out over more than three hundred pages.[81]

It is no wonder, therefore, that when the FDJ issued its first decree on the establishment of uniform group libraries for its local chapters in mid-1949, Goethe headed the list of German personalities whose portraits should be made available for display at lectures and *Heimabende.* He took precedence over Schiller, Beethoven, Marx, Engels, Liebknecht, Luxemburg, Thälmann, and Robert Koch (the list of foreign personalities to be honored this way included, in descending order, Lenin, Stalin, Franklin D. Roosevelt, Henry Wallace, Mao Tse-tung, and many others). But among the list of books to be procured Goethe did not figure even once except in the form of Resch's Marxist-Leninist study. Three Heine volumes were included (*Deutschland—ein Wintermärchen, Harzreise,* and *Nordsee*), as were three prose texts by Schiller: *Uprising in the Netherlands, The Thirty Years' War,* and the *Letters on Aesthetic Education.* But the Schiller works were hardly his most memorable, and their political and ideological subject matter was more useful for *parteilich* indoctrination purposes. Topping the list were the Soviet writer Nikolai Ostrovsky's Komsomol melodrama, *How the Steel Was Tempered,* and Howard Fast's *Road to Freedom.* The rest consisted of antifascist novels, Marxist-Leninist primers, pro-Soviet propaganda pamphlets, Stalin's works, and various technical manuals.[82] Of course, the mere fact that the *Zentralrat* drew up and published such a list did not mean that the regulations were actually carried out to the letter. The organization regularly criticized the group

---

80. Heymann, "(Brief) An die Sozialistische Einheitspartei Deutschlands, Kreisvorstand Leipzig," 31 March 1949, SAPMO BArch IV 2/906/70, Bl. 118.

81. Johannes Resch, *Goethe. Vermächtnis und Aufruf. Eine Einführung* (East Berlin, 1949). For more of the same see Alexander Abusch, "Goethe und unsere Jugend," *JG* 3 (1949): 129–31. Gerhard Baumert attempted a humorous approach (unthinkable a few years later) in his article "'Mit Stelzen durch die Jahrhunderte,'" *JG* 7 (1949): 330–31. In this article, a melancholy young FDJ member is approached by a mysterious stranger (none other than Goethe himself) who responds to the young man's doubts about his own work and the future of Germany with carefully selected Goethe quotations.

82. "Entschliessung zur Verbesserung der ideologischen Arbeit der Freien Deutschen Jugend vom 16./17. Juli 1949: Plan für den Aufbau der Gruppenbüchereien," *DGV* 8 (1949): v–vi.

libraries, and *Junge Generation* once described in detail a particularly messy library whose shelves were packed with old cookbooks, old-fashioned German potboilers, American *Schundliteratur,* and even Nazi era bestsellers. The local members had thrown out their sole copy of Ostrovsky because the cover was slightly damaged (at least that is what they told *Junge Generation!*).[83] Thus, the fact that Goethe's *Faust* was not included on the list does not mean that some libraries did not dig up a copy somewhere and put it on the shelf. It instead reflected the SED's new priorities in mid-1949 and especially after the proclamation of the German Democratic Republic in October. For now that the Party was genuinely in control of the Soviet sector, it could abandon its caution and move toward wholesale Marxist-Leninist indoctrination.

The FDJ's first major change occurred with the *Zentralrat*'s announcement in December 1949 of a new "badge for knowledge" (*Abzeichen für Wissen*) to be awarded in connection with the first *Deutschlandtreffen.* Beginning in 1950, all FDJ members could compete for this badge in bronze, silver, or gold after an examination on political, ideological, and cultural issues of interest to the FDJ.[84] Members prepared for the examination through FDJ learning circles and through the new primer, *The ABC of the FDJ Member.* The exact content of the examination does not concern us here. However, the new competition is important in the development of myth-building since for the first time the actual significance of the classical heritage was now standardized. For example, Heine's actual works were no longer of particular importance, but rather his views on German unity and his friendship with Marx. The quality of Grotewohl's "Hammer or Anvil" speech was no longer a matter of individual taste, as it had been in 1949. Now, a year later, detailed study of the speech was one of the requirements for the award. "Thus," a functionary stated, "the award for good knowledge will contribute to the even more comprehensive and rapid completion of the great ideological transformation process of the young generation."[85]

In 1950 the campaigns against formalism and cosmopolitanism were in full force. The GDR was swept by a wave of Party purges and show trials against "terrorists," "saboteurs," and other "agents of U.S. imperialism." The SED was also gripped in a bitter struggle against the Protestant

---

83. Ulrich Beer, "Und Euere Heimbücherei?" JG 2 (1950): 94. This is an extreme example, but the *Zentralrat* made it clear from the beginning that local members were to assemble their libraries themselves. Cf. Jochen Stief, "Gruppenbücherei—allen ein Begriff?" JG 9 (1949): 423.

84. "Stiftung eines Abzeichens für gutes Wissen," DGV 12 (1949): iv–v.

85. Hans Schönecker, "Mit der 'Auszeichnung für gutes Wissen' zum Deutschland-treffen," JG 12 (1949): 570.

Church and its youth group, the *Junge Gemeinde.* The cold war turned into open warfare in Korea. In the midst of this atmosphere the SED proclaimed a "National Bach Celebration" to commemorate the two hundredth anniversary of Johann Sebastian Bach's birth. The idea to organize a national celebration of this date did not originate with the SED but instead with the venerable Leipzig *"Bach-Gesellschaft,"* which remained the official sponsor. The SED gained control over both the society and the festivities by arranging the admission of the *Bach-Gesellschaft* into the *Kulturbund,* itself a Marxist-Leninist mass organization. Now, by coordinating the society and coopting its name, the Party was in a position to secure the cooperation of West German and international scholars and musicians who would otherwise have been suspicious of taking part in an SED event. This last point was essential. The SED then set up a Berlin-based "German Bach Committee," which took over actual control. The new committee set up a panel of Marxist-Leninists, including Ernst Hermann Meyer of the University of Berlin and Jürgen Kuczynski, to reinterpret Bach for the event. This new interpretation then found its way into the Party's official proclamations in the Bach year.[86]

According to the SED's "National Declaration for Bach," Germany's democratic renewal "can only take place on the basis of the great German *Kulturerbe,* the free and progressive *Kulturtraditionen* of the German people. Only in the most bitter struggle against all influences of the corrupting American *Kulturbarbarei* can and will the democratic renewal of our cultural life be realized." Since Bach was "a great pathbreaker in the field of music," "to declare oneself for Bach means to declare one's self for the free and progressive cultural traditions of our people."[87] Such a declaration was only possible coming from the working classes, since the bourgeoisie had never understood Bach and never would. Indeed, the American imperialists were trying to falsify Bach and "to declare him, in the interests of their cosmopolitan propaganda, to be a 'supranational' church

---

86. Transcript from the article "Herein mit J.S. Bach in die 'Nationale Front,'" in the West Berlin newpaper *Der Tag,* 19 March 1950, SAPMO BArch IV 2/9.06/70, Bl. 83–86. This article and the related articles in this file provide a fascinating behind-the-scenes look at the workings of the "German Bach Committee." The authenticity of the contents are vouched for by Karl-Heinz Tetzner, secretary of the "German Bach Committee," in a letter to Stefan Heymann, director of the SED's Office of Party Indoctrination, Culture, and Propaganda on 24 March 1950: "This essay, which was published without a name or pseudonym, was with the greatest certainty written by Eberhard Gelbe-Haussen, formerly the district secretary of the *Kulturbund* in Leipzig, or based on information given by him or documents stolen by him. This is proven by the intimate knowledge of the Leipzig situation, literal quotations from the protocols of the previous discussions, and the breaking off of this chronologically structured concoction with the resolutions which were announced on the day of his escape." Bl. 82.

87. "Nationales Bekenntnis zu Bach," *Dokumente der SED*, vol. 2, 464–65.

composer or formalist." "Only the defeat of the German Imperialists with the smashing of German Fascism through the armies of the Socialist Soviet Union cleared the way for a genuinely *objective* evaluation and appreciation of Bach. . . . The great cultivation, which especially the Soviet people bestow upon Bach's music, is evidence for the recognition of the world importance and *effectiveness* of this great national composer by the most free and progressive country in the world, the land of perfected Socialism"[88] (emphasis added).

But the Bach cult was not mere agitprop. Underlying the entire campaign was an earnest belief in the therapeutic powers of Bach's music to renew Germany and perhaps the SED itself. In his keynote speech at the official state ceremony in Leipzig in July 1950, Wilhelm Pieck's invocation of Bach's life sounded like an incantation: "He embodies the best and noblest qualities of our people. Emotion and admiration grip us when we consider how, from the narrow, petty conditions of a Germany left miserable and disunited through the barbarism of the Thirty Years' War, this wondrous genius arose."[89]

The SED also reinterpreted Bach as both an instrument of the class struggle and an antireligious force. He now became a "popular composer" who had been compelled to compose church music as an employee of the church. "Bach's great importance lies in the fact that he burst the ecclesiastical shackles of music and, in the place of dead formulas, set human experience and feeling, in which the bourgeois humanist opposition against the declining feudal society was expressed. Bach's great national importance lies in the fact that he, closely linked with the people, wove folk songs and folk dances into his treasury of melody and, through his adaptation of folk songs and other secular melodies into chorales and other church music, 'secularized' this music." According to SED aestheticians, Bach's religious music was vastly inferior to his secular pieces. Thus in one of the most bizarre quirks of the cold war, Bach's light-hearted "Coffee Cantata" and above all his obscure "Peasant Cantata" were reinterpreted as his greatest works.[90]

The latter piece was indeed about peasants, but it was hardly the ode to collectivized agriculture that the SED made it out to be. Instead, Bach had written it as a tongue-in-cheek musical tribute to the Saxon chamberlain Carl Heinrich von Dieskau in 1742. In the cantata, a peasant man and

---

88. Ibid., 466.
89. "Ehren wir Bach, indem wir seinem Werk den Frieden erhalten. Die Rede des Präsidenten der Republik, Wilhelm Pieck, auf der Nationalfeier in Leipzig anlässlich der 200. Wiederkehr des Todestages von Johann Sebastian Bach," ND 29.7.1950.
90. Karl-Heinz Tetzner, "Die Werke Bachs für uns entdecken. Unsere Aufgabe im Jahr des 200. Todestages J.S. Bachs," JW 17 March 1950.

woman outdo each other in paying homage to von Dieskau upon his inheritance of the manor of Klein-Zschocher near Leipzig (hence the cantata's opening aria: "We have a new lordship"). In the original version of the finale, whose melody and rhythm really are reminiscent of old folk dances, the couple sings:[91]

> Now we go where the dudelsack,
> The dudel-, dudel-, dudel-, dudel-, dudel-, dudelsack
> Drones in our tavern,
> And gladly we proclaim:
> Long live Dieskau and his house,
> May he be granted what he desires,
> And what he himself may wish!

For the SED, the music represented the very essence of Bach's creative genius. It was sung repeatedly during the Bach year and found its way into the FDJ songbook *Live-Sing-Fight,* remaining there in every new edition until 1989. Unfortunately, the original text did not match Bach's alleged progressive intentions. This problem was solved when the SED poet Paul Hermann penned a new text for this tune and the entire cantata.[92]

> Now we go where the dudelsack, etc.
> Long live the peasant and his class,
> Long live the broad, free land,
> May he be granted, in goods and value,
> What he creates with his hand!

The opening aria, which was also included in the FDJ songbook, was similarly expurgated. The original text reads:

> We have a new lordship
> In our Chamberlain.
> He gives us beer, that goes to our heads,
> That is the clear kernel.
> Let the pastor do his worst;
> You musicians, stay nimble, etc.

---

91. Werner Neumann, "Das Schaffen Johann Sebastian Bachs, Kantaten," *Archiv Produktion des musikhistorischen Studios der Deutschen Grammophon Gesellschaft* (Hamburg, 1960).

92. *Leben-Singen-Kämpfen. Liederbuch der FDJ,* 12th ed. (Leipzig, 1973), 238–39.

This was replaced by "Today we're celebrating our parish fair / With dance and cheerfulness, / There's good food of the very best kind / And beer and cool wine." The following line about the straitlaced pastor, rendered meaningless outside of its original context, remained unchanged in the new version and served as evidence of Bach's anti-Church sentiments.[93] The performance of the "Peasant Cantata" by a "National *Kultur* Group of the FDJ" formed the climax of the DEFA's Bach film in 1950, at the end of which the following words appeared on the screen: "The works which Johann Sebastian Bach left behind are a priceless national heritage . . . Be proud of him, fatherland, be proud of him, but also be worthy of him."[94]

As with the Goethe celebration of 1949, the Bach celebration of 1950 consisted of two parts: first a "Bach Commemoration of Youth" in March, to be followed by the "Bach Ceremony of the GDR" to be held in July. According to *Junge Generation,* "it is more than a symbolic act that first and foremost the German democratic youth and with it the progressive youth of the entire world declares itself for one of the most spiritually powerful [*geistmächtigsten*] creative geniuses of mankind." After all, "the declaration for Bach is a declaration for truthfulness, purity, and integrity of the character, is a declaration for the harmony of the polyphonic community, for the active life and [for] belief in an ordering power."[95]

All of this was reflected in the "Bach Celebration of German Youth" in Eisenach from 19 to 21 March 1950, which was attended by several thousand eastern and western German youths. During the festivities the youths attended a concert of the Leipzig *Kreuzchor,* which performed a program of Bach's secular songs, modern choral works, and FDJ "youth songs." This was followed the next evening by the Berlin *Rundfunkorchester*'s performance of the "Coffee Cantata" and the expurgated "Peasant Cantata." The climax of the event took place on the third and final evening, when the eastern and western youths took part in a torchlight procession up to the Wartburg. In the courtyard of the castle the FDJ functionary Horst Brasch delivered his keynote speech. "To commemorate Bach," Brasch told the youths, "today means to defend German *Kultur* against the attacks of American imperialism. We do not allow the imperialist *Kulturbarbaren* to perform a Bach concert for the unemployed in which they play the works of the great German in jazz style [*verjazzen*]. We also do not allow them to hawk hand-painted neckties with Bach's portrait. In the same way that we protest against the dismantling of our German peace industry"—by which he referred to Allied actions in the

---

93. Ibid., 238.
94. Ernst Dahle, dir., *Johann Sebastian Bach,* DEFA, 1950.
95. Karl Schönewolf, "J.S. Bach und die Jugend," JG 3 (1950): 137.

Ruhr region, not to the dismantling of SBZ industry by the Soviet Union—"we fight against the contamination of German youth by the *Unkultur* of U.S. imperialism. The Bach tribute of German youth," Brasch concluded, "is thus a pledge to German *Kultur* and to the unified and indivisible German Democratic Republic."[96]

In July 1950 the *Zentralrat* formally admitted that its haphazard indoctrination programs were not showing the expected results among the FDJ rank and file, and proclaimed a new propaganda system designed to complement the "Good Knowledge" program. The "Indoctrination Year of the FDJ" was scheduled to begin in January 1951.[97] "The indoctrination takes place according to a unified established plan of instruction on the basis of instructional books, in self-instruction and in circles on indoctrinational days, which are determined by the Secretariat of the Central Council and are carried out twice monthly—three times monthly in the countryside during the winter—after work and after school."[98] The main areas of study were to be the policies of the SED and the FDJ, love of Stalin and the Soviet Union, and the "unmasking" of Western imperialists. The resolution also called for more intensive indoctrination at the FDJ academies, for an even heavier ideological content in the FDJ's publications, and for stricter control over the group libraries.

In the new ideological climate *Kultur* lost nearly all its therapeutic qualities in the youth organization and was reduced to a weapon of the cold war—much to the dismay of SED ideologues, who had genuinely hoped to create a new "*Nationalkultur*" and now feared ridicule. Typical of this phenomenon was the way in which Heine's most famous song, *Die Loreley,* was used as an anti-American tool after press reports that the U.S. Army was planning to plant mines on the Loreley rock and blow it up in the event of a Soviet invasion in order to block the Rhine River.[99] This campaign was also propagated through the Ernst Busch/Hanns Eisler youth agitation song "*Ami* go home," the third verse of which went: "*Ami,* learn the melody / Of the maiden Loreley, / Who sits above and combs her golden hair. / He who breaks her comb in two / Will break his own neck. / Ancient is the tale, sad, but true: / Go home, *Ami, Ami* go

96. "Ehrung eines grossen Deutschen. Bachfeier der deutschen Jugend in Eisenach," JW 24 March 1950; Irma Nawrotzki, "Eindrücke am Rande der Bach-Tage, Gespräche mit westdeutschen Teilnehmern," JW 28 March 1950.

97. The German name was "*Schuljahr der FDJ.*" While *Schulung* can also be translated as "instruction" or "training," "indoctrination" reflects the FDJ's intentions more accurately.

98. "Entschliessung der 6. (26.) Tagung des Zentralrates der FDJ zur Verbesserung der politischen Aufklärungsarbeit der FDJ" (13 July 1950), DGV September 1950, vi.

99. E.g., "Hände weg von der Loreley," JW 23 June 1950.

home, etc."[100] As one concerned ideologue wrote in the SED journal *Einheit:* "Not long ago a daily newspaper published an article about the FDJ Indoctrination Year. A youth friend, so it is reported, responded to the question 'What do you think of when you hear the name *Loreley?*' [with the words] 'I think: *Ami* go home!' "[101]

To be sure, the organization did offer solid instruction in actual cultural interest groups, where "already graphic artists are again learning from such masters as Dürer, the young composers are creating electrifying, persuasive songs because they are building them upon the works of such great masters as Bach and Beethoven."[102] (This doubtless explains the neoclassical style of many statues of steel workers and the curiously baroque flavor of many FDJ "youth songs.") Furthermore, such mass events as the "Theater Day of Youth" on 12 January 1952, in which a total of sixty-five theaters throughout the GDR presented a wide range of classical and modern plays, operas, and operettas, did indeed introduce thousands of young people to Goethe, Schiller, Lessing, Wagner, Kleist, Mozart, Lortzing, and many others, alongside Brecht, Gorki, Ostrowski, and other *parteilich* authors. Even if, according to the organizers, these works "actively reflect the boldness, the affirmation of life, the love of fatherland, the creative strength and the striving for peace and progress" of modern youth, the young people could still form their own opinions.[103] But the propagandistic quality of most cultural events, the narrow ideological indoctrination offered at the FDJ academies, the constant pursuit of propagandist awards and badges "for good knowledge," and the feverish culture of "plan fulfillment" made a narrow vision only natural. This outlook is expressed in the propaganda guidelines issued to the FDJ in 1952. When agitating with classical and modern literature, the Soviet author of the guidelines writes, "the work, or the excerpt from it, must completely correspond to the thought that the propagandist wants to illustrate. It must be fully and completely understandable to the course taker in regard to language and must not be lengthy."[104] It is hard to imagine a new *Nationalkultur* arising from such a system.

---

100. *Leben-Singen-Kämpfen,* 83.

101. Johanna Rudolph, "Heines Werk dem Volke! Zur Heine-Ausgabe des Aufbau-Verlages 1951," *Einheit* 6 (1952): 569.

102. Rudi Raupach, "Die Auswertung der Festspiele auf dem Gebiet der Kulturarbeit," *JG* 8 (1951): 7–8.

103. Hans Rodenberg, "Jugend und Theater," *JW* 8 January 1952.

104. N. Kusin, "Wie man den Unterricht in der politischen Grundschule durchführt," *Bibliothek des Propagandisten* 2 (1952): 49. The propagandist should further attempt to popularize the literature "so that the course takers develop a taste for the systematic reading of the fictional literature" (50).

The year 1952 was especially turbulent in the GDR. With its slogan "Germans at one table!" the SED was intensifying the campaign it had begun the year before against the Federal Republic's application to join the "General War Treaty" and for the reunification of Germany, a campaign that intensified after the publication of the "Stalin note" of 10 March 1952, offering the Western Allies a united and democratic German state in exchange for German neutrality. The Western Allies' rejection of this offer led the SED to seal and fortify the inner German border (but not yet in Berlin) in May, followed soon after by a resolution by the Second Party Conference to begin "the systematic construction of the foundations of Socialism," that is, the full-scale reorganization of all of GDR society on the Soviet model.

Amid the furious propaganda activity these events generated, the functionaries' journal *Junge Generation* ran a series of biographical articles entitled "We are learning from the great Germans," which included Goethe, Lessing, Ferdinand Freiligrath, Heine, Büchner, and the heroes of the War of Liberation against Napoleon in 1813. But the greatest German of all in 1952 was Ludwig van Beethoven. According to the SED's official proclamation, the events commemorating the 125th anniversary of Beethoven's death took place "in a time in which the American Imperialists are preparing another war and militarism in West Germany is rising again. . . . Beethoven's work belongs to the indestructible treasures of our national *Kulturerbe*. Its cultivation and further creative development are the concern of the entire German people. His work is a tremendous source of strength in the struggle for the unity of our fatherland and the preservation of peace."[105] Whereas the Americans, as usual, were attempting to "poison the German national consciousness, to destroy German *Kultur*," the SED honored "in Beethoven the inspired son of our people, the fearless fighter for progress, the singer of the brotherly solidarity of peoples, the passionate ambassador of peace." In these trying times the German people had only one ally. "What Beethoven fought for and what he foresaw and strived after for the future has become a reality through the Great Socialist October Revolution, through Soviet power. When in the year 1936 the peoples of the Soviet Union adopted the Stalinist Constitution, Beethoven's Ninth Symphony rang out." By contrast, "The American *Kulturbarbaren* and their lackeys desecrate Beethoven's memory by misusing Bonn, his birthplace, for the most depraved national degradation."[106]

The FDJ press concentrated on Beethoven's noble personal qualities and presented him as a model of hard work and study. Beyond that, his

---

105. "Zum 125. Todestag Ludwig van Beethovens am 26. März 1952," *Dokumente der SED,* vol. 3, 751.

106. Ibid., 751, 754, 756, 757.

greatest contributions to *Kultur* were his closeness to the people, his pro-gressiveness, and his patriotism. As the "leader of the realistic epoch in music" he still had "a great deal to say to us today in the struggle against formalism and the American *Kulturbarbarei,* for realism in art and litera-ture."[107]

Of course, many of these fine ideological points were too abstract for the masses, who were only now becoming fully acquainted with Marxism-Leninism and its *Kulturerbe.* FDJ functionaries and future SED leaders, at whom most of this was directed, drew their own conclusions. "It is a true pleasure," one FDJ journalist wrote, "to see how these simple people exchange their opinions on musical issues, how they begin to assimilate the *Kulturgüter* of their homeland." When the journalist asked a group of FDJ secretaries why they liked Beethoven's music, youth friend Jürgen replied: "'How should I put it, it's so hard to express. . . . What I like about Beethoven is the militant element. We recently heard his Fifth Symphony . . . '—and now the eyes of the youth friends light up.'"[108]

For the journalist, Beethoven's message was in his music.[109]

What is it that we like about Beethoven? His immense strength, his struggle for what is good, for what is noble in the world, and finally the victory of light over darkness in his music.

Unfortunately, the fact that Beethoven was born in Bonn and had no link to the territory of the GDR prohibited elaborate wreath-laying cere-monies and torchlight parades. Thus the SED did not organize a special youth ceremony for Beethoven, but concentrated its efforts on a national Bach festival in Berlin with FDJ participation. On 26 March, following the playing of the GDR national anthem, Wilhelm Pieck placed himself before a gigantic Beethoven portrait in the Berlin State Opera and delivered a speech declaring the cultivation of Beethoven's legacy to be a "national task." The festivities consisted mainly of concerts in theaters and factories, lectures, FDJ *Heimabende,* radio broadcasts, and visits by Soviet cultural officials.[110]

The SED institutionalized this ideological line in the "National Research and Memorial Center" in Weimar, founded at the behest of Cul-

---

107. Egon Rentzsch, "Die Freie Deutsche Jugend ehrt Beethoven," JG 6 (1952): 28–30.

108. Sigfried Mühlhaus, "Wie stehen unsere Funktionre zur ernsten Musik?" JG 20 (1952): 34–35.

109. Mühlhaus, 35.

110. W. P. Claever, "Zu Ehren Ludwig van Beethovens," JW 22 March 1952; Claever, "Festakt zu Ehren Ludwig van Beethovens," JW 28 March 1952; see also other articles from this period.

tural Minister Johannes R. Becher in 1952. Until their reorganization in
1990, the research institute, the classical publishing house, and the museums in Weimar sought, "guided by the principles of Marxist-Leninist
scholarship and Socialist cultural policy, to foster . . . the adoption of this
heritage by the working class, youth and the entire toiling *Volk* and contribute to the training of all-around educated and convinced builders of
Socialism, filled with the spirit of Socialist patriotism and proletarian
internationalism." Equally important was their "contribution to the international representation of the GDR. They defend the humanistic values of
the *Erbe* of classical German literature and art against their misuse, their
falsification and destruction through Imperialism as well as against all
varieties of reactionary bourgeois ideology."[111]

Friedrich Schiller's memory was also put to interesting new uses during this period. He differed from the other cultural figures in that he was
accorded no therapeutic value whatsoever. For example, in 1952 SED
chief ideologue Fred Oelssner explained to FDJ peasant youths in a lecture on agricultural production that "in Schiller's drama *Kabale und
Liebe* you can read how a few hundred years ago German princes sold off
their '*Landeskinder*' by the thousands to America in order to buy jewels
for their courtesans with the blood money. In order to increase the profits
of his family company, Adenauer wants to sell off the entire male population of West Germany to America, [he] wants to drive them into a frat-
ricidal war against Germans."[112] It was this criterion, and presumably
this criterion alone, that made *Kabale und Liebe* Schiller's most frequently
performed play in the 1950s and a prerequisite for the "good knowledge"
award in silver.

The ceremonies marking the 150th anniversary of Schiller's death in
1955 fell together with the SED's final offer to the West of nationwide elections, Adenauer's signing of the Treaty of Paris bringing the Federal
Republic into NATO, the founding of the Warsaw Pact, Khrushchev's de
facto renunciation of German reunification, and the preparations for the
creation of a "National People's Army," which was formally created in
January 1956. The ceremonies reflected this atmosphere by celebrating
Schiller's "struggle for the development of a democratic national consciousness and a unified German nation state. . . . Schiller formed heroes
out of the simple toiling people, who place themselves at the head of the

---

111. "Statut der 'Nationalen Forschungs- und Gedenkstätten der klassischen
deutschen Literatur in Weimar' (1975)," in Peter Lübbe, ed., *Dokumente zur Kunst, Literatur-
und Kulturpolitik der SED 1975–1980* (Stuttgart, 1984), 85.

112. Fred Oelsner, "Die Aufgaben der Freien Deutschen Jugend im Dorf," in
Schriftenreihe der FDJ 12 (1952): 3. Adenauer owned stock in the Messerschmidt aircraft
company.

national liberation struggle and lead it to victory." Schiller was especially important for youth: "The searing breath and the future-pointing ideas of his heroes made them into a model for German youth. That is why his work was especially effective in the struggle of the German people for national unity and democratic freedom. . . . May the Schiller Year 1955 serve to strengthen the unity of our fatherland and its humanistic *Kultur* in thought and deed!"[113]

In the FDJ press Schiller was "the poet of youth." "Our generation in particular has been given the sacred task not just to quote the poetic fire of patriotism which burned within Schiller and lives on in his works, but also to use them as a weapon against those who attempt to tear apart our fatherland."[114] Or, as another author put it even more succinctly, Schiller's importance for youth lay in his "genuine patriotic *Pathos.*"[115]

As usual the FDJ put on a "Schiller Ceremony of German Youth in Weimar" on 2–3 April 1955. It opened with a joint contingent of eastern and western youths laying wreaths at the Schiller mausoleum and the Goethe–Schiller monument. The main ceremony took place in the National Theater and began with the playing of the overture to Wagner's *Meistersinger,* followed by speeches by Honecker and Grotewohl. The latter emphasized Schiller's "humanism" and called upon German youth to realize Schiller's slogan from *Wilhelm Tell:* "We want to be a single people of brothers." The next day visitors could choose between a tour of Weimar's monuments or a trip to the former Buchenwald concentration camp, where the great antifascist monument was under construction. In the evening the young people attended a performance of Schiller's *Jungfrau von Orleans* and took part in the standard torchlight parade. The event concluded in an atmospheric ceremony in the courtyard of the Weimar Castle, where amid the fading torches SED dignitaries urged the youths to keep the flame of their love of Germany alive. The progressive young West German visitors were to continue their fight against imperialism and the East German young people to join the People's Police, which was soon to develop into the National People's Army.[116]

But a few years later it had become clear to Ulbricht and the Politburo that reunification was not imminent. Although plans for German–German

---

113. "Zum 150. Todestag Friedrich Schillers am 9. Mai 1955," *Dokumente der SED,* vol. 5, 219, 220, 222, 223.

114. "Seid einig einig einig. Zum 150. Todestag Friedrich Schillers," JG 4 (1955): 33.

115. Hans Jürgen Geerdts, "Schillers Ringen um die einige Nation," JG 5 (1955): 25.

116. "Schillers Vermächtnis liegt in den Händen der Jugend," JW 4 April 1955; "Nicht verlöscht die Flamme eurer Liebe," JW 5 April 1955; "'Wir sind ein Volk.' Richtungsweisende Rede unseres Ministerpräsidenten Otto Grotewohl an die deutsche Jugend," JW 5 April 1955.

confederations, demands for peace treaties, and the like continued all the way to Ulbricht's removal from power in 1971, the main emphasis was now placed on consolidating socialism within the GDR. The GDR's halfhearted "de-Stalinization" process also discredited the personality cults of the era, and this included the personality cults around cultural figures, which now seemed slightly foolish.[117]

In the meantime, Western popular culture, spread by the plague-*Amis* and their imperialist radio stations, had become a real epidemic among GDR youth. Thousands of youths were taking advantage of the open border in Berlin to watch western films and to dance in western youth clubs. Since melodramatic appeals to German cultural ideals were not working, the FDJ shifted to a campaign of threats and gentle reasoning. For example, at a printing shop in Halle the local FDJ secretary was horrified to find that the apprentices were not only listening to the swinging tunes of Radio Luxembourg, but also printing and passing around pictures of Elvis Presley and Bill Haley. Knowing that a simple condemnation of the two entertainers would be useless, the secretary and other FDJ functionaries put together a wall newspaper.[118]

> On the right side of the wall newspaper we tacked up the pictures of top athletes . . . ; in addition we presented two former apprentices, one of whom is today an engineer, the other an officer of the National People's Army; we further added the farewell letter of [the antifascist] Walter Husemann and introduced Prof. Dr. Baade of our aviation industry. We presented all of these personalities as role models.
>
> On the left side of the newspaper we derided the screaming devil Presley, and showed how concerts with Haley end [i.e., in a riot]. From this we drew the conclusion that these ruffian singers as well as Rock'n Roll are being used by [West German defense minister Franz Josef] Strauss, [John Foster] Dulles, and others for psychological warfare.

But more important was the new cultural policy called the "Bitterfeld Path," so named after the Bitterfeld Conference of April 1959. Under the slogan "Buddy, grab your pen!" the conference laid out a new cultural policy that reaffirmed the cultivation of classical German *Kultur,* the develop-

---

117. It is important to note that the personality cult around Ulbricht was not affected by "de-Stalinization," nor were the cults surrounding Lenin and the martyrs of the antifascist resistance. These, in fact, increased in intensity.

118. Horst Freigang, "Radio Luxemburg, Westschmöker und der kalte Krieg," JG 5 (1959): 4–5.

ment of an activist aesthetic dedicated to plan-fulfillment and the strengthening of socialism, the incorporation of workers and other groups into the artistic process, and finally the unification of art and entertainment. It formally ended the overt campaigns against "formalism" and "cosmopolitanism," even though these notions lived on in spirit throughout the Ulbricht era and many traces remained until 1989. The goal was a new socialist *Nationalkultur,* rooted in German classicism and socialist realism, that would encompass the entire society and in which the working class would actively participate in the development of a culture both surpassing the classics and rooted in daily life. This was part of the SED's overall strategy of closing the gap between state and society, Party and people.[119]

This cultural policy corresponded with the resolutions of the Fifth Party Convention of the SED and the Sixth Parliament of the FDJ, which likewise demanded the "adoption of the cultural legacy and the new socialist *Kultur* as well as the development of the artistic self-activity of young people."[120] The key word was *humanism,* which had by now become interchangeable with *Kultur* and which the SED defined as the essence of "Socialism." Humanism was the quality Otto Grotewohl celebrated in his speech marking the GDR's comparatively low-key Handel Year of 1959, in which a series of concerts and lectures was designed to open up Handel's works to the masses.[121] Aside from minor adjustments over the years, this cultural policy and the SED's new slogan "Plan with us, work with us, govern with us" remained in place for the next thirty years of the GDR's existence.

Under the new policy, *Kultur* was no longer particularly useful as a weapon, but was needed again for its therapeutic qualities. As West Germany strengthened its economy and embedded itself ever further into the Western Alliance, the GDR took an increasingly defensive position. Since the Party and FDJ press were stirring up war hysteria with daily warnings of an imminent NATO invasion, inner unity and the resolution to defend the Socialist fatherland were demanded. This was reflected by the events marking Schiller's two hundredth birthday in 1959. Appeals to unity were a mere formality this time, and denunciations of American *Kulturbarbarei* absent. According to the "Schiller Committee of the GDR," the events of the year "are an example of how the state of the workers and peasants and the Socialist society unlock and carry on the cultural assets of past cen-

---

119. Volker Gransow, *Kulturpolitik in der DDR* (West Berlin, 1975), 89–98.

120. *Geschichte der FDJ,* 337.

121. Karl Schönewolf, "Das Händel-Jahr beginnt," JW 1 January 1959; "Händels Werk in guten Händen. Aus der Fest-Ansprache Otto Grotewohls," JW 16 April 1959; Hermann Kähler, "Tage der Musik," JW 17 April 1959.

turies."[122] The state unlocked and carried them on in 1959 through scholarly conferences with international guests, theater productions, a DEFA film version of *Kabale und Liebe,* various exhibitions and other activities throughout the entire GDR, wreath-laying ceremonies, and the inevitable torchlight parade through the nighttime streets of Weimar.[123]

As usual, according to the official manifesto, the main thrust of the celebration was aimed at "the youth of our time, who have the task to build with us the peaceful future of their fatherland and to stand in the front line of the pathbreakers of a new Socialist world, [and] will take in the flaming *Pathos* and the progressive thoughts of Schiller's poetic works and will let themselves be inspired by them to [perform] the deeds of today."[124]

In 1958, the SED and the FDJ, in connection with the Weimar city council and the *Nationale Forschungs- und Gedenkstätten,* agreed upon the need to "create a new tradition" of a Schiller Festival of Youth that could pick up on an older tradition that had ended in 1933. This new tradition was launched in August 1959 with rotating three-day Schiller programs for shifts of one thousand FDJ members, nonorganized GDR youths, and western visitors. Each of the programs began with attendance at a performance of Schiller's *Fiesco* at the National Theater. The second day was taken up by a six-hour visit to the new Buchenwald monument. The visit included the showing of three antifascist films: *Night and Fog, Never Again,* and a documentary on the monument itself. In the National Theater that evening the young people attended a production of Brecht's *Fear and Misery of the Third Reich.* On the last day, the young people visited Weimar's monuments.[125] The following year the event was renamed "Theater Days of Youth" and offered performances of Schiller's *Don Carlos* and Friedrich Wolf's *Professor Mamlock,* alongside visits to Buchenwald and to the historical sites of Weimar. It became a firm FDJ institution that lasted until 1989.[126]

The Schiller Festivals of 1959–60 marked a turning point in the *Kultur* myth in the FDJ and in the GDR as a whole. By this time the myth of *Kultur* had become largely subsumed under general GDR cultural policy and was pursued according to the demands of the "Bitterfeld Path" within

122. "Stenographisches Protokoll der 2. Sitzung des Schiller-Komitees der DDR," 20 March 1959, SAPMO BArch IV 2/906/71, Bl. 94.

123. Ibid.; "Direktive zum Schillerjahr 1959," SAPMO BArch IV 2/906/71, Bl. 183–84.

124. "Erklärung des Schiller-Komitees der Deutschen Demokratischen Republik, 1959," SAPMO BArch IV 2/906/71, Bl. 90.

125. "Ablauf und Programm für die Schiller-Festspiele der Jugend in Weimar vom 19.8. bis 30.8.1959," SAPMO BArch IV 2/906/71, Bl. 213.

126. "Erlebnisreiche Tage in Weimar," JW 19 August 1960.

the schools, whose teachers by this time were nearly all products of the FDJ. What is more, the new scientific and technical demands of the Sputnik age made the obsessive acquisition of the *Kulturerbe* seem just a bit old-fashioned. Finally, the construction of the Berlin Wall on 13 August 1961 slowed down the large-scale East–West youth exchanges, and the cultural events consequently lost half of their purpose. Now that GDR youth had no means of escape, *Kultur* in the melodramatic style of the 1940s and 1950s stood in the way of the even more melodramatic myth-building strategies of antifascism, German–Soviet friendship, and the "Socialist fatherland."

Kultur for Kids

The use of classical *Kultur* in the FDJ's agitation and propaganda made sense among the older members, who either still attended or had completed school and university courses based upon the classical heritage, were regularly bombarded with Marxism-Leninism and *parteilich* lectures on Beethoven, and perhaps had even begun participating in the *Kulturerbe* themselves in their free time. But Young Pioneers and nonorganized GDR children were simply too young to enjoy, say, *The Sorrows of Young Werther,* let alone to identify a Marxist-Leninist moral in it. The FDJ, the Young Pioneer leadership, and the entire educational and propaganda apparatus of the GDR were compelled therefore to use the one aspect of *Kultur* that was and still is readily accessible to all children: fairy tales.

This idea was not original with the Young Pioneers and the FDJ. In fact, Marxist-Leninists have long believed that fairy tales represent genuine folk culture, and hence are really about them. Already in 1925 the Young Spartacus League had discovered that "the most important vehicles for popular mass propaganda" among the youngest fighters were "the children's theater, speech choirs, brass and drum corps, social games, moreover the political puppet show, and *Kasperletheater* [Punch and Judy shows]."[127] The Young Pioneers used all of these tools and above all fairy tales to illustrate the principles of capitalist exploitation and popular resistance in keeping with the issues of the moment. "Kasper will be the teacher, the critic," an SED functionary wrote in 1949, "he will enlighten and agitate, he will be everywhere that a free sturdy word has to be spoken."[128] On the one hand this was an example of general SED propaganda, but on the other a typical use of the *Kulturerbe* for modern needs. There was also a much more prosaic reason for the renaissance of fairy

---

127. "Reichskonferenz der JSB.-Leiter, kommunistische Lehrer und Elternbeiräte vom 10.–13. Oktober in Halle," SAPMO BArch I 4/1/81, Bl. 287.
128. Ulrich Baer, "Wo bleibt das Handpuppenspiel?" JG 10 (1949): 474.

tales and Kasper puppets in these years: *parteilich* children's books were still hard to find, and the writings of non-Marxist children's authors like Erich Kästner and Johanna Spyri were severely frowned upon (charged with "reaction" in the first case, "*Kitsch*" in the second). Soviet children's literature, hastily translated into German, could not fill the gap. Just like Goethe and Schiller, Hans Christian Andersen and the Brothers Grimm were free of formalism and served as a surrogate *Kultur* until the development of a new domestic socialist variety.

The most elaborate expression of this strategy came in the form of the GDR's fairy-tale films, which are still shown today and which offer a fascinating contrast to the Walt Disney films of the same period. Since the films were intended to be not only entertaining but also instructional, the DEFA coordinated its production activities closely with the Young Pioneers and the Ministry of Education. DEFA, which had a monopoly on film production in the GDR from 1945 until 1989, was created as a state propaganda instrument. Its most important tasks, according to the Soviet military authorities, who first created it before passing over full control to the GDR in 1949, were "the struggle for the education of the German people, above all youth, in the cause of genuine democracy and humanity, and thus to awaken respect for other peoples and countries."[129]

DEFA's first full-length color fairy-tale film reflected this general "humanistic" orientation, and while it did point prophetically to the founding of the GDR as the fulfillment of the common people's supposed age-old longing for a socialist state free of exploitation, it still refrained from open agitation. This film was DEFA's 1950 adaptation of the story "The Cold Heart" by the nineteenth-century German Romantic writer Wilhelm Hauff.[130] In this tale the poor young charcoal-burner Peter seeks out an evil forest spirit with whom he exchanges his warm working-class heart for a cold capitalist heart granting him a life of wealth and power at the cost of his humanity. The Black Forest (i.e., West German) setting is significant here, as is Peter's journey down the Rhine to decadent Cologne and Amsterdam where he makes a quick profit at his companions' expense. In the end Peter realizes the terrible damage he has done, retrieves his warm heart, picks up his old axe, and, as the music swells, rejoins the toiling masses building rafts on the banks of the river.

Soon afterward the SED's propaganda war with the West made it

---

129. Quoted in Heinz Kersten, *Das Filmwesen in der sowjetischen Besatzungszone* (Bonn and Berlin, 1963), 8–9. On GDR children's films in general, see Steffen Wolf, *Kinderfilm in Europa* (Munich, 1969), 143–99.

130. Paul Verhoeven, dir., *Das kalte Herz,* with Lutz Moik and Hanna Rucker, DEFA, 1950.

necessary to transform these implicit messages into explicit regulations. In 1951 a Party statement demanded that "in the forefront of the political mass propaganda lies the development of a broad popular movement against the remilitarization of West Germany and for the conclusion of a peace treaty in the year 1951, for the formation of an All-German Constituent Council with the goal of the unification of Germany."[131] At a film conference organized by the SED Central Committee in 1952 the Party demanded that filmmakers contribute to "heightened watchfulness against agents, spies, and saboteurs, to the defense of our homeland and hatred against the imperialist arsonists, militarists, and traitors to their fatherland," as well as to help bring about "the construction of Socialism and the successful execution of our Five Year Plan."[132]

All of these elements found their way into DEFA's 1953 adaptation of the fairy tale "Kleiner Muck," which was also based on a story by Hauff.[133] While the film followed Hauff's story closely, it also added new elements that fit the issues of the time. For example, the greedy and jealous viziers at the sultan's court plan a war of conquest for the sole purpose of increasing their revenues, a plan that little Muck foils with the help of the common people. Furthermore, after winning a footrace against the sultan's messenger with the help of his magic slippers and then taking his place at the court, Muck deeply regrets his rival's fall into destitution and denounces a society in which such things are possible. Finally, after making his escape from the evil kingdom, Muck is so disgusted with the opulent but merciless world he has left behind that he smashes his magic cane and buries it and his magic slippers and returns to a humble but honorable life among simple working people.

Despite the obvious *Parteilichkeit* of these films, many SED members were deeply disappointed in the DEFA's efforts so far. Official guidelines appeared in 1955. Henceforth the filmmakers were "to emphasize those aspects in particular which serve the democratic education and development of the child in the interests of a true humanism, [and which] help mold his will and character correspondingly." The fairy tale to be filmed was to be selected according to these criteria, and "the recognizable socially critical aspects of the fairy tale text require serious attention. . . . To the extent that it corresponds to the character of the fairy tale, the inherent societal conflicts are to be presented realistically, and the critical aspects, which reflect the attitude of simple people to the oppressive con-

---

131. ND, 18 February 1951.

132. ND, 27 July 1952.

133. Wolfgang Staudte, dir., *Die Geschichte vom kleinen Muck,* with Thomas Schmidt and Johannes Maus, DEFA, 1953.

ditions of their time, are to be accentuated. Thus in the fairy tale film the resistance of the broad masses of the people against the ruling system and the longing of the oppressed for a better, happier future become clear."[134]

Typical of this agitprop ideal were "Der Teufel vom Mühlenberg" (1954), "The Bold Little Tailor" (1956), and "Rumpelstilzchen" (1960), which were explicitly antifeudal. Not all the films are as blatant as these. In the DEFA version of the Andersen fairy tale "The Tinderbox" (1959) the soldier is merely depicted as a generous righter of social wrongs in an unjust, parasitic kingdom reminiscent of the SED's view of the Federal Republic.[135]

All in all, "the fairy tale and the fairy tale film [can] contribute decisively to the fufillment of the educational goal of the schools in the German Democratic Republic and its humanistic mission to raise our youth to independently thinking and consciously acting human beings, who love their people and their fatherland, and who devote their entire strength to its preservation and to progress."[136] Nevertheless, the SED was still generally dissatisfied with fairy-tale films since most of them "limit *Parteilichkeit* in art to taking sides with general humanistic strivings and goals . . . Socialist morality and ethics can in no way be limited to general humanistic ideas which are left over from the bourgeois or even pre-bourgeois era."[137] But the films did introduce several generations of future socialists to the GDR's *Kulturerbe.*

Kultur as Stabilizer

As the fronts of the cold war hardened and an immediate resolution of the German question became less and less likely, the SED took a less confrontational posture on *Kultur.*

The construction of the Berlin Wall in 1961 eliminated the GDR's critical brain drain, and this measure, combined with the new Soviet policy of peaceful coexistence, gradually defused *Kultur* without diminishing its importance. The propagandistic use of Goethe, Schiller, and other "humanistic" figures continued in the schools and political academies in much the same style until 1989. A partial, random list of the GDR's later official state-sponsored mass *Kultur* events in these years would have to

---

134. Werner Hortzschansky, "Das Märchen im Film," special supplement to *Deutsche Filmkunst,* 5 (1955): 19–20.

135. Siegfried Hartmann, dir., *Das Feuerzeug,* DEFA, 1959.

136. Hortzschansky, 20.

137. Anton Ackermann, "Zur Parteilichkeit in der Filmkunst," in *Einheit* 4 (1958), quoted in Wolf, *Kinderfilm in Europa,* 161.

include the Heine Tribute of 1972, the Kleist Tribute of 1977, the Semper-Tribute of 1979, the Lessing Tribute of 1981, the Goethe Tribute of 1982, the Richard Wagner Days of 1983, and the grandiose 750th anniversary celebration of Berlin in 1987.[138] The tremendous rebirth of Berlin under SED leadership, Honecker proclaimed, symbolized the proud achievements of "a free people on free soil."[139]

Under Erich Honecker cultural policy underwent important changes. In 1971 the Eighth Party Convention of the SED declared the existence of a "Socialist nation" on the soil of the GDR.[140] The Federal Republic as a continuation of the "bourgeois nation" had thus become a foreign country. This formal renunciation of reunification introduced a new policy of "demarcation" that coincided with the détente policy of the United States and the Soviet Union. The GDR had in effect become a Germany in its own right. East Germans were now called upon to cultivate the entire *Kulturerbe,* both progressive and reactionary, to cultivate an independent cultural profile, and to try to forget the Federal Republic. Thenceforth, GDR propagandists emphasized the country's "humanist legacy," which they claimed was rooted in the works of the classics and expressed by the progressive social policies of Honecker's GDR.

But the most important cultural areas throughout the GDR's remaining decades were historical preservation and classical music. Historical preservation began in earnest in the 1970s and served two main purposes. First, the restoration of historic buildings and the centers of key GDR cities was "intended to draw the historically developed environment into the life of Socialism in such a way that the citizens feel good, so that they meet their cultural need for identification with the unmistakable, historically developed social environment, and so that they can utilize the traditional zones of communication with state and societal institutions, production plants, trade and gastronomic establishments in their productive activity, in relaxation, in recreational activities, and in family life."[141] Second, and more important, was the propagandistic value of carefully restored monuments and individual streets in selected historic towns such as Berlin and Dresden. As with the commemorative years, these restoration projects provided the GDR with a positive public relations boost by linking the letters *GDR* with the rich German cultural heritage in the minds of foreign guests. Equally important, they brought the state valu-

---

138. For a complete listing, see *Unsere Kultur—DDR-Zeittafel 1945–1987* (East Berlin, 1989).
139. ND 27/28 September 1986.
140. *Bericht des Zentralkomitees an den VIII. Parteitag der SED* (Berlin, 1971), 31–32.
141. *SED und kulturelles Erbe,* 478–79.

able foreign currency through the flood of Western tourists who arrived to attend performances at the lavishly restored Dresden *Semperoper* or the Berlin *Schauspielhaus*.[142] Visits to these *Kultur* monuments had a profound nostalgic quality in those days, since the anachronistic and dilapidated appearance of GDR towns vividly evoked earlier ages. (This aesthetic aspect was the happy by-product of "really existing Socialism.") But at the same time, these selected prestige projects covered up the desolate condition of residential areas outside of the restoration zones and drew attention entirely away from such devastated provincial towns as Stendal and Greifswald. These cities, like so many others virtually untouched by "Anglo-American bombers," were saved from almost complete decay and demolition by the events of 1989.

The GDR's heavy emphasis on classical music was one of the regime's most successful propaganda instruments both at home and abroad. Such renowned musical groups as the Dresden State Orchestra and the Choir of the St. Thomas Church in Leipzig helped fulfill the aesthetic needs of the better-educated East German citizens, earned valuable foreign currency, and spread the GDR's reputation as a land of poets, philosophers, and musicians to concert halls throughout the world.

The FDJ participated in all of these activities, either actively or as audience. Its members were always on hand when a new opera house was dedicated to hear a political speech and give a cheer for Honecker and Socialism, but they no longer played the central role they had in the 1940s and 1950s. The new FDJ cultural policy as represented by the folksy *"Singebewegung"* and the highly political FDJ youth festivals encompassed all four myths into a new "progressive" synthesis. The SED and the FDJ also toned down somewhat their campaign against *Kulturbarbarei* beginning in the early 1960s. Beatlemania did not stop at the Berlin Wall, and continuing the complete ban on "poisonous" music was more dangerous to the regime's legitimacy than legalizing it. Once again, the purpose of the FDJ was not to ban fun, but rather to control it. In any case, the Wall relieved much of the internal pressure, and the Party no longer had to worry about FDJ members sneaking over to West Berlin jazz clubs. At a conference of the FDJ's Central Council in December 1962, First Secretary Horst Schumann openly denounced the Party's policy of trying to make GDR youth into, in his words, "square prigs" (*"spiessbürgerliche Musterknaben"*). Schumann even went so far as to dance the dreaded Twist in public.[143] After the FDJ's remarkably liberal *Deutschlandtreffen*

---

142. "Tourismus," in Hartmut Zimmermann, ed., *DDR-Handbuch* (Cologne, 1985), 480.

143. Hermann Weber, *DDR. Grundriss ihrer Geschichte 1945–1990*, completely revised and expanded edition (Hannover, 1991), 108.

of 1964 and the creation of the youth radio station "DT 64," the Party gradually allowed the formation of GDR rock bands provided that they balanced western songs with a set minimum of wholesome, moralizing songs from the East. The Honecker government liberalized popular culture considerably, and partially succeeded in coopting pop music for its own aims. In the 1980s the rock band Puhdys received state honors. In the last years of the GDR it was common to see young FDJ members in their FDJ-sponsored youth clubs, their blue shirts stuffed into their blue jeans, dancing to the music of Michael Jackson and Bruce Springsteen—American *Kulturbarbarei* in its purest form.

The last great *Kultur* event of the GDR was the "Bach-Handel-Schütz Tribute" of 1985. It was an anomaly in the last decades of GDR cultural policy and reflected Honecker's desire for full international acceptance. It differed from the earlier *Gedenkjahre* through its high professionalism and relative freedom from Marxist-Leninist hairsplitting. For example, instead of insisting that Bach was a secular composer and developing a cult around the "Peasant Cantata," the SED encouraged the production of a first-rate record set of all of Bach's cantatas.

As in old times, the FDJ participated in a special youth ceremony for Bach. On 21 March 1985, 15,000 FDJ members were assembled on the Eisenach *Frauenplan.* Selected members laid a wreath at the Bach monument while others performed festive music on trumpets and trombones. In a speech by FDJ chairman Hartmut König, they were told that Bach's works meant peace and that in view of the increasingly complex demands of the 1980s "it is natural that youth will ever more consciously reach for the treasures of *Kultur* and art, for the progressive artistic *Erbe.*"[144] The youths did not conduct a torchlight parade (that honor was by this time reserved for antifascist and pro-Soviet ceremonies), but instead proceeded in an orderly manner to attend their choice of five FDJ and professional concerts held both in Eisenach and in the Wartburg. Although the event was covered heavily in the *Junge Welt* and on GDR television, it is unlikely that most FDJ members took much notice. The old melodrama was gone, and the concerts—as professional as they were—had become a routine aspect of life in the GDR.

A few days after the Bach ceremony an FDJ functionary, reflecting on the famous photograph of Soviet soldiers uncovering the Goethe–Schiller monument in Weimar and all that had happened since that day, summed up the FDJ's role in the *Kultur* myth and its current normality as follows.[145]

---

144. Irene Tüngler, "Ein Werk, das Menschen bis heute erhebt," 20 March 1985; "Bachs Werk ist uns Verpflichtung, den Frieden zu erhalten," JW 22 March 1985.

145. Peter Kroh, "Wichtigeres in Weimar?" JW 25 March 1985.

What began on the *Theaterplatz* of Weimar with the liberation of Goethe and Schiller from Fascist imprisonment found its sequel in many events organized by the FDJ: the Schiller Festival of the FDJ, the Theater Days of Youth, the founding of Youth Theater Rings. . . . Youth and *Kultur*—with us they belong together just like Goethe and Schiller.

Nevertheless, four years later hundreds of thousands of East German youths were fleeing the GDR by any means they could. A year after that, a majority of those who remained voted for unification with the Federal Republic.

Conclusion

As we have seen, the myth of *Kultur* developed from bourgeois cultural notions and was adopted by Marxist-Leninist theorists who themselves originated from the educated middle classes. They hoped to use bourgeois *Kultur* as a stepping-stone to a higher socialist *Kultur* that would be created by a postrevolutionary classless society. The KPD, the SED, and the FDJ first used *Kultur* as an antidote to National Socialism and then as a means to win over non-Marxists for Marxism-Leninism. High culture represented a source of identification for SED members and helped forge a link between the working class and the "intelligentsia." In later years the SED used *Kultur* as a weapon against American imperialism and the Federal Republic, as an argument for German reunification under a socialist regime, and then increasingly as an ingredient of a new "Socialist *Nationalkultur.*" Under the Honecker regime *Kultur* served mainly as a source of GDR pride and identity.

The myth of *Kultur* could not save the GDR in 1989–90. Does that make it a failure? There is no statistical information with which to measure the myth's effectiveness, and even if such statistics existed they would not be helpful. No doubt thousands of young East German Communists discovered the Marxist-Leninist "classics" after being taken the long way through the *Kulturerbe.* Many East Germans were certainly proud of the way their state cared for selected historical monuments, just as they were proud of the GDR's athletic achievements. So was the SED's systematic use of *Kultur* nothing more than a cynical ploy, as some scholars argue, or did it in fact reflect the Communists' idealistic wish to abolish class barriers and open up *Kultur* for all Germans and thus make them into still better Germans?[146] The

---

146. Wolfram Schlenker in *Das Kulturelle Erbe in der DDR. Gesellschaftliche Entwicklung und Kulturpolitik 1945–1965* (Stuttgart, 1977) argues that the emphasis on classical culture in SBZ and GDR cultural policy was aimed mainly at placating the "intelligentsia" even

unsatisfying answer is that both views are correct, and the principle of *Parteilichkeit* enabled the GDR's leaders to pursue both goals at once. The Marxist-Leninist intellectuals behind much of the cultural myth-building (such as Johannes R. Becher, Alfred Kurella, or Alexander Abusch) were after all trying to help build a society in which they themselves would feel comfortable and where their own personal myths would find a home.

The myth probably had its greatest impact on East German intellectuals. As we have already observed in chapter 1, Marxism-Leninism and the *Parteilichkeit* principle reduced human experience to a collection of black–white clichés. The modern world boiled down to the confrontation between "socialism" and "imperialism" and little else. According to this view, to live in the West meant to wallow in a slough of exploitation, consumerism, and sheer bad taste. Americans and their "West German lackeys," if no longer explicitly "plague-*Amis*," were in any case *Kulturbarbaren* and embodied the destructive principle, whereas socialism represented cultural preservation and rebirth.[147] The decision to dedicate one's self to "the cause of the working class" and serve the GDR thus came more easily and was also ennobled.

It is hardly necessary to discuss the myth's success abroad. While the militant *Gedenkjahre* of the early 1950s likely frightened off as many westerners as they attracted, the strategy of the Honecker regime was a smashing success. Granted, West Germany was undeniably the center of contemporary German culture: it was the home of internationally respected figures like Günter Grass and Jürgen Habermas, and the refuge for such eastern renegades as Wolf Biermann or the flamboyant rock star Nina Hagen. But the world tours of East German choirs and symphony orchestras and the splashy rededications of the Leipzig *Gewandhaus,* the Berlin *Schauspielhaus* and the Dresden *Semperoper* firmly established the GDR—and not the "Americanized" FRG—as the true home of the classical *Kulturerbe* among *Bildungsbürger* and would-be *Bildungsbürger* the world over.

An SED scholar wrote in his dissertation that he[148]

himself experienced after 1945, and relived through his research, that these humanistic works, which often rise above the ideological hori-

---

at the expense of the workers who would have preferred to supplant the intellectuals (75–77). Manfred Jäger, in his *Kultur und Politik in der DDR* (Cologne, 1982), rejects this position as unconvincing, arguing that "for the leading functionaries of the first hour, including and above all those of proletarian background, it was a self-evident goal to make the received culture of humanity accessible to as many as possible" (16).

147. See Richard Herzinger, "Die obskuren Inseln der kultivierten Gemeinschaft. Heiner Müller, Christa Wolf, Volker Braun—deutsche Zivilisationskritik und das neue Antiwestlertum," *Die Zeit,* 4 June 1993.

148. Pfeiffer, 10–11.

zons of the bourgeoisie, opened [youth's] eyes to scientific Communism, which represents the quintessence of all the progressive thought of mankind. It proved to be correct to allow youth to find the path from Heine to his friend Marx, from the Russian poet Pushkin to the theoretician of the Russian working class, to Lenin.

Whether this was indeed the correct thing to do to German youth remains a question that can only be answered according to the observer's own degree of *Parteilichkeit.* But it is hard to imagine how the GDR ever could have been created or have found recognition abroad without this strategy. At the same time, the myth of *Kultur* also helped bring the regime down, once again because of the thoroughness with which it was carried out. Any *Kultur* deserving the name does not lend itself to facile Marxist-Leninist categories. Thus the popularization of the German classics not only helped lead several generations of young Communists to Marxism-Leninism, it also led a minority of Communists and noncommunists to independent thought, dissent, and finally revolution. Knowledge of the classics only highlighted the appalling taste of official state *Kultur.* Genuine connoisseurs of Schinkel's architectural style could only shake their heads over the imitation Schinkel style of the monstrous Berlin *Stalinallee.* Music students who were forced to endure lectures on Louis Fürnberg's song "The Party Is Always Right" before proceeding to Bach and Handel quickly drew their own conclusions as to the state of the *Kulturerbe.* Theater lovers who had grown up on Schiller's "genuine patriotic *Pathos*" were dismayed by Honecker's long-winded praises of the aging leaders of the Soviet Union and the People's Republic of China. In the hearts of many GDR intellectuals, these obvious contradictions eventually helped awaken dreams of a democratic GDR or, indeed, a genuine "socialist cultural revolution" that would sweep away the conservative SED and create a regime far more radical than anything Ulbricht and Honecker would ever have dared attempt. For the rest of the population, cheap concert tickets, while welcome, were simply not reason enough to pledge their loyalty to the SED as soon as they had an alternative. Thus, despite its many successes, by 1989 *Kultur* had become a liability. After all, the last thing a good Marxist-Leninist needs—assuming he wants to remain one—is a solid liberal arts education.

CHAPTER 3

"In the Spirit of Ernst Thälmann": The Antifascist Myth

*Horst Menzel fell during the assault on Gandessa on 29 August 1938. . . .
He died for freedom, for progress, [for] all that is new and better in the
entire world! And that elevates him to the ranks of those whom we
proudly call Our Own. Horst Menzel is one of us.*
—Junge Welt article, 1948[1]

If the myth of *Kultur* was useful in gaining supporters for the SED in its
early years, the myth of the GDR's "antifascist legacy" was the raison
d'être of both the Party and the state from beginning to end. At first
merely the strongest argument among others, the role of this legacy grew
in importance until by 1989 antifascism became, in fact, the only argument
for the continued existence of an SED-run GDR. It alone had the power
to arouse fanaticism and justify the killing of one's fellow citizens upon
command. Membership in the GDR's antifascist elite was perhaps the
greatest of all privileges, and one that was shared by SED functionaries
and loyal non-Party members alike. But what did this "double negative"
of antifascism actually mean? The "antifascist myth"[2] basically claims that

---

1. "Zeugen deutschen Widerstandskampfes—Horst Menzel," JW 27 October 1948.
2. On the GDR's antifascism, see Manfred Hantke, "Zur Bewältigung der NS-Zeit in
der DDR. Defizite und Neubewertunge," Friedrich-Ebert-Stiftung, ed., *Die DDR. Real-
itäten—Argumente* (Bonn, 1989); Konrad Jarausch, "Das Versagen des ostdeutschen
Antifaschismus. Paradoxien von Wissenschaft als Politik," *Initial* 2 (1991), 114–24; Günter
Fippel, "Der Missbrauch des Faschismus-Begriffs in der SBZ/DDR," DA 10 (1992):
1055–65; Hans-Helmuth Knütter, "Antifaschismus und politische Kultur in Deutschland
nach der Wiedervereinigung," *Aus Politik und Zeitgeschichte* 9 (1991): 17–28; Antonia
Grunenberg, *Antifaschismus—ein deutscher Mythos. Essay* (Reinbek, 1993); Ralph Giordano, *Die zweite Schuld oder von der Last, Deutscher zu sein* (Hamburg, 1987); Ralf Kessler
and Hartmut Rüdiger Peter, "Antifaschisten in der SBZ. Zwischen elitärem Selbstverständ-
nis und politischer Instrumentalisierung," in *Vierteljahresheft für Zeitgeschichte,* vol. 43, no.
4 (October 1995): 611–33.

the GDR was the direct product of a popular anti-Nazi resistance struggle carried out with tragic loss of life under the leadership of the KPD. The bloody struggle against Nazism had had a purifying and unifying effect on the new socialist society emerging in the Soviet Zone of Occupation. The SED, as successor to the KPD, was a thoroughly antifascist party whose credentials in the German resistance movement provided it with the legitimacy it needed to assume the leadership of German society. Antifascism legitimated the GDR's leaders and their policies. The SED's policies of denazification and land reform had "eradicated the roots of Fascism and militarism," thus transforming the GDR into an "antifascist society." The alternative to the GDR, namely the capitalist FRG, represented at heart a continuation of Fascism, both in regard to leadership and policies. Thus the choice to support the GDR and fight against the FRG was not just a choice between two states, but a choice between war and peace, Fascism and freedom. The struggle against both the FRG and opposition within the GDR itself was a direct continuation of the antifascist resistance struggle. A decision for the GDR—which no longer was a real decision— was a moral imperative.

Before proceeding, it is important to make clear that this chapter is not about the individual or collective merits of actual resistance fighters or Nazi victims who either lost their lives and were commemorated by the SED, or who survived and later made their homes in the GDR. For them, antifascism was and is very much a lived reality. Their story goes far beyond the parameters of this study. Instead, this chapter deals with the antifascism—or, more accurately, the ex post facto antifascism—of the GDR. It examines the ways in which the resistance fighters' legacy was adopted by the SED in its forty-year attempt to mold young people in the spirit of an "antifascist legacy" of its own making.

It is a sad fact that active resistance to the Third Reich was both rare and ineffective in any part of Germany, and even though the various antifascists were united in their opposition to Hitler, their future goals differed widely.[3] So how does one develop a state-supporting myth of antifascism if very little of it actually existed? Once the original Fascists and their capitalist accomplices have been driven away, how does one perpetuate antifascism for over forty years? Who benefits by doing so? For the GDR was not founded by actual resistance fighters within Germany, but instead by the exile KPD leadership in Moscow, who upon its return removed thousands of Communist and noncommunist resistance fighters from their

---

3. On antifascist resistance, see Horst Duhnke, *Die KPD von 1933 bis 1945* (Cologne, 1971); Detlev Peukert, *Die KPD im Widerstand. Verfolgung und Untergrundarbeit an Rhein und Ruhr 1933–1945* (Wuppertal, 1980); Beatrix Herlemann, "Der deutsche kommunistische Widerstand während des Krieges," *Beiträge zum Widerstand 1933–1945,* 35 (Berlin, 1989).

newly gained positions of authority, imprisoned some of them, and proceeded to build up a new elite of obedient young "uncontaminated"
cadres. It was in the interest of both the émigré apparatus and the new generation of functionaries and professionals to play up the alleged Fascist
threat emanating among non-*parteilich* East Germans and from the West,
not least when it came to convincing the Soviets of the benefits of a strong,
Marxist-Leninist GDR.[4] The old Communists and Social Democrats did
not understand the changes that had occurred in the Soviet Union since
1933, often had their own ideas about how to construct Socialism, and had
not survived twelve years of National Socialism only to take orders from
Ulbricht and Pieck.[5] The presence of prominent exceptions—such as Erich
Honecker, who spent most of the Third Reich in the Nazi penitentiary in
Brandenburg, or Hermann Axen who survived Auschwitz—confirms the
rule that by 1949 actual power was wielded by the Moscow émigrés.[6] This
seemed unfair at the time considering the dangers the resistance fighters
had faced inside Germany. Nevertheless, there was a certain justice when
one considers that at least three thousand German Communists met death
in the Soviet purges, and that more top KPD leaders were killed off by
Stalin's NKVD secret police than by the Gestapo.[7] Ulbricht, Pieck, and
their associates were merely claiming their dues.

The way in which they and their successors claimed these dues by
means of the myth of the "antifascist legacy" is the subject of this chapter.

Aspects of the Antifascist Myth

The antifascist myth was generally represented by the symbolism of the
oath and the covenant. According to the SED, antifascism was a popular
movement of "Communists, Social Democrats, trade unionists, Chris-

---

4. The extent to which the creation of the GDR can be traced to the machinations of
the SED itself—often at odds with the Soviet leadership, which was anxious to strike a deal
with the West—has so far received little serious attention. A good starting point for this discussion is Wilfried Loth's controversial *Stalins ungeliebtes Kind. Warum Moskau die DDR
nicht wollte* (Berlin, 1994).

5. As Dietrich Staritz writes, "At every functionaries' conference where Ulbricht spoke,
the old comrades always spoke up and criticized the new course of their party." *Die Gründung
der DDR. Von der sowjetischen Besatzungsherrschaft zum sozialistischen Staat* (Munich,
1984), 82.

6. Karl-Heinz Jahnke has told me that Hermann Axen once approached him and told
him his entire life story. The Nazis persecuted Axen as both a Communist and a Jew, and
forced him to wear a yellow star at Auschwitz. Axen complained bitterly that no one in the
SED ever showed the slightest interest in his fate as a Holocaust victim. Interview with Karl-
Heinz Jahnke, Rostock, 1 December 1992.

7. Hermann Weber, "Kommunistischer Widerstand gegen die Hitler-Diktatur
1933–1939," *Beiträge zum Widerstand 1933–1945,* 33, 2d ed. (West Berlin, 1990), 17.

tians, and bourgeois democrats," who "stand up for peace, democracy, friendship among peoples, and humanity; against militarism, imperialist war, terror, race-baiting, and mass murder."[8] In the GDR all of these groups were gathered together in the "National Front" under SED leadership. The SED viewed the GDR as a covenant among these groups and between the generations.

The oath and the covenant were well chosen. They are religious in origin and are used in nearly every modern society. They symbolize unity in any organization. The Socialist Unity Party depicted the unity of the working class that it claimed to embody with an emblem consisting of a handshake superimposed upon a red banner. The oath and the covenant are used as the symbolic foundation of nearly all modern states, whether Switzerland's legendary "Rütli oath" celebrated in Schiller's *Wilhelm Tell* (*"Wir wollen sein ein einig Volk von Brüdern"*) or the American Declaration of Independence, at the conclusion of which the Founding Fathers "mutually pledge to each other our lives, our fortunes and our sacred honor."[9] The antifascist covenant of the GDR was symbolized by the "Oath of Buchenwald."

Unlike a simple contract, which may contain escape clauses, a covenant is usually open-ended and may last either for eternity or until the passing of its makers. Sacred oaths can be repeated with great dramatic effect at mass events, at which the covenant is symbolically renewed. The SED presented its antifascist covenant in very simple terms in its youth propaganda and public symbolism. But the way in which this supposed covenant came into being was extremely complex.

The relationship of the KPD and later the SED to National Socialism had always been ambivalent. While Communist propaganda always proclaimed its uncompromising resistance to all manifestations of "Fascism," the reality was much more complex. One of the greatest weaknesses of Marxist-Leninist analysis lies in its fixation on class conflict and its inability to accept the role of the irrational in human behavior, even though, as we have seen, Communist propagandists regularly exploited myths and irrational emotions in their own work. If they are taken seriously at all, unwelcome irrational beliefs are simply classified as "false consciousness" and ascribed to faulty indoctrination. The Communists' confusion about the nature of National Socialism arose from their ideological interpretation of it, which beginning in 1922 emphasized only its economic aspects

8. "Antifaschismus," *Taschenlexikon für Zeitungsleser,* 3d ed. (East Berlin, 1988), 16.

9. Cf. Hans Kohn, *The Idea of Nationalism: A Study in Its Origins and Background* (New York, 1944), 15–16.

and characterized all right-wing extremist regimes (in Germany, Italy, Poland, Japan, and later Spain) as "Fascist" without any consideration of national differences. From the beginning, the Communists wavered in their policies toward the National Socialists and alternately fought them and cooperated with them in their mutual struggle to overthrow the Weimar Republic. According to a formula developed in the 1920s and then proclaimed as official Comintern policy by Georgi Dimitroff in 1933, Fascism was the "open terrorist dictatorship of the most reactionary, the most chauvinistic, the most imperialist elements of finance capital."[10] As such its rise to power throughout Europe did not represent a break with bourgeois rule, but rather a continuation of it by other means. Thus it was an unpleasant but not necessarily negative phenomenon, since it represented the final stage of capitalism and was a decisive step toward the centralization of capital and production. In other words, it represented the jumping-off point for Socialism.[11] The Communists saw the Social Democrats ("social Fascists"), and not the Nazis ("national Fascists") as their principal enemy according to a theory first discussed at a Comintern conference held in 1922.[12] At the Seventeenth Party Congress of the Communist Party of the Soviet Union in 1934, Stalin analyzed the Nazi seizure of power as[13]

> not only a sign of the weakness of the working class and as a result of the treachery against the working class on the part of Social Democracy, which paved the way for Fascism. One must also view it as a sign of the weakness of the bourgeoisie, as a sign that the bourgeoisie is no longer able to rule with the old methods of parliamentarism and bourgeois democracy, and as a consequence is forced to reach for terroristic governing methods in its domestic policy.

This interpretation took into account neither Hitler's wildly irrational anti-Semitism nor the Nazis' "blood and soil" ideology. For understandable reasons it also disregards the terroristic governing methods of the

---

10. "Faschismus," in *Kleines politisches Wörterbuch,* 7th rev. ed. (East Berlin, 1988), 248.

11. Andreas Dorpalen, *German History in Marxist Perspective: The East German Approach* (Detroit, 1988), 393–94.

12. Wolfgang Wippermann, *Faschismustheorien,* 13. While this theory appears grotesque in light of the events after 1933, it is important to remember that the Communists were basing their judgment on the repressive actions of the European Social Democratic Parties after World War I. The Communists' main grievance was, of course, the murder of Karl Liebknecht and Rosa Luxemburg by military officers under either direct or indirect orders from the SPD-led provisional government.

13. Josef W. Stalin, *Fragen des Leninismus* (East Berlin, 1951), 522.

Stalinist system itself. Although Stalin was nominally de-canonized in 1956 and GDR historiography made considerable progress in its "Fascism" research in its later years, this interpretation remained more or less in place until 1989 and still has many supporters today.[14] It provided in good faith the ideological basis of all GDR antifascist propaganda. The implications were clear: imperialism and fascism were varieties of capitalism. The capitalist Federal Republic was in essence a Fascist state that could become openly Fascist at any time. Fascism was an instrument of capitalist rule imposed from above and lacking a solid popular base. The actual "Fascists" were a relatively small group: capitalists, big landowners, the nobility, portions of the officer corps, and much of the Prussian bureaucracy. The German people had been "blinded" by Fascist propaganda and were thus not completely to blame for their actions. By collectivizing agriculture and nationalizing most industries, the SED had, according to the GDR constitution, "eradicated German militarism and Nazism on its soil."[15]

As for the Third Reich itself, it was not so much a story of mass murder as it was a class struggle. The victims of National Socialism were above all resistance fighters who, under the leadership of Ernst Thälmann and the KPD underground, were fighting for an "antifascist/democratic" Germany. Jews, Gypsies, the disabled, and other victims—when they were mentioned at all—were of interest only as auxiliaries to this struggle, or at best as supplemental examples of Fascist barbarity. Even if historians did begin to pay more attention to these victims in the 1980s, they were always subordinated to working-class victims in antifascist propaganda.[16] Mass murder through gas chambers and firing squads was thus given a heroic (if deeply tragic) quality. The Nazi terror was symbolized in almost all antifascist monuments, not by the yellow Star of David, the symbol of the

---

14. Cf. Werner Bramke, "Der antifaschistische Widerstand in der Geschichtsschreibung der DDR in den achtziger Jahren. Forschungsstand und Probleme," *Aus Politik und Zeitgeschichte,* 8 July 1988, 23–33.

15. "Verfassung der Deutschen Demokratischen Republik, 6. April 1968," *Gesetzblatt der DDR,* part 2 (Berlin, 1968), 337.

16. In order to appreciate the discrepancy between GDR historiography aimed at Western historians and historical propaganda aimed at the East German masses, it is worthwhile examining the SED's definition of the word *Holocaust* in its popular political dictionary, *Taschenlexikon für Zeitungsleser,* as late as 1988 (97–98): "Translatable as 'sacrifice, fire, complete,' today this term is used as a synonym for genocide. It gained entry into political usage in connection with the mass extermination of Jews by Hitler-Fascism. 'Holocaust' is also occasionally used to describe the extermination campaign of the Israeli imperialists against the Palestinian people, or the danger of the atomic extinction of mankind brought about by the imperialist hyper-armament and confrontational policies."

Holocaust, but by the red triangle—the insignia for political prisoners on concentration camp uniforms.[17]

This view is deeply problematic. For even if the sufferings of the Communist resistance fighters are beyond question, it is now clear that their behavior in the concentration camps was far more complex than the public myth admitted, as a secret SED commission discovered as early as 1946. In Buchenwald, for example, Communist inmates systematically collaborated with the SS in order to save the lives of their comrades. This meant, among other things, that Communist *Kapos* (gang bosses under SS command) routinely replaced the names of KPD members with those of noncommunist inmates on execution or deportation lists in order to preserve the KPD camp committee. In return for such privileges, Communist *Kapos* frequently assisted the SS in torturing and executing prisoners. Thus in order to carry on the antifascist resistance struggle, many Communists saw no choice but to become part of the Fascist terror machinery themselves.[18] Moreover, Stalinist purges and the liquidation of political enemies were not suspended with the Nazi seizure of power and the mass arrests of German Communists, but continued unabated behind barbed wire.

But the antifascist myth was based upon an ideal unity of the oppressed. This interpretation of the Third Reich was expressed by the profoundly contradictory monument to the "victims of Fascism and militarism" in the *Neue Wache* in East Berlin. There, defended by a gray-uniformed, goose-stepping honor guard, an eternal flame flickered over the tombs of the unknown resistance fighter and the unknown soldier. The remains of the unknown resistance fighter were from an unidentifiable concentration camp inmate who was executed by an SS guard during a death march in April 1945. It will never be known whether he really was a resistance fighter, or a Jew, a Polish slave worker, a Jehovah's Witness, or some other victim of National Socialism. The wearing of a concentration camp uniform automatically made him into a "resistance fighter" in the eyes of the SED.[19] Whether the unknown

---

17. On the treatment of National Socialism and the resistance to it see Hans-Ulrich Thamer, "Nationalsozialismus und Faschismus in der DDR-Historiographie," *Aus Politik und Zeitgeschichte,* 13/87, 27–37; Andreas Dorpalen, *German History in Marxist Perspective. The East German Approach* (Detroit, 1988), 393–464; Peter Steinbach, "Vom Vorurteil zum Urteil?" *Initial* 5 (1993): 3–10.

18. See Lutz Niethammer et al., *Der gesäuberte Antifaschismus. Die SED und die roten Kapos von Buchenwald* (Berlin, 1994).

19. Thomas Leinkauf, "Der Junge war kaum zwanzig Jahre alt. Spuren des unbekannten Soldaten und des unbekannten Widerstandskämpfers in der Neuen Wache, Unter den Linden," *BZ* 1 November 1993; Birgit Spies, "Aus einem unabgeschlossenen Kapitel," in Daniele Büchten and Anja Frey, *Im Irrgarten der deutschen Geschichte. Die Neue Wache 1818–1993* (Berlin, 1993), 37–44.

soldier was also a victim of militarism or perhaps a war criminal himself is equally unknowable.

It is only logical that for all the antifascist rhetoric they were exposed to, young people were taught virtually nothing about Fascism itself, except that it meant killing Communists and waging war on the Soviet Union. The actual ideology of National Socialism was taboo, as was any real discussion of Hitler and why millions of people supported him and not the Communists. It was enough to know that the Fascists were wrong and the antifascists were right, without being asked to consider why this should be so. Any other approach would have been "objectivist" and hence counterproductive.

All of this is perfectly reasonable if one takes the Dimitroff-Stalin theory of "Fascism" seriously, and why shouldn't a good Marxist-Leninist do so? For without this understanding, nothing in the twentieth century makes sense—neither the extraordinary popularity of Hitler and National Socialism (even among workers), nor the KPD's and SPD's failure to check Nazism's growth, nor the Hitler-Stalin Pact, nor the millions of otherwise meaningless victims of Nazism, nor the postwar division of Germany. Without the myth of the antifascist legacy two facts above all lose their justification: the very existence of the German Democratic Republic and the dictatorship of the Socialist Unity Party.

In 1958, the city of Weimar erected a statue of KPD leader Ernst Thälmann on the "Square of the Fifty-Six Thousand" to commemorate his murder at the nearby Buchenwald concentration camp.[20] But what of the other 55,999?

Antifascist Youth Indoctrination in the SBZ

On 31 July 1945 the Soviet Military Administration approved the formation of "antifascist youth committees," which would be the only youth organizations allowed. The analysis of "Fascism" and World War II offered in the committees was made remarkably simple and was extremely attractive to disoriented Hitler Youths and young soldiers. As Walter Ulbricht stated in a speech to KPD functionaries on 25 June 1945, "Surely German youth has heard nothing but the evils of Nazi propaganda. But within German youth, too, there are forces that took part in the anti-Fascist struggle. And even many members of the Hitler Youth have recently expressed their opposition to the Nazi leaders. We have

---

20. Volker Frank, *Antifaschistische Mahnmale in der DDR. Ihre künstlerische und architektonische Gestaltung* (Leipzig, 1970), 16–17.

confidence in German youth that with the help of experienced anti-Fascists they will learn from the catastrophe which Hitler drove Germany into."[21]

The concept of forgiveness through "learning from the catastrophe" soon applied to the entire society. It is important to remember this fact when trying to understand the GDR's view of the antifascist tradition. The Soviet Military Administration and the GDR government clearly expelled, imprisoned, and executed far more Nazi war criminals than the Western Allies and the Federal Republic. Virtually all Nazi judges and teachers lost their jobs. Even so, the GDR's understanding of "learning from the catastrophe" sometimes meant that former Nazis could absolve themselves of their past and begin new careers by denouncing other alleged Nazis.[22] In individual cases, former *Wehrmacht* officers helped build up the People's Police and the National People's Army, former Nazi propagandists became SED newspaper editors, and former SS and Gestapo officers helped organize the *Stasi,* the Ministry for State Security.[23] However, far too much has been made of this sort of thing in the Federal Republic, which itself accepted many more former Nazis into its service, including almost the entire Nazi judiciary. Moreover, thousands of Nazis, aristocrats, industrialists, and other "reactionary" elements fled to the West in 1945. Thus, there was considerable truth to the SED claim that the Federal Republic was "Fascist" from a Marxist-Leninist viewpoint. But while revelations of former Nazis among its own membership were always embarrassing for the SED, they were part of its policy from the beginning. Only a year after the German capitulation it formally invited nominal Nazi Party members who had demonstrated loyalty to the new regime to participate in the "democratic reconstruction" of the Soviet Zone and join the SED.[24]

Through the antifascist myth, repentant Germans were offered a great and unexpected gift by the SED and the Soviet authorities: actually to become that which they now wished they had been all along—antifascists. Stalin himself blessed this transformation in his celebrated telegram congratulating Pieck and Grotewohl on the founding of the GDR: "The formation of the peace-loving German Democratic Republic," Stalin

21. Walter Ulbricht, *Zur Geschichte der deutschen Arbeiterbewegung,* vol. 2 (East Berlin, 1963), 441.

22. For an example of this practice, see Rüdiger Knechtel and Jürgen Fiedler, eds., *Stalins DDR. Berichte politischer Verfolgter* (Leipzig, 1991), 25–27.

23. Hundreds of such cases are documented in Olaf Kappelt, *Braunbuch DDR. Nazis in der DDR* (West Berlin, 1981).

24. "SED und nominelle PGs. Beschluss des Parteivorstandes vom 20. Juni 1946," *Dokumente der SED,* vol. I, 52–53.

wrote, "is a turning point in the history of Europe."[25] GDR propagandists interpreted this vague statement as a transcendent new beginning. All eastern Germans had to do was join the SED or one of its subordinate block parties, or a mass organization, or even just accept the leading role of the Party and start clearing away the rubble. In any case, both Fascism and liberal democracy with its injustice and instability were utterly discredited. "The new life must be different," Max Zimmering wrote in a poem at this time. This notion was especially appealing to young people, most of whom had no real responsibility for the horrors of the war and who were fascinated by the possibility of helping to build a new society and doing a better job of it than their parents. Confused young soldiers in reeducation seminars, Antonia Grunenberg writes, "understood that they were being offered the opportunity to shift from the side of the losers to the side of the victors. . . . Against this background even the Stalinist party history (the *Short Course*) was read by knowledge-hungry young people as a revelation of a new world."[26]

In order to grasp the attractiveness of Stalin's policy toward eastern Germans, it is necessary to look at the situation in the western zones where, as the historian Gregory Sandford writes, "the Americans in particular tended to see Nazism primarily as a moral evil arising out of some deep-seated perversion in the German psyche. Mass media in the U.S. Zone bombarded the German public with evidence of Nazi atrocities and with insistent reminders that they were all collectively responsible for these horrors. But no possibility of atonement or rehabilitation was offered: with all political initiatives still regarded as suspect, the average citizen's safest course was still, as under the Nazis, passive obedience."[27] While the Communists did not deny the existence of guilt, they tempered it with the opportunity for redemption. Until 1949 much of the rhetoric within the FDJ admitted a collective German guilt for the war. At this time, to be sure, most members had been Hitler Youths or BDM members, and many had been soldiers. In an article for *Junge Generation* in January 1949 an FDJ functionary wrote: "We can only pay off the heavy guilt which we have laid upon ourselves if we place ourselves fully and without reservations on the side of progress, and eliminate the remnants of Fascism,

25. "Aus dem Telegramm J.W. Stalins zur Gründung der DDR, 13. Oktober 1949," in Hermann Weber, ed., *DDR. Dokumente zur Geschichte der Deutschen Demokratischen Republik 1945–1985,* 3d ed. (Munich, 1987), 163.

26. Antonia Grunenberg, *Antifaschismus—ein deutscher Mythos. Essay* (Reinbek, 1993), 135–36.

27. Gregory W. Sandford, *From Hitler to Ulbricht. The Communist Reconstruction of East Germany, 1945–46* (Princeton, 1983), 226–27.

which still remain among us, from our midst, and at the same time make sure that the opponents of peace . . . within our people find no new followers."[28] With the founding of the "peace-loving" GDR in October 1949 there would be no more talk of guilt, except in regard to West Germany.

The antifascist indoctrination in the youth committees differed little from the *Kultur* indoctrination going on at the same time. As we have already seen in the preceding chapter, both were key elements of what Johannes R. Becher in his *Erziehung zur Freiheit* called the "anti-Fascist-democratic consciousness." The committees offered *Heimabende* aimed first at informing utterly uninformed young people and only then in presenting an appropriate "antifascist/democratic" interpretation. They offered such programs throughout the entire SBZ and, at first, in all sectors of Berlin. From the beginning, antifascism also encompassed the Republican cause in the Spanish Civil War. In an interview given in 1975, the FDJ's cofounder Horst Brasch recalled *"Heimabende* in Berlin-Charlottenburg, where we wanted to learn the song *'Spaniens Himmel'* [The sky over Spain—the song of the KPD's "Thälmann Battalion" in the Spanish civil war]. Back then it took us three *Heimabende* to do it. That wasn't because of the limited musicality of the friends, but stemmed from the fact that the content of the text first had to be explained to the young people. We talked about Ernst Thälmann, the role of the international brigades and the Fascist 'Condor Legion,' the concept of heroism, and many other things. There were similar clarifying discussions on, for example, the writings and activities of Heinrich Heine and Georg Büchner."[29]

From the beginning the KPD and SED centered its antifascist propaganda around selected heroic figures. The antifascist, anti-imperialist myth-building strategy of the FDJ traces its origins to a programmatic speech given by Ernst Thälmann at a plenary meeting of the KJVD in Prieros near Berlin on 19 November 1932. In his remarks Thälmann denounced the standard slogan "Smash the Fascists wherever you encounter them." Instead, the KJVD (like the FDJ in the late 1940s) should attempt to win over disillusioned young Nazis by learning from the Hitler Youth's success and adopting its methods. Like the Fascists, the Communists should adopt sports, discipline and comradery, scouting games and marches. "Why don't we pick up on the romantic-revolutionary sentiments of the masses of young workers? Why are we so dry and

---

28. Klaus Rosenthal, "Stalingrad," JG 1 (1949): 24.

29. Interview protocol, Horst Brasch and Günter Schwade, in Günter Schwade, "Die Kulturarbeit der FDJ und ihre Rolle bei der ideologischen Erziehung der Jugend in der Zeit der antifaschistisch-demokratischen Umwälzung von 1945/46 bis 1949" (Diss. Rostock, 1979), 3.

dull in our work? More vitality, more enthusiasm, more drive belong in our working methods. We have to create magnets to draw the proletarian youth into the KJVD!" Thälmann saw the Nazi propaganda style as essential to the KJVD's success and evoked the "Schlageter course" of the 1920s. "National Socialism used another means to enthrall its young masses of followers: the glorification of certain persons who were celebrated as heroes. I ask you: Why don't we celebrate our revolutionary heroes? The Nazis, for example, have their Leo Schlageter. Why don't we celebrate our revolutionary heroes who fell in the battle for freedom? Why don't we celebrate our youth comrades Demare and the other young proletarians assassinated by French imperialism during the Rhein-Ruhr occupation? The example of these fighters, the brave risking of their lives for the cause of the proletarian freedom struggle—those are facts which can enthrall and inflame each and every young Communist and young proletarian. Here is a great task for the Communist Youth Organization. Here there are great possibilities to anchor the spirit of proletarian internationalism in the hearts and minds of our young class fighters."[30]

The awarding of antifascist symbols to exceptional FDJ groups was the preferred method used to demonstrate the continuity from the older generation of KPD and antifascist fighters to the new. The first SBZ-wide antifascist myth-building campaign of this kind began in 1948. At the Third Parliament of the FDJ in Leipzig in 1949, the winners of the various organizational and propagandistic competitions that always accompanied such events were to be awarded "assault banners" bearing the names of fallen antifascists such as Ernst Thälmann, the Social Democratic leader Rudolf Breidscheidt, and the young Communist antifascists Artur Becker, Ernst Knaack, Horst Menzel, Werner Seelenbinder, and many others. During the months leading up to the Leipzig Parliament, the FDJ newspaper *Junge Welt* carried weekly articles introducing these fallen fighters to young East Germans. The FDJ student organization in Leipzig was granted the "assault banner Sophie Scholl" for "exemplary work at a university." This latter selection is remarkable considering the profoundly religious and thoroughly noncommunist motives behind the actions of the White Rose resistance group.[31]

In October 1949 the FDJ Central Council issued formal guidelines for the granting of names to FDJ units, active groups, brigades, cultural groups, schools, district organizations, and FDJ institutions. A unit, district organization, and so forth could apply for a specific name if it had shown outstanding achievements in realizing the constitution of the FDJ

---

30. "Rede des Genossen Ernst Thälmann auf der Plenartagung des KJVD, am 19. November 1932," JA, IzJ A 11.712, 15–17.
31. *Geschichte der Freien Deutschen Jugend,* 171–73.

or other FDJ resolutions, in plan fulfillment in industry, agriculture, and at educational institutions, as well as for "progressive cultural work." If the application was approved by the regional FDJ authorities and by the Secretariat of the Central Committee, a group or institution could "name itself after the great models of progressive world youth, who have distinguished themselves through their fearless struggle for peace, national independence, and societal progress against imperialism, warmongers, and the colonial oppression of the peoples." Names could be chosen first from among "the fearless resistance fighters against Fascism," and second from among "personalities who stand at the head of our German Democratic Republic." In third place were "outstanding personalities who stand at the head of the peoples in the great camp of peace." These were followed up by pioneers of production, science, technology and culture, and finally by progressive figures of German history.[32]

The FDJ also applied Thälmann's suggestions to the organization's public image. Adoption of the antifascist myth was made easy in the late 1940s by the SED's direct imitation of familiar Hitler Youth organizational forms and symbols. This phenomenon is a classic example of passive myth-building in the GDR. By 1949—all the antifascist rhetoric to the contrary—the FDJ had become an organization with striking structural and visual similarities to—as East Germans like to say—"what came before." In his memoirs, Hans Mayer suggests that these similarities arose from the fact that the overwhelming majority of young eastern Germans had had no personal experience of "antifascism" or of anything besides Nazism and militarism. "Thus the imitation of Komsomoldom on German soil inevitably led to the resuscitation of former Hitler Youth rituals. All the more so, since the senseless and reality-blind opinion of the people in the Politburo earnestly took for granted that, if the Germans are really to like a regime, they once again have to be prescribed a military-militaristic ceremonial. Review marches, goose-stepping, fanfares, fife and drum corps, flag consecrations, pledges of allegiance, speech choruses of the common will."[33]

These similarities became especially obvious in the mammoth youth parade of the FDJ "Peace Day" on 24–25 September 1949, or the evening of 11 October 1949 when thousands of uniformed FDJ members marched in a torchlight procession along Unter den Linden in honor of the founding of the GDR on 7 October. The visual parallel to 30 January 1933, when Nazi storm troopers marched in a torchlight procession through the Brandenburg Gate and on to the Reich Chancellery, was too unsettling

---

32. "Richtlinien für die Verleihung von Namen" (27 October 1949), JA IzJ A 2.391.

33. Hans Mayer, *Der Turm von Babel. Erinnerung an eine Deutsche Demokratische Republik* (Frankfurt am Main, 1991), 67.

even for the largely coordinated eastern press. The satire magazine *Ulenspiegel* discreetly pointed out these similarities and suggested that the FDJ looked too much like the Hitler Youth and the German *Wehrmacht.* "The gray columns were pulled, directed. The blue columns move according to their own will. And, God damn it, they don't need a drummer. And furthermore, they have a cute little responsibility toward the very youngest. And these very young ones have no need whatsoever for a drummer and drums, forward, march!, quickstep, hup-two-three-four."[34]

The SED's response was quick and bitter. "In the best case," a functionary wrote to the magazine's editors, "it is not yet clear to the author that today it is essential to mobilize youth by all available means for the struggle for the securing of peace, that it is essential to beat the drums for the struggle against war, that it is essential to levy the masses of the people for a counterattack against the war arsonists." The "democratic press," the letter continued, must "explain to our people and above all to our youth that 'marching, drumming, and trumpeting' are not reactionary [or] subversive in general, but that it all depends on *what* one trumpets, marches, and drums *for,* and the important thing is that only those persons are drumming, trumpeting, and marching who also know that they are doing it for peace."[35]

Thus the symbolic continuities of life from the Third Reich to the GDR were striking. Making allowances for the tricks of the aging memory, it is hardly surprising that older East Germans recalling the early days of the GDR regularly confuse such abbreviations as the HJ (Hitler Youth) and the FDJ, the NSDAP (Nazi Party) and the SED, the Gestapo and the *Stasi.*[36]

The "Oath of Buchenwald" and "Day X"

Considering that it understood itself as an atheistic and rationalist state, the GDR spent a great deal of energy promoting the religious notions of resurrection and redemption.[37] Of course, Marxist-Leninists reject both

34. *Ulenspiegel* 21 (1949): 8.
35. Letter, "An die Redaktion des 'Ulenspiegel,'" 9 November 1949, SAPMO BArch IV 2/16/102, Bl. 145–46.
36. Dorothee Wierling, "Is There an East German Identity? Aspects of a Social History of the Soviet Zone/German Democratic Republic," *Tel Aviver Jahrbuch für deutsche Geschichte* 19 (1990): 199.
37. On the use of pseudoreligious symbolism and liturgy in the GDR and other communist societies, see Gerd Rabbow, "Pseudosakrale Symbole in der SBZ," *Deutsche Studien* 12 (1965): 443–58; Klemens Richter, "Jugendweihe und andere profane Symbolhandlungen. Ein kritischer Vergleich," *Diakonia* 7 (1976): 38–44; Klemens Richter, "Ritenbildung im gesellschaftspolitischen System der DDR," *Liturgisches Jahrbuch* 27 (1977): 172–88; E. B. Koenker, *Secular Salvations. The Rites and Symbols of Political Religions* (Philadelphia, 1965).

the concept of a deity and a resurrection as a fraud. The sole meaning of life, they argue, lies in the construction of the communist society. One's good deeds in the current society will be continued by others and will find fulfillment in that future society. "Religion," one Party functionary explained, "feeds people with hopes of overcoming the earthly vale of tears in the Beyond, and thus distracts them from changing this world." It makes people "into a tool of those who require the existence of a God to maintain their feudal rule. He who lives in Socialism needs no consolation of a life after death."[38]

This secular notion of resurrection was the central theme of the Johannes R. Becher/Hanns Eisler 1949 national anthem, *"Auferstanden aus Ruinen"* (Arisen from ruins). It was also the underlying theme of Stephan Hermlin's moving book *Die erste Reihe* (The front line), which told the stories of thirty young resistance fighters and underground youth groups who were murdered in Spain and in World War II. With the sole exception of the Catholic "White Rose" group surrounding the Munich students Hans and Sophie Scholl, for whom Hermlin shows only grudging admiration, all of these martyrs were Communists. For years this book stood at the center of antifascist myth-building in the youth organization. Hermlin dedicated his book to "the millionfold second line, the Free German Youth." As Hermlin put it, "The heirs of Artur Becker and Hans and Sophie Scholl, the heirs of the executed underground fighters and the fallen German partisans in the Soviet Union and in Greece and France, the heirs of the dead in the Spanish freedom struggle are in all of Germany marching under the blue flag into a future which will finally, finally be life."[39]

Few East Germans did more to build the antifascist myth than Hermlin. An influential Party member and one of the GDR's most celebrated writers, Hermlin had always presented himself as the classic antifascist author, having spent time in the Sachsenhausen concentration camp, losing a father to the Nazi gas chambers and a heroic pilot brother to German antiaircraft, and having fought in both the Spanish civil war and the French Resistance. Hermlin's image was severely deflated by revelations made in 1996 that none of these claims was true and that he in no way could be counted among the "first line" of GDR antifascists.[40] He died soon after. Whether his prevarication was mere opportunism or whether it had more profound psychological motives is unclear. Neverthe-

---

38. "Weil die Religion die Menschen lähmt," *Neuer Tag* 10 April 1958, cited in Klemens Richter, "Ritenbildung im gesellschaftspolitischen System der DDR," 185.

39. Stephan Hermlin, *Die erste Reihe* (East Berlin, 1951), 10–11.

40. Karl Corino, *Außen Marmor, innen Gips. Die Legenden des Stephan Hermlin* (Düsseldorf, 1996).

less, Hermlin's delusion highlights the power of GDR antifascism as both a motivating principle and a key to fame and success.

With the dedication of the Buchenwald monument in 1958, East Germans were given a central memorial at which to commemorate the sacrifices of the antifascists. It stood at the center of the antifascist myth, and literally millions of Young Pioneers, FDJ members, and National People's Army recruits took part in antifascist ceremonies there. For this reason it is worth close attention.

The Buchenwald concentration camp on the Ettersberg near Weimar was one of the most brutal of the Third Reich, although hardly comparable to extermination camps like Auschwitz and Treblinka. Some fifty-six thousand people were murdered, or died of starvation, disease, exposure, or exhaustion behind its gates. In April 1945, when most of the camp's SS guards had already fled and American tanks were within earshot, a secret camp committee under Communist leadership distributed a secret cache of weapons and briefly took control of the camp. Whether this action by a tiny group of armed activists once the liberation was a foregone conclusion can be considered a "self-liberation" is doubtful, although its participants certainly viewed it as such. This, however, was the interpretation of the KPD and SED as popularized in the novel and film *Naked among Wolves*.[41] It was one of the central founding myths of the GDR for reasons that will become clear later on.

At a memorial ceremony performed a few days later, on 19 April 1945, several hundred survivors assembled on the camp's parade ground and remembered their fallen comrades. At the climax of the ceremony a member of the camp committee recounted the terrible history of the place and then delivered this appeal, which has gone down in history as the "Oath of Buchenwald."[42]

> We will only halt our struggle when the last perpetrator stands before the judges of the peoples!
> The extermination of Nazism with its roots is our slogan. The building of a new world of peace and freedom is our goal.
> We owe this to our murdered comrades and their families.
> As a sign of your readiness for this struggle raise your hand and repeat after me:
> WE SWEAR!

---

41. Bruno Apitz, *Nackt unter Wölfen* (East Berlin, 1958). See also the memoirs of one of the participants in the uprising: Robert Leibbrand, *Buchenwald. Ein Tatsachenbericht* (Stuttgart, 1945).

42. *Buchenwald. Mahnung und Verpflichtung. Dokumente und Berichte* (East Berlin, 1961), 587–88.

But the Buchenwald cult had a slow start. After the Soviet occupation of Thuringia in July 1945, the camp was reopened as a Soviet internment camp where tens of thousands of former Nazis were imprisoned along with uncounted Social Democrats, union officials, and other rivals of the KPD and SED (a few of whom had already done time at Buchenwald under the Nazis). Thousands died from starvation and disease. Thus the SED could not begin the construction of a Buchenwald museum and memorial until the final disbanding of the Soviet camp in 1951.[43]

The memorial was built just outside the actual camp on a prominent slope of the Ettersberg hill overlooking a broad expanse of the Thuringian landscape. The site measures 600 by 520 meters. The lower section consists of three ceremonial round spaces (*Ringgräber*) connected by a long "Street of the Nations" flanked by large stone blocks labeled with the names of the countries whose citizens were imprisoned in the camp. Upon each block stands a ceremonial brazier that was lit for special events. The steps leading up the slope are flanked by a series of stone relief sculptures depicting the history of Buchenwald, from the construction of the camp to the "illegal Thälmann celebration" to the "self-liberation." At the center of a broad square on top of the hill stands the larger-than-life Fritz Cremer sculpture of the self-liberation. The faces and bodies of the eleven bronze male figures are ravaged by their struggle. In the center a resistance fighter raises his right hand in the "Oath of Buchenwald." Near him a man raises his rifle symbolizing the self-liberation. One fighter is wearing a Basque cap, symbolizing the Spanish civil war. One falls in the struggle, some stand helplessly in despair, one cynic stands aside and scoffs. Most significant of all, a small boy stands bravely at the far right end, symbolizing the new antifascist generation. Above the entire ensemble waves the banner of the working class. Behind the sculpture stands a fifty-five meter tall bell tower bearing the year "1945" in Roman numerals. Inside is a bronze plate engraved with the names of other Nazi concentration camps. At the top of the tower hangs a giant "liberty bell."[44] Inside the actual camp compound several hundred meters away, a small bronze column marks the spot in the camp crematorium where Ernst Thälmann was murdered.

---

43. On some of the ironies of the Buchenwald camp and monument, see Eve Rosenhaft, "The Legacy of Communist Resistance in the GDR," in Francis R. Nicosia and Laurence D. Stokes, eds., *Germans Against Nazism: Resistance in the Third Reich* (New York, 1990), 369–88; Manfred Overesch, "Thüringen 1945—Das Ende der antifaschistischen Gründungslegende in der SBZ/DDR," *Deutsche Studien,* December 1990, 348–59.

44. Frank, *Antifaschistische Mahnmale,* 12–16; H. Koch, "Nationale Mahn- und Gedenkstätte Buchenwald. Geschichte ihrer Entstehung," *Buchenwald Heft* 31 (Weimar-Buchenwald, 1988).

The memorial was dedicated on 14 September 1958 in a ceremony presided over by Otto Grotewohl. Grotewohl's presence and Ulbricht's absence are highly significant, since Grotewohl, unlike Ulbricht, had spent the Nazi years in Germany and did time in prison.[45] Despite its tendentiousness, the memorial was not much different from other tendentious war memorials.[46] However, the Buchenwald memorial was just as much about the present as it was about the past. The Cremer sculpture represented the resurrection of the antifascist resistance fighters in the new GDR. From the SED's standpoint, Fascism did not end in 1945 but continued on in the guise of "imperialism." The thousands of Young Pioneer and FDJ delegations, youth consecration groups, and young recruits swearing their oaths of allegiance before the sculpture, and hence renewing the antifascist covenant that was the foundation of the GDR, always did so with an eye to current events.

The concept of resurrection—in this particular case decrying American militarism—was propagated by the song "The Bell of Buchenwald," which was imported from the Soviet Union and translated into German.[47]

> Over Buchenwald, with dark richness,
> Drones the peal of the bell.
> Thousands, who found bitter death here,
> Are awakened by the call, to fight renewed murder.
> They have arisen from the ashes,
> And their word admonishes us.
> Those who perished in fire and dungeon,
> Line up, line up in columns,
> And we have heard their call,
> Through the entire world, through the entire world.

A standard symbol on the GDR's antifascist memorials was a red triangle upon which was superimposed a raised hand pointing to the state emblem of the GDR—the oath and its fulfillment.

The methods by which Buchenwald and the hundreds of lesser antifascist memorials were used in GDR myth-building are illustrated by the following experience of a youth consecration group in 1962: "The excursions to the former concentration camps Sachsenhausen and Ravensbrück deeply impressed the participants. The Fascist cruelties were

---

45. Manfred Overesch emphasizes this point in his article "Thüringen 1945," 349, 359.

46. On war monuments in general, see George L. Mosse, *Fallen Soldiers. Reshaping the Memory of the World Wars* (New York, 1990).

47. A. Soboljew and W. Muradeli, German by Heidi Kirmsse, "Die Glocke von Buchenwald," *Leben Singen Kämpfen,* 81–82.

inconceivable to them. Thus following the visit, young people from the 25th *Oberschule* in Lichtenberg [East Berlin] asked: 'Why did people allow that to happen and not do anything about it?' In the clarifying conversation the girls and boys were forced to recognize the danger which comes from the West of Germany, where a Globke [a controversial adviser and accused war criminal in the Adenauer cabinet] and many infamous Nazi blood judges can live and spread slander with impunity. In this connection and through the comparison with the GDR the participants realized why the GDR is the fatherland of German youth."[48]

This judgment of Globke and others may have been justified, but the myth of antifascism and its monuments early on found uses that most of the fallen resistance fighters never could have imagined. The GDR's "real" antifascist legacy was rapidly devalued by the uncontrollable inflation of the term "Fascist." In 1948 the Yugoslav government became "the Fascist Tito regime," beginning in 1949 the Federal Republic and all of its actions were likewise declared "Fascist," and the U.S. involvement in Korea was classified as a return to the "Fascist war" and to "barbarism." As we saw in chapter 2, faced with a poor harvest in 1950 the SED spread the story that the U.S. airforce was dropping potato beetles onto East German fields. Young Pioneers were given tin badges in a nationwide competition to collect and destroy as many potato bugs and potato bug larvae as possible. In typical SED style the competition against these vermin was presented as a junior version of the antifascist resistance struggle. According to one poster from 1950, showing an American bomber dropping a load of hideous bugs onto a collective farm, "*AMI*-BEETLES ARE SET TO DESTROY OUR HARVEST. / THEY THREATEN YOUR LIVELIHOOD! Destroying the potato beetle is a way of fighting the war plans of the imperialists. Your struggle against the pernicious plague from the USA is a STRUGGLE FOR PEACE!"[49] The Berlin workers' uprising of June 1953 predictably turned into a "Fascist coup attempt," and in 1955 FDJ propagandists pointed to "the historical parallels between the *Reichstag* fire trial and the trial of the Federal Constitutional Court against the KPD in West Germany."[50] In 1961 the GDR's most famous monument, the Berlin Wall, received the name "antifascist defensive wall."

Berlin's most famous landmark was constructed at the height of the "Berlin crisis" of 1958–61. According to the SED, the Wall did not start going up on 13 August 1961 to stanch the flow of hundreds of thousands

---

48. "Auszüge aus den Jahresabschlussanalysen 1961/1962 der Bezirksausschüsse für Jugendweihe," SAPMO BArch IV 2/905/138, Bl. 106–7.

49. "The Image of America as the Enemy in the Former GDR," *Deutsches Historisches Museum Magazin* 7/3 (1993): 11.

50. "Rahmenplan für die Lektionspropaganda für das Jahr 1953," JA IzJ A 341.

of East Germans trying to leave the country (159,730 had escaped by way of Berlin between January and August 1961 alone, and nearly 200,000 the year before),[51] but instead to protect the GDR from "Day X": a supposedly imminent invasion by the Fascist Federal Republic led by a "march through the Brandenburg Gate with drums beating."[52] In a national television address five days later, Ulbricht justified the construction of the Wall in a speech filled with antifascist rhetoric and claimed that by taking this action he was protecting the world from a repeat of 1933 and 1939. If the German working class had been as well prepared in 1933 as it was in 1961, Ulbricht stated, "what misfortune would the German people and the world have been spared!"[53]

The youth organizations played a key role as extras in the antifascist melodrama the Party was enacting. Young Pioneers and FDJ members were used in photo opportunities in which they were shown giving bouquets of flowers to the bricklayers and soldiers. Thousands were called together into great mass demonstrations to cheer Ulbricht's decision. As it happened, 13 August 1961 coincided with the Fourth Pioneer Meeting, which some thirty thousand children were attending in Erfurt. The SED officials on the spot proclaimed the official justification for the Wall, "the Pioneers unanimously proclaimed their support for this decisive step of the Party and the government," and the Pioneer Organization lit "peace fires" on the evening of 14 August to celebrate. The climax of the Pioneer Meeting occurred four days later, the anniversary of Ernst Thälmann's murder, when a three thousand-member Pioneer delegation traveled to the

---

51. Hermann Weber, *DDR. Grundriss der Geschichte 1945–1990*, completely revised and expanded edition (Hannover, 1991), 304–5.

52. Manfred Paul and Horst Liebig, *Grenzsoldaten* (East Berlin, 1981), 147.

53. "Ansprache des Vorsitzenden des Staatsrates der Deutschen Demokratischen Republik, Walter Ulbricht, im Deutschen Fernsehfunk am 18. August 1961," in *Unser Staat rettet den Frieden in Deutschland. Dokumente zur Einschätzung der Massnahmen vom 13. August 1961 und über die Perspektive der Hauptstadt der DDR, Berlin* (*Schriftenreihe des Staatsrates der Deutschen Demokratischen Republik*, 15/1961), 12. It is important to note that the victims of the Wall were only mentioned in SED propaganda as instruments of West German anticommunist propaganda. As Ulbricht stated in his speech of 18 August 1961, West German politicians "did not demonstrate any special inventiveness in their attempt to rub out the German Democratic Republic. After all, there are plenty of people who can remember exactly how Hitler planned his invasion of Czechoslovakia and then Poland. Back then the radio, the *Völkischer Beobachter,* and the whole mob of the Nazi press brought, for weeks and months, every single day reports on the poor miserable refugees, on the old granny, who jumped over border creeks and other hindrances with a whole flock of little children, just to rescue herself home to the *Reich,* to 'freedom.' That was joined by a lying propaganda about self-determination, namely self-determination according to the recipe of the German imperialists, who wanted to determine for themselves which country they would loot next" (9).

Buchenwald monument to endorse the Wall and to participate in a ceremonial roll call under the slogan "Your peace deed for our peace state!"
(*"Eure Friedenstat für unseren Friedensstaat!"*).[54]

Many people believed Ulbricht. But the half-truths contained in this
justification were obvious even to many *parteilich* Communists who wel-
comed the Wall's construction for the good of Socialism. This explains
the almost complete public taboo that surrounded the Wall in the 1960s,
and the technocratic quality and the belabored heroism of the later
official commemorations of 13 August 1961 as the day of the "securing of
the state border of the GDR to Westberlin." But in 1971 the Party went
on the offensive. Ironically, 13 August 1971 was both the tenth anniversary of the Wall and the one hundredth birthday of the revolutionary and
KPD founder Karl Liebknecht. In its official ceremonies and parades
marking both events, SED made the most of this coincidence and portrayed the Wall as a hallmark of the GDR's revolutionary tradition. The
Kampfgruppen (workers' militia) members who sealed off the border in
1961 had acted as if Liebknecht "had been in their midst," the *Junge Welt*
proclaimed.[55] In the central parade on Unter den Linden in East Berlin,
workers marched in both their regular *Kampfgruppen* uniforms and in the
traditional uniform of the Red Front Fighter League of the 1920s and
1930s. Thousands of National People's Army soldiers marched as well,
their gray uniforms decorated with bouquets of flowers representing the
people's thanks for the army's role in this victory against the Fascists. Six
border guards who had been shot by West Germans at the Wall over the
past ten years were consequently honored as the latest victims of Fascist
aggression.[56]

But the dilemma of feeling compelled to lock up and even shoot at
one's own people for their own good—Marxist-Leninists call this sort of
thing *dialectics*—had disastrous effects on the quality of pro-Wall propaganda. For instance, in one of the few FDJ "youth songs" composed in
direct celebration of the Wall, the author hopelessly mixes his metaphors,
evoking both the old patriotic song "The Watch on the Rhine" (trans-

---

54. *Thälmanns Namen tragen wir* (East Berlin, 1988), 124–28; *Geschichte der Freien
Deutschen Jugend. Chronik* (East Berlin, 1976), 180.

55. *Junge Welt* wrote on this anniversary: "On that 13 August 1961 probably none of
the comrades of the *Kampfgruppen,* who at first sealed off the state border to Westberlin with
only their armed bodies, thought of Karl Liebknecht's ninetieth birthday. But they acted as
if he had been in their midst. And that has nothing to do with the fact that two memorable
events come together on one 13 August. It comes from the revolutionary spirit which prevails
in our Marxist-Leninist Party of the working class." Zeno Zimmerling, "Zusammenhang im
Zufall zweier Jahrestage am 13. August," JW 13 August 1971.

56. See the heavy press coverage in ND and JW, 13 and 14/15 August 1971.

muted into "the Watch on the Spree") and the old *no pasaran* ("they shall not pass") slogan of the Spanish civil war.[57] To most Westerners, of course, the construction of the Wall and the subsequent posting of a goose-stepping honor guard a few hundred meters away at the East Berlin monument to the "victims of Fascism and militarism" did more damage to the GDR's antifascist, humanitarian image than all of its other human rights violations combined. As Konrad Jarausch has written, "the proud anti-Fascist legacy in the GDR contributed to the justification of a new kind of tyranny."[58] The Berlin Wall was a clear example of failed myth-building. But in fairness to the SED, it is hard to see how it could have done better under the circumstances.

As far as the public image of antifascist events is concerned, most East German Communists genuinely knew nothing besides the symbolic forms of the Weimar Republic, the Third Reich, the Soviet Union, and the GDR itself. The sculptor Fritz Cremer was a typical case. He sculpted countless antifascist statues and monuments, including the massive Buchenwald monument. As such he was largely responsible for the visual form of the antifascist myth, that is, contorted bodies, small heads, and enormous fists. He himself did not openly resist the Nazis during the Third Reich, and that sense of shame seems to have driven his work in the GDR. In an interview given in 1976, Cremer described his motives as follows.[59]

> I really believe that if anybody who as a German does not feel responsible for what the Germans have done, both to themselves and to the other peoples of the world—I feel sorry for that person. . . . When I know that twenty million Soviet citizens or six million Jews had to die because the Germans thought they had a better view of the world and

---

57. Siegried Berthold and Kurt Greiner-Pol, "Jung sind die Linden," *Leben Singen Kämpfen,* 358–59. The first verse runs as follows:

Es war in den Tagen des August, die Rosen erblühten im Garten,
Da haben wir unseren Schutzwall gebaut, wir konnten nicht länger warten.
Wer das Leben stört und die Warnung nicht hört, spürt die Faust unsrer starken Armee.
So lang man aus Bonn noch mit Kriegsbränden droht, stehn wir auf der Wacht an der Spree.
CHORUS:
Jung sind die Linden, und jung bleibt Berlin,
Weil wir auf Wache zum Spreeufer ziehn.
Uns weht die Fahne des Sieges voran,
Wir halten stand—no pasaran!

58. Jarausch, "Das Versagen des ostdeutschen Antifaschismus," 114.
59. "Gespräch mit Fritz Cremer," *Sinn und Form,* 1976/5: 908.

could improve the world, then I can't close my eyes. I can't simply, in the name of art, look away and say I'm an artist. Yes, I don't know what kind of artist that would be who would say such a thing in times like these.

And what of the SED leadership? Perhaps the question of cynicism is wrong. It is more accurate to speak of survival. Pieck, Ulbricht, Honecker, and others had only barcly escaped Fascism and "Stalinism" with their lives. The East German dramatist Heiner Müller, reflecting on the biographies of the former SED leadership, argued in 1993 that "only intellectuals can be cynical. . . . The persecuted and the vanquished always have a more exact view of history than the victors. Victors have illusions, the persecuted cannot afford illusions, [but] only lies and clichés, which they need in order to make it through the day."[60]

"Ernst Thälmann Never Fell"

Although the SED honored hundreds of antifascists in school names, on street signs, on commemorative plaques, and elsewhere, no hero received more attention than Ernst Thälmann. Thälmann was born to a Social Democratic workers' family in Hamburg in 1886 and became active in leftist politics at an early age. He worked at odd jobs in Germany and America before joining the KPD in 1920. He helped organize the abortive Hamburg uprising of 1923 and was elected chairman of the KPD in 1925. As KPD leader and a member of the Presidium of the Executive Committee of the Communist International, Thälmann consistently followed the Stalinist course and transformed the KPD into a "party of a new type" upon the model of the CPSU. He was arrested by the Gestapo in March 1933 and spent eleven years in various Nazi prisons.[61] The irony of Thälmann's sad fate was that during the period of the Hitler-Stalin Pact, when relations between the two dictatorships were at their best and when Stalin was delivering thousands of German Communists to the Gestapo as a goodwill gesture, the KPD's exile leadership under Ulbricht and Pieck saw to it that no attempt was made to free their leader. Thälmann was consequently murdered by the SS in the Buchenwald concentration camp in August 1944, and Ulbricht and Pieck took over the leadership of the KPD. To be sure, whether Stalin or the KPD actually wanted Thälmann to die, and whether intervention would have saved Thälmann's life at a cost acceptable to the

---

60. "Stalingrad war eigentlich das Ende der DDR. Interview mit Heiner Müller," *Der Freitag* (Berlin), 18 June 1993.
61. Cf. Willi Bredel, *Ernst Thälmann* (East Berlin, 1961); Hermann Weber, *Die Wandlungen des deutschen Kommunismus* (Cologne, 1969).

Soviet Union, remains speculation.[62] But it was obvious that Thälmann was far more valuable to the cause dead than alive.

The organized Thälmann myth preceded the GDR and began even before the leader's arrest. As the Hitler cult continued to grow and the KPD seemed unable to do anything about it, there is evidence that the Communists deliberately developed a personality cult around Ernst Thälmann.[63] He was not so much portrayed as a German Stalin, but instead as a kind of Marxist-Leninist "*Führer.*" During his imprisonment communists and intellectuals the world over mounted a massive propaganda campaign demanding the release of this "representative of the Other Germany."[64]

Thälmann's life and martyrdom were a feature of GDR youth propaganda from the very beginning. Thus in the "assault banner" campaign of 1948–49 the Thälmann banner was the most prestigious of the lot and was to be awarded to the most active FDJ group in the entire SBZ. It was won by the FDJ organization of the Wismut uranium conglomerate in Saxony. This is especially significant, since Wismut was mining uranium for the Soviet atomic weapons industry and was hence perhaps the most important industrial installation in the East. After receiving this honor the local organization introduced an indoctrination program under the title "Ernst Thälmann—Our Model." Making the usual allowances for the excessive optimism of FDJ progress reports, the program looked something like this: "Even before the festivities in Leipzig were over, the two thousand participants and delegates of the Wismut district passed a resolution to hold on to the Ernst Thälmann assault banner by all means, to defend it and never to let it out of their hands. They committed themselves to raise further their production output in the months of June and July, moreover to become members of the Society for the Study of the Soviet Union, since they recognized that it is worthwhile to study the culture and the life of the Soviet Union in order to draw the necessary consequences for their further work. Every one of them also committed himself to recruiting within a month one new FDJ member each and to take part regularly in the functionaries' indoctrination. Already in July they managed to recruit 1,500 new members."[65]

---

62. Günter Hortzschansky, personal letter to the author, 2 January 1994. I am indebted to Hortzschansky, the leading Thälmann expert in the former GDR, for sharing his knowledge of this issue with me. My thanks also to Hermann Weber for sharing his thoughts with me on Thälmann's fate.

63. Otto Flechtheimer, *Die KPD in der Weimarer Republik* (Frankfurt am Main, 1969), 256.

64. On the "Free Thälmann" campaign, see the extensive document collection on permanent display at the "Gedenkstätte Deutscher Widerstand" in Berlin.

65. Gerhard Zadek, "Wismut—kümmert sich um den Menschen," JG 8 (1949): 353.

The Thälmann cult grew rapidly and soon took on a blatantly religious character. On 18 August 1949, the fifth anniversary of Thälmann's murder, Ulbricht spoke of the leader's character and martyrdom in terms reminiscent of the Crucifixion, and at the same time offered a possibility to redeem German war guilt.[66]

We Germans have an especially high obligation. We did not find the strength to drive away the war criminals in time to protect Ernst Thälmann and thousands of other peace fighters. If we want to preserve his memory it is not enough only to speak of his heroic life. We must strive to fight as heroically as he, as boldly as he, as uprightly as he for peace, for the happiness of the people.

Despite the gruesomeness of the story, Thälmann's life and death were made into a veritable children's religion in the Young Pioneers. This was foreshadowed by the motto of the predecessor organization to the Young Pioneers in the late 1940s, the "Children's Association of the FDJ": "*Keines zu klein—Kämpfer zu sein*" (None too small to be a fighter). In keeping with the spirit of the "anti-Fascist democratic upheaval," the Pioneer Organization itself, founded in 1949 and from the beginning an almost exact duplicate of its Soviet counterpart, was ostensibly created to raise German children to be "progressive, studious, work-happy, industrious, honest, happy, democratic young people."[67] Upon admission to the Young Pioneers, each child was ceremoniously given a blue neckerchief, symbolizing the blue flag of the FDJ that the children themselves should strive one day to carry. The neckerchief's three corners represented "school–parents–Pioneer Organization."[68] They were also taught the over-the-head Pioneer salute and the responsive Boy Scout–style Pioneer greeting: "Be prepared!—Always prepared!" At first the organization was mostly concerned with food distribution, physical fitness, school reform, and vacation camps. Antifascist indoctrination and visits to former concentration camps were not particularly important.

In 1950, when the worst of the war damage had been dealt with and the cold war had begun in earnest, the Pioneers began detailed study of Thäl-

---

66. *Ernst Thälmann. Vorbild der Jugend als wahrer Patriot und Kämpfer für den Frieden* (East Berlin, 1952), 10.

67. "Der Aufbau des Verbandes der Jungen Pioniere. Beschluss der 18. Tagung der FDJ vom 6. Februar 1949," *Seid bereit—für die Sache Ernst Thälmanns. Dokumente und Bilder zur Geschichte der Pionierorganisation "Ernst Thälmann" 1945 bis 1952* (East Berlin, 1968), 86.

68. "Gesetze der Jungen Pioniere," JG 3 (1949): 141.

mann's life. In June 1950 in the course of the first *"Deutschlandtreffen,"* the "Pioneer Republic Ernst Thälmann"—a vacation park complete with parade grounds, playing fields, and a narrow gauge "Pioneer Railroad"— was dedicated in Berlin. A month later, the Third Party Congress of the SED proclaimed the formation of a "national resistance" to the imperialist occupiers and the introduction of "patriotic education" in the schools and mass organizations.[69] Thälmann was to be built up as a "national" figure of resistance. But despite the increased attention shown Thälmann, he was still only a shadow of the idolatrous treatment given Lenin, Stalin, Marx, Engels, Karl Liebknecht, and Wilhelm Pieck at this time.

Then, at the Second Party Conference of the SED in July 1952, Walter Ulbricht proclaimed the "systematic construction of the foundations of Socialism in the GDR."[70] This meant not only complete control over the country and its people, but also the full-scale introduction of the Soviet political and propaganda system in the GDR. The Politburo consequently announced that, following the tradition of the "Pioneer Organization V.I. Lenin" in the Soviet Union, the GDR Young Pioneers would be given Thälmann's name, with all the honors and duties that went with it. They had ostensibly earned this name through hard work at school, helping old people, collecting money and scrap metal, and above all by combating the dreaded potato beetle.[71] The formal ceremony was to take place during the "First Pioneer Meeting" in Dresden from 19 to 24 August 1952 to coincide with the eighth anniversary of Thälmann's murder. The choice of Dresden was extremely symbolic: destroyed by "Anglo-American bombers" in 1945, by 1952 its energetic reconstruction campaign had made it into a symbol of the new German Democratic Republic, which had itself "arisen from ruins."

Otto Grotewohl opened the festivities with a keynote speech explaining the significance of Thälmann's life and sacrifice. As at all later "Pioneer Meetings," the following days were filled with games, dances, parades, "youth songs," and solemn rituals with flags and torches. The actual ceremony took place at a rally of some twenty-five thousand Young Pioneers in central Dresden on 23 August. In the presence of Rosa Thälmann (Ernst's widow) and Erich Honecker, Politburo member Hermann Matern delivered a dramatic speech on Thälmann's martyrdom and presented the Pioneer Organization with a special "red flag of the working class," bearing the likenesses of Ernst Thälmann and Wilhelm Pieck. With this red flag

---

69. *Protokoll des III. Parteitages der SED* (East Berlin, 1950).

70. *Protokoll der II. Parteikonferenz der SED* (East Berlin, 1952).

71. "Grussadresse des Zentralkomitees der SED," *Der Jungpionier* (special edition), 19 August 1952.

they were to "fight for the red neckerchief," which they would one day be permitted to wear. The genuine emotion of the ceremony is obvious from contemporary newsreel footage. Finally a selected Young Pioneer functionary, Gisela Wessely, her voice choked with tears, saluted Matern Pioneer-style and read aloud the new "Pledge of the Young Pioneers."[72]

> We Young Pioneers, sons and daughters of the German people, by our Pioneer honor, pledge to our President Wilhelm Pieck that we will always show ourselves worthy of the name of Ernst Thälmann, who fought and gave his life for the happiness of our people.
> This we swear!
> [ALL:] This we swear! . . .
> We promise to live and learn in an exemplary way in order to become worthy citizens of our German Democratic Republic.
> [ALL:] This we swear!

The evening concluded with a tremendous display of fireworks—"the most beautiful fireworks display of my life," Wessely recalled more than three decades later.[73] The Pioneer Meeting closed the next day with an elaborate parade of nearly eighty thousand uniformed Young Pioneers before President Wilhelm Pieck, Erich Honecker, and other dignitaries. In front of the usual slogan banners and array of uniforms and symbols representing the different interest and hobby groups within the organization, three Young Pioneers led the parade with the consecrated "red flag of the working class."[74] It would thenceforth be used in the organization's solemn flag consecration rite, by which the banners of new Pioneer "friendships" (local groups) were touched against the sacred Thälmann–Pieck banner.

Over the next decade the solemnity of the Thälmann cult grew tremendously until it reached a plateau in the early 1960s. Children cultivated Thälmann's memory with the arcane rituals and incantations surrounding their pennants and blue neckerchiefs ("whoever dirtied his neckerchief had, so to speak, symbolically dirtied the idea of the liberation of humanity and had to be reprimanded accordingly," as one former Pioneer recalls),[75] "the Pioneer salute," the ceremonial kissing of the red flag, the

---

72. "Gelöbnis der Jungen Pioniere anlässlich der Namensverleihung in Dresden," *Der Junge Pionier,* 23 August 1952; see also Gisela Wessely's (admittedly biased) recollections of the event in *Thälmanns Namen tragen wir,* 56–66.

73. *Thälmanns Namen tragen wir,* 66.

74. "Gewaltige Demonstration der Thälmann-Pioniere vor dem Präsidenten Wilhelm Pieck am 24. August 1952," JW 26 August 1952.

75. "Thälmann, Thälmann—und was noch?" in Thomas Flierl et al., *Mythos Antifaschismus,* 79.

decoration of red-draped, altar-like Thälmann "tradition corners" in their club houses, relentless indoctrination at school, in the vacation camps, and in their "friendships," visits to memorials and talks with border guards and (Communist) resistance fighters. No Pioneer or FDJ member could get on with his life without attending the two full-length Thälmann films produced in the 1950s, followed by the mandatory set lecture and discussion. At the Third Pioneer Meeting in Halle in August 1958, Matern unveiled the cumbersome new Pioneer greeting: "Forward in the spirit of Ernst Thälmann! For peace and Socialism! Be prepared!"—"Always prepared!"[76]

In Halle Thälmann was joined by a new model for children: "The Little Trumpeter," a young Red Front Fighter League member who in the 1920s, while attending a rally at which Thälmann was to speak, was shot dead by police and who inspired the League's later fight song. The Pioneers visited his new monument in Halle and a year later were presented with an illustrated children's propaganda book on the struggle and death of their new model.[77] By the early 1960s East German children had grown used to constant appeals exhorting them to be worthy of Thälmann's life and—ominously—"worthy of his death."[78]

If "Teddy" Thälmann had been presented at first as a warm, cozy father figure (much like "our beloved President Wilhelm Pieck" and as such a spiritual substitute father for the thousands of East German war orphans), his unavenged murder quickly grew in importance. Central to the myth was the notion that Thälmann, like Joe Hill, had never really died. The SED was relentless on this point. In his speech at Dresden, Matern had proclaimed to his young listeners: "Ernst Thälmann did not live to see the final victory of the Soviet Army over Fascism. But the spirit of Ernst Thälmann lives on in the deeds of our toilers in the Socialist reconstruction. The spirit of Ernst Thälmann will live on in the columns of

---

76. *Thälmanns Namen tragen wir,* 104.

77. Inge and Gerhard Holtz-Baumert, *Der kleine Trompeter und sein Freund* (East Berlin, 1959). The clichés in this story are typical of the class-war children's propaganda of the time. For example, on page 14 young Fritz describes a capitalist he sees on the sidelines of a Communist demonstration: "Fritz cast him an evil glance. He saw the white collar of the fine gentleman glow. The back of his neck shone like a slab of bacon." This book was the first in a new series of militant books for Young Pioneers, the "*Kleine Trompeterbücher.*" When I returned a copy of the book to the Humboldt University Library in eastern Berlin in 1993, the librarian picked up the book, smiled, and said fondly: "Ah yes, *Der kleine Trompeter*! That was a beloved children's book in the GDR."

78. Robert Lehmann, foreword to *Thälmann ist niemals gefallen. Geschichten und Berichte* (East Berlin, 1961), 8.

the Pioneer Organization, which will bear his name with pride."[79] This was expressed in the "Thälmann Song" of the SED poet "Kuba" (Kurt Bartel): "Thälmann and Thälmann before all others, / Germany's immortal son, / Thälmann never fell, / Voice and fist of the nation."[80] More to the point was Max Zimmering's poem "Legacy," which the SED recommended for Thälmann ceremonies in the 1950s.[81]

As if Ernst Thälmann could ever die.
Thälmann died yet did not die.
For that which he, while he lived, taught,
That for which he, without rest, propagandized,
Lives as an admonition in millions of hearts,
Lives as knowledge in millions of brains.
Do you see the millions of toiling hands
Fearlessly grasping for the stars?
Thälmann lives in all tractors
Which drive the seedcorn onto the fields,
Thälmann lives in all the open-hearth furnaces,
Which were yesterday still without fire.
Thälmann lives in all airwaves,
Which spread the love of peace among the people,
Until the bowed backs stretch themselves once more, etc.

The Thälmann cult strongly resembled the Horst Wessel cult in the Third Reich and represented a fulfillment of Thälmann's Prieros speech in 1932. But the real model for the Thälmann cult was, of course, the Lenin cult in the Soviet Union. The principal difference was that Lenin did not achieve immortality through martyrdom, but through the skill of his embalmers. (It is intriguing to speculate on the possible development of the Thälmann cult in the Stalin era had his remains been preserved.) In contrast to the godlike Lenin and Marx, beginning in the early 1950s Thälmann himself appeared as a sort of secular, *parteilich* Christ figure. This was not a coincidence. This pseudoreligious myth-building appeared with the full-scale introduction of Marxist-Leninist indoctrination in the schools, universities, and mass organizations, a purge of Christian SED

79. "Vorwärts, 'Thälmann-Pioniere,' für eine glückliche Zukunft. Aus der Rede Hermann Materns vor den Jungen Pionieren in Dresden," in *Seid bereit—für die Sache Ernst Thälmanns* (East Berlin, 1969), 187.

80. Kuba and Eberhard Schmidt, "Thälmannlied," *Leben Singen Kämpfen*, 58.

81. Max Zimmering, "Vermächtnis," *Ernst Thälmann. Vorbild der Jugend als wahrer Patriot*, 25.

members, the periodic banning of Protestant and Catholic newspapers, and the active repression and even the temporary banning of the independent Protestant youth group *Junge Gemeinde* (young congregation), which the FDJ in 1953 denounced as a "front organization for warmongering, sabotage, and espionage in the pay of the U.S.A."[82] But the active veneration of Thälmann's memory was only cultivated intensively among children, less intensively among youths, and the Party never seriously attempted to create anything more than a rhetorical Thälmann cult among adults. To have done more would have ultimately contradicted the pseudorational basis of Marxist-Leninist ideology and the "scientific" quality of the GDR's civic religion as summed up in the official youth consecration book, *Universe-Earth-Man.*[83] In any case, this explicitly supernatural quality was fulfilled by the Lenin-Stalin cult, which the SED imported from the Soviet Union and which had supremacy (minus Stalin after 1956) until the GDR's collapse. But even if it had done more, the cult's sterile transcendence—that is, resurrection as a tractor—simply lacked the depth of emotion contained in the Easter story. The Thälmann cult was a mass cult, and in mass events it was successful. But the martyred Thälmann, the "hero of his class," offered no hope of personal redemption. Partly as a result of the repression of the churches and the listlessness of civic culture, by the 1980s more than half of all East German burials and cremations took place without any ceremony at all. It was partly to remedy this situation that in 1989 the SED launched a new Marxist-Leninist mass organization, a "League of Freethinkers of the GDR," designed to revamp all GDR ceremonies in a worthy, secular, and *parteilich* form.[84]

Why did the SED and the Young Pioneers expend so much time, effort, and money on the memory of a murdered KPD leader? Blind imitation of the Lenin cult was only one reason. Just as important was Thälmann's example in getting young people to work harder. In fact, Pioneer and FDJ leaders mostly used Thälmann to persuade school children to raise their grades. Thälmann's unconditional "friendship to the Soviet Union" was also important. Beyond these profane purposes, the religious quality of the Thälmann cult was aimed at replacing Jewish-Christian

82. Special edition of JW, April 1953. On the suppression of the churches in general and of the *Junge Gemeinde* see Robert F. Goeckel, *The Lutheran Church and the East German State: Political Conflict and Change under Ulbricht and Honecker* (Ithaca, 1990), 44–47; and Christian Stappenbeck, "Zur Kampagne gegen die Junge Gemeinde 1952/53," lecture delivered at Kloster Banz, 8 May 1991, JA IzJ B 6189.

83. Gisela Buschendorf et al., *Weltall-Erde-Mensch. Ein Sammelwerk zur Entwicklungsgeschichte von Natur und Gesellschaft* (East Berlin, 1954). It was followed by many later editions.

84. Alan Nothnagle, "The League of Freethinkers of the GDR," *Free Inquiry,* winter 1989/90, 46–48.

ethics with a militant Socialist ethical system. Thälmann's life was a model of Marxist-Leninist morality. In children's books, Thälmann was depicted in the "sweet Jesus" style of the Lutheran Sunday school sermon. It should be noted that the Thälmann story did not include a Sermon on the Mount. Thälmann never preached reconciliation. Nowhere in the ocean of Thälmann pamphlets does one find an exhortation to love one's enemies, nor does a Good Samaritan or a Good Imperialist fit into Thälmann's grim fighting image. The "Ten Commandments of Socialist Morality," which Walter Ulbricht proclaimed in 1958, had much the same purpose. They contained many admirable sentiments, including the commandments "Thou shalt love thy fatherland and be always prepared to devote thy entire strength and ability to the defense of the workers' and peasants' power" and "Thou shalt raise thy children in the spirit of peace and Socialism to all-round educated human beings, strong in character and physically steeled." But the commandment "Thou shalt not kill" would just have gotten in the way.[85]

Already in March 1953 the FDJ functionaries' journal *Neue Generation* described the new ideal youth as follows.[86]

> Now, upon the rubble of the war which was unleashed by the Fascists
> . . . a new generation is arising which takes the life of Ernst Thälmann
> as its example. It is characterized by its love of the German homeland,
> by its unshakeable will to victory in the construction of Socialism. It
> is convinced of the invincibility of the Socialist Soviet Union and
> appreciates and respects the peoples of the people's democracies
> along with all peace-loving people, and is prepared when necessary to
> defend its homeland gun in hand against the revanchist and rapacious
> cravings of the imperialists.

But the early Thälmann cult was most important as the foundation of the Ulbricht cult. Thälmann's significance was carried over onto the old antifascist resistance fighters, who regularly appeared at official GDR ceremonies. They served the same function as the "Old Bolsheviks" in the Soviet Union, who according to Nancy Heer "act as living icons, whose very appearance at selected public occasions links the present political leadership with the founders of the system. Lacking a blood line, religious ordination, or popularly elected party leaders, this ideological legitimation

---

85. Walter Ulbricht, "10 Gebote der sozialistischen Moral, 10. Juli 1958," Hermann Weber, ed., *DDR. Dokumente zur Geschichte der Deutschen Demokratischen Republik 1945–1985,* 3d ed. (Munich, 1987), 237.

86. Kurt Grützner, "Was gibt der Brief Ernst Thälmanns an einen Kerkergenossen unserer Jugend?" part 2, JG 7 (1953): 22.

is of considerable symbolic importance."[87] A leader who exalted Thälmann automatically exalted himself. Ulbricht, whose bureaucratic genius
saved him from the fate of many an old antifascist fighter, lacked the
heroic element, and GDR propaganda never seriously denied this.[88]
Instead, the Pioneer and FDJ press consistently depicted Ulbricht as the
"teacher" of youth. "He . . . shows them the true heroes of the German
people, acquaints them with the life and the struggle of the leaders of
the German working class and the heroes of the anti-Fascist resistance
struggle, above all with the life and struggle of Ernst Thälmann, whose
pupil and close associate he himself was."[89] Ulbricht thus built his own
myth upon the heroism of Thälmann, just as Stalin had done with Lenin.
Here, Ulbricht was just as circumspect as his Soviet mentor, for Thälmann
(although thoroughly loyal to Stalin, as the Party continually pointed out)
also called to mind the antifascists who spent the war either in Nazi prisons or in Western exile. Ulbricht had purged most of these often unreliable
cadres by the early 1950s, and this fact probably explains many of the
byzantine features of the Thälmann cult. For, as a scholar of the Soviet
Union writes, if "a cult of Lenin that evoked a *nostalgia* for Lenin could
inspire a critical attitude toward the current 'idiot ruler,' then that devotion was harmful to the stability of his rule. The idealized Lenin could only
be tolerated if he were marching hand in hand with his 'faithful compan-
ion,' Stalin."[90]

This changed in 1971 with the succession of Erich Honecker to power.
Honecker was a genuine antifascist resistance fighter in the sense that as a
youth he continued to administer the underground KJVD in the early
years of the Third Reich and subsequently spent ten years in a Nazi prison.
Honecker appears to have been obsessed by these years. He spoke of it
repeatedly in his speeches and made frequent visits back to the Brandenburg penitentiary. In his apologia of 1992, Honecker felt compelled to
include a lengthy essay on his underground work, on the terrors of the
penitentiary with its constant executions, and on the Allied bombing of
Berlin, which he witnessed as a forced laborer. "I could never forget all of
that for one moment of my life," he wrote.[91]

---

87. Nancy W. Heer, *Politics and History in the Soviet Union* (Cambridge, MA, 1971),
16–17.

88. An exception to this is the series of articles appearing in the youth press in June
1953, presenting Ulbricht as a war hero because of his propaganda feats on the Russian front
during World War II. These articles appeared in preparation for Ulbricht's sixtieth birthday
on 30 June, but also were used to counter the extreme popular hatred of Ulbricht, which
exploded in the popular uprisings of that month.

89. Hannes Keusch, "Walter Ulbricht—Lehrer und Erzieher der Jugend," JG 10
(1953): 24.

90. Nina Tumarkin, *Lenin Lives!* (Cambridge, MA, 1983), 251.

91. Erich Honecker, *Erich Honecker zu dramatischen Ereignissen* (Hamburg, 1992), 76.

But this trauma did not make Honecker skeptical of dictatorship, but instead deepened his loyalty to the Soviet Union, which had saved his life. He consistently sought to coordinate the GDR even more closely with Soviet policies and values. Under Honecker, the already well-worn Thälmann myth underwent a renaissance. The renewed Thälmann cult was symbolically begun in August 1972 at the lavish "First Central Council Meeting of the Pioneer Organization 'Ernst Thälmann'" in Dresden, which coincided with the twentieth anniversary of the rousing "First Pioneer Meeting" in that same city. Its opening ceremonies included the exhibition of a huge Thälmann portrait, assorted pledges to Thälmann, and a performance of Beethoven's Ninth Symphony.[92] In December of the following year, the twenty-fifth anniversary of the organization, Honecker renewed the SED's covenant with the Pioneer Organization by conferring upon the "Thälmann-Pioneers" (the older group, grades four through seven, who were preparing for admission to the FDJ) the red neckerchief, which symbolized the red banner of the working class. The ceremony symbolically took place in the building of the State Council of the GDR in East Berlin. This honor had been outlined already at the "First Pioneer Meeting" in 1952. The "Red Young Pioneers" of the 1920s, to which Honecker himself had belonged as a child, had also worn such red neckerchiefs. Thus Honecker was not just bringing the Thälmann-Pioneers more in line with the Soviet "Lenin Pioneers" (who started this whole business with the neckerchiefs in the first place), but also with his own generation.[93]

Beginning in 1979, FDJ members in the "Socialist Circles"—alongside their ongoing indoctrination with Marxist-Leninist theory, the laws and political system of the GDR, and the life of Karl Marx—embarked on the systematic study of Thälmann's life by means of the new, closely supervised, and thoroughly *parteilich* Thälmann biography.[94] "Occupation with the life and work of Ernst Thälmann, with the historic path of the KPD," the FDJ district administration in Berlin claimed in 1980, "shall enable [young people] to work with confidence of victory and militant optimism for the realization of our current and future tasks, and irreconcilably to fight the policies and ideology of imperialism."[95] Beyond reading and discussing the book, this goal could be obtained by visiting local sites where Thälmann had been active and by talking with workers there about "what characterizes a Communist in our present?"

The cultivation of the spirit of Ernst Thälmann became an obsession

---

92. *Geschichte der FDJ*, 260.

93. *Thälmanns Namen tragen wir*, 211–31.

94. Günter Hortzschansky et al., *Ernst Thälmann* (East Berlin, 1979).

95. "Massnahmen zur Vorbereitung und Durchführung des FDJ-Studienjahres 1980/81, Beschluss des Sekretariats der FDJ-Bezirksleitung Berlin vom 16.4.1980," JA IzJ A 10.255.

during the Honecker era. In 1974, the Tenth Meeting of the Central Council of the FDJ decreed the establishment of "Thälmann cabinets," that is, memorial corners, in all district organizations of the FDJ.[96] But aside from the small monument in the crematorium of Buchenwald where Thälmann was murdered, there still existed no central memorial to the great antifascist's memory in the GDR. Honecker himself stated in 1976 that "the formation of Socialism in the German Democratic Republic" was monument enough, and the Pioneer Organization bearing Thälmann's name certainly was as well. But in 1981 the SED announced the construction of a genuine Thälmann monument that would finally do justice to this great fighter. It would consist of a vast combined high-rise housing development/shopping and recreation center to be built on the site of an old gas works in the traditional Berlin workers' district of Prenzlauer Berg. With a Thälmann sculpture erected on a broad ceremonial square and an antifascist museum to go with it, the complex would be called *"Ernst-Thälmann-Park."*[97]

Both the monument and the housing development were formally unveiled on 16 August 1986, Thälmann's one hundredth birthday. The monument reduced Thälmann to the essentials: a gigantic bald head gazing resolutely into the future, a huge clenched fist, and above it all a giant flag bearing a hammer and sickle. For the last three years of the GDR's existence, this monument was the central site of the Thälmann cult and was regularly visited by Young Pioneer and FDJ groups, school classes, youth consecration groups, old antifascists paying their respects, and a variety of other organizations that met there for antifascist and pro-SED demonstrations on holidays. Newlyweds in Prenzlauer Berg were encouraged to stop off there after leaving the registry office to lay a wreath and have their picture taken. The present author and his bride were offered the opportunity at their own wedding in Prenzlauer Berg in August 1988, but politely declined.[98]

To be sure, by West German standards the *Ernst-Thälmann-Park* was at best a mediocre subsidized housing complex, reminiscent of giant human beehives. This observation brings us to what was perhaps the most important aspect of the "spirit of Ernst Thälmann," but one that the Party never enunciated. Thälmann's spirit was, after all, the spirit of the 1920s and 1930s: of the proletarian fight against capitalist exploitation and utter poverty, against Fascism and imperialism. This was the only world that Honecker and many of his generation knew. The *Ernst-Thälmann-Park*

---

96. *Geschichte der Freien Deutschen Jugend. Chronik,* 327.

97. *Ernst-Thälmann-Park Aufbau 1983–1986* (East Berlin, 1986).

98. Nevertheless, the ceremony could not go through without at least one reference to Thälmann: "'A life without love is like a sky without stars.' Thus wrote Ernst Thälmann to his wife from prison. . . ."

represented the fulfillment of Thälmann's dream, and the fulfillment of the "Oath of Buchenwald." This modest but comfortable complex represented the new Socialist utopia, in contrast to the bombastic and by this time ramshackle *Stalinallee,* which we will encounter in the next chapter. Compared with the living and working conditions of workers in Thälmann's time, *Ernst-Thälmann-Park* was an architectural triumph and a source of tremendous pride for the SED. It summed up Honecker's massive nationwide apartment-building program and his slogan of "everything for the good of the people!" The younger generation of the Honecker era was going to have everything that Honecker's generation lacked. Thus education in the "spirit of Ernst Thälmann" really amounted to learning to view the world from Thälmann's perspective, not from the perspective of the Federal Republic, whose social and cultural advances had long ago left the strict "right–left," "cannons or butter" dichotomy of Thälmann's time behind them. For many Communists, Thälmann's mythic world lived on in the GDR, untouched by the frantic changes taking place in the mysterious Western world on the other side of the Wall. Cultivating the spirit of Ernst Thälmann meant using modern technology to fulfill the values and ideals of the 1920s and 1930s in the 1970s and 1980s.

Youth Heroes

The Thälmann cult was the foundation for a pantheon of antifascist (Communist) youth heroes. Artur Becker was a young German Communist and *Reichstag* member who served as a political commissar in Spain, where he was captured and tortured to death by Gestapo agents in 1938.[99] Becker was to the FDJ what Thälmann was to the Young Pioneers. He was commemorated early on in *Heimabende* and a variety of ceremonies. The Central Council named its highest award the *"Artur-Becker-Medaille."* The Becker myth was centered around the *"Jugendkraftwerk* [youth power plant] Trattendorf 'Artur Becker.'" The Trattendorf plant had been built by FDJ members in the early 1950s and a decade later was awarded the name "Artur Becker" in recognition of its high productivity and important propagandistic function. Upon this occasion, a Trattendorf FDJ functionary reported in 1962, "we expounded upon Artur Becker's life in party meetings, union and FDJ assemblies, in the consultations of the economic functionaries of the brigades—everywhere where our factory personnel comes together. . . . It was especially important to us to keep Artur Becker's life's work alive in our plant and to establish a genuine relationship to Artur Becker's struggle in our activities. After all, only in this way can the

---

99. Hermlin, *Die erste Reihe,* 157–64.

name-giving become the point of departure for higher production; only in this way can we really do justice to Artur Becker's legacy."

The functionary goes on to point out that while most of the workers admired Becker's achievements and liked to think they would have performed similarly heroic feats had they lived at that time, they saw little connection to their own lives in the 1960s. "We took this discussion as an opportunity to make clear to the young people of our plant that today in our German Democratic Republic the true heroes are those who give all their strength, all their skill, all their ability in the struggle for the fulfillment of our plan assignments, in the struggle to carry through our production mobilization." He concludes by stating that the plant's propagandists based this argument on Becker's lifelong fight against imperialism and militarism, as well as his experience as a political commissar in Spain. "We have explained to the young people of our plant that the same forces which bestially murdered Artur Becker as a severely wounded prisoner— the imperialists and militarists—still govern in West Germany today."[100]

The FDJ commemorated the thirtieth anniversary of Becker's murder in 1968 with a flood of lectures, newspaper and magazine articles, radio and TV programs, name givings, demonstrations, plaque installations, an "Artur Becker Matinee" at the "Theater of the Young Guard" in Leipzig, and a "Youth Week" in Trattendorf.[101] The commemoration of Becker's seventy-fifth birthday on 12 May 1980 began with the laying of a wreath at the "Memorial of the Socialists" in Berlin-Friedrichsfelde attended by a delegation of the Central Council under FDJ chief Egon Krenz (who would briefly succeed Honecker as leader of the GDR in October and November 1989) and a group of twenty surviving resistance fighters. The whole group then drove to Trattendorf where they attended an extended ceremony and banquet in Becker's honor. There, Krenz awarded FDJ groups bearing Becker's name with the consecrated "Artur Becker Honor Banner." An FDJ choir from Cottbus accompanied the event with workers' and fight songs.[102]

Hans Beimler was another young German Communist who was killed in Spain. Beginning in the 1960s, the FDJ organized annual "Hans

100. Klaus Cober, "Wir erziehen die Jugend nach dem Vorbild Artur Beckers!" in *Wenn wir gemeinsam kämpfen sind wir unüberwindlich. Protokoll der wissenschaftlichen Konferenz "Erfüllt das Vermächtnis der Helden des antifaschistischen Widerstandskampfes— kämpft für die Überwindung des westdeutschen Imperialismus und Militarismus!" Veranstaltet vom Historischen Institut der Ernst-Moritz-Arndt-Universität Greifswald am 24. und 25. Januar 1962* (Berlin, 1962).

101. "Massnahmen zur Würdigung des Kampfes von Artur Becker in Vorbereitung des 30. Jahrestages seiner Ermordung am 16. Mai 1939," JA IzJ A 10.523.

102. "Veranstaltungen des Zentralrats der FDJ aus Anlass des 75. Geburtstages von Artur Becker am 12. 5.1980," JA IzJ A 10.523.

Beimler Competitions" as part of the mandatory paramilitary training (*Wehrerziehung*) for eighth-graders. Beimler was the very model of an antifascist fighter. The Communist singer Ernst Busch wrote a remarkable song about Hans Beimler in which he took the traditional German song for fallen soldiers, Ludwig Uhland's "The Good Comrade" ("I had a comrade, you will never find a better one . . ."), which had been sung by the German army all the way up to 1945 and especially within the Nazi Party, and put new lyrics to it in honor of Beimler ("Before Madrid on the barricades, / In the hour of danger, / In the International Brigades, his heart loaded full of hate, / Stood Hans the commissar, stood Hans the commissar").[103]

The FDJ also built the myth of antifascist continuity by elevating contemporary heroes into antifascist resistance fighters in their own right. As one former Communist who did time in a West German prison wrote, "Because in Stalinist journalism the Federal Republic is depicted as a Fascist state . . . , the political imprisonment of a Party member is transformed into a sort of substitute for a stay in a concentration camp and is rewarded with all the marks of individual heroism."[104] The FDJ got its first real taste of antifascist resistance during the Third World Youth Festival held in East Berlin in August 1951. Two million GDR young people attended, and the mayor of West Berlin, Ernst Reuter, invited the participants to visit his part of the city and see "freedom" first hand. On 15 August one hundred thousand uniformed FDJ members followed Honecker's suggestion to march into West Berlin and take Mayor Reuter up on his offer. The march was intended as a provocation and Honecker gave instructions to link arms and break through the West Berlin police line. Nine hundred seventy-six FDJ members were injured in the ensuing clash with the police, and the organization promptly celebrated the FDJ incursion as an act of antifascism.[105] A few months later, the East German sculptor Felix Krauser created a statue in honor of this event, showing a group of bloodied but determined FDJ boys and girls defending their blue flag. Strongly reminiscent of the Buchenwald sculpture and other antifascist monuments, the monument was simply called "15 August 1951."

Another example of this latter-day antifascism was the short-lived cult developed around Philipp Müller, a young West German Communist who was shot dead by the police at an anti-European Defense Community demonstration in Essen in 1952. The FDJ declared the date of his death,

---

103. *Leben-Singen-Kämpfen. Liederbuch der FDJ,* 12th ed. (Leipzig, 1973), 116.

104. Ralph Giordano, *Die Partei hat immer recht. Ein Erlebnisbericht über den Stalinismus auf deutschem Boden* (Freiburg im Breisgau, 1990), 68.

105. *Geschichte der FDJ. Chronik,* 84–85; see also Heinz Lippmann's memoirs, cited in Ilse Spittmann, ed., *Die SED in Geschichte und Gegenwart* (Cologne, 1987), 202–9.

11 May, to be the "Day of Struggle of German Youth" and organized memorial ceremonies in all FDJ groups throughout the GDR. To this purpose the Cultural Department issued poems, plays, stories, and other propaganda materials through the organization's publications. According to these guidelines, FDJ club rooms were to be decorated with a gigantic portrait of Müller above the words "Philipp Müller—Our Role Model," flanked by smaller portraits of Marx and Stalin. At the memorial services, demonstrations, parades, and so on, young East Germans were to think about the heroic patriots of Essen "with holy hatred against the Adenauer regime and its imperialist taskmasters in their hearts, prepared to defend the peace by any means necessary, and determined to fight for the national unity of our homeland." Müller was to be presented as a German counterpart to the Komsomol hero in Nikolai Ostrovsky's *How the Steel Was Tempered*. "Of Philipp Müller can be said: He dedicated his entire young life to the cause of the German working class, to the struggle for the liberation of our homeland from the American intruders, and bravely and decisively sacrificed it for our people."[106] And yet only two years later Philipp Müller, like so many other GDR heroes, had been reduced to one of those thousands of mass-produced tin badges, this time honoring "extraordinary achievements in the preparation and execution of the people's elections on 17 October 1954."[107]

The constant emphasis on the heroic and violent deeds of such macho figures as the fearless Ernst Thälmann and "Hans the commissar" implied a man's society—in fact, the militant male *"Kampfbund"* ideal of the 1920s—and the FDJ had to work hard to make the "antifascist resistance struggle" attractive to girls and women. To be sure, the SED put great emphasis on gender equality, and by the late 1950s female FDJ members preparing to enter traditionally male careers were certainly justified in stating that Clara Zetkin and Rosa Luxemburg would be proud of what they had achieved in the GDR.[108] The Marxist-Leninist perception of human beings called for women to be fighters, industrial workers, engineers, tractor drivers, intellectuals, party secretaries, and so on, *and* traditional mothers and housewives at the same time. In order to mold the young women into this prefabricated image, the FDJ was forced to blend all of these dissonant elements together. Thus, in one FDJ girls' group, a female functionary wrote in *Junge Generation,* "through excursions and visits to exhibits, as well as in discussion evenings, the girls are made acquainted with the life and struggle of such female role models as Jenny Marx, Clara

---

106. "11. Mai 1953. Kampftag der deutschen Jugend," *Sonderdruck der Schriftenreihe Heim und Klub* (n.d.), 2, 14.

107. *Geschichte der FDJ,* 270.

108. See *Dokumente der Mädchenkonferenz der FDJ,* vol. 1 (Berlin, 1958), 64.

Zetkin, Rosa Luxemburg, Grete Walter, [and] Raymonde Diem. Infant care circles, fashion circles, cooking circles, and similar interest groups are formed and represent a good supplement to the lectures. The cultural work is also strongly tied to the lecture circles, for example through common theater attendances to such plays as *The Diary of Anne Frank.*"[109] Such reports are interesting not only for the anemic revolutionary spirit they evoke, but also for the fact that these female role models otherwise received very little attention in the public rhetoric and ceremonies of the GDR, appearing chiefly as street names and as names for female work brigades in the ubiquitous "Socialist name competitions." The real models for girls in the Young Pioneers and in the FDJ were Ernst Thälmann and Artur Becker respectively. Jenny Marx, for example, was celebrated for the ways she supported her husband. Clara Zetkin, although a fascinating figure in her own right, was presented as little more than a female sidekick of the greatest fighter of all, Ernst Thälmann. And Rosa Luxemburg, an unsettlingly independent thinker and one of the founders of the KPD, was important only as a martyr and a female counterpart to the heroic Karl Liebknecht. The more interesting of her writings were chronically "out of print," especially her critical essay "On the Russian Revolution." FDJ members were given only her warm *Letters from Prison* to read. She probably received her highest honor in the GDR when the central academy for East German border guards at Plauen was named after her—an ironic end for a revolutionary whose most famous slogan was "Freedom is always the freedom of those who think differently"![110]

If the building of the Berlin Wall stifled the GDR's antifascist dynamism and if the cult of the young resistance fighters quickly settled into a routine inside the GDR, it experienced a renaissance in the GDR's aid to developing countries. Beginning in 1964, the FDJ sent dozens of "friendship brigades" (a sort of Marxist-Leninist Peace Corps) to build Socialism in Cuba, Vietnam, Nicaragua, Angola, and other countries. The friendship brigades in Algeria were named after Becker and Beimler.

The spirit of Becker and Beimler was summed up in the FDJ youth song "Build the Roads of the Future," whose incongruously cheerful refrain went as follows: "We stride in the marching step of the Ruhr Army, / And in the assault pace of the International Brigades. / The flag for which Karl Liebknecht fell / We young fighters are carrying to its goal. / Forward to new deeds!"[111]

109. Gert Rebelski, "Massenpropaganda—aber wie?" JG 1/1959, 28. Raymonde Diem was a young French woman who organized blockades of American military transports through France.

110. David Childs, *The GDR: Moscow's German Ally,* 2d ed. (London, 1988), 281.

111. Fritz Krakeel and Karl Greiner-Pol, "Baut die Strassen der Zukunft," *Leben Singen Kämpfen,* 357.

One Youth—One Class

After constructing the Berlin Wall in 1961, Ulbricht could concentrate on consolidating his rule. Now that he had youth where he wanted them, and now that Stalin had been nominally dethroned, he combined the antifascist myth with a campaign to break down all remaining class barriers in the GDR and to make all young people nominal members of the ruling working class. The ideological appeal of such a strategy to the SED is obvious. And since Ulbricht viewed himself as the quintessential labor leader, the celebration of the German workers' movement was a celebration of his rule. But a deepened proletarianization was also essential to keeping the GDR Socialist. For how could the antifascist and anticapitalist struggle be continued now that the roots of Fascism had been exterminated and capitalism itself was kept from sight behind barbed wire and cement walls? It is ironic that the triumph of Socialism in the GDR had actually become a liability for the future.

Ulbricht solved this problem by moving the history of the German working class and of the proletarian youth movement into the center of the school curricula and the indoctrination programs of the Young Pioneers and the FDJ. This heightened emphasis was accompanied, as always, by a steady stream of Marxist-Leninist and political indoctrination. Over the entire history of the GDR, nearly all young people were put to work in the fields and factories at some point, usually during summer vacation and harvest time. This was not done merely to raise lagging production levels. It also ensured that all East Germans got a taste of manual labor and thus theoretically came to feel a part of the working class.

This proletarian myth-building strategy culminated in the mass events in 1968 surrounding the fiftieth anniversary of the November Revolution. At the central rally, Ulbricht spoke to 150,000 FDJ members on the East Berlin Marx-Engels-Platz. The twentieth anniversary of the founding of the GDR in 1969 was the justification for a huge paramilitary event, "Signal DDR 20." Hundreds of thousands of Young Pioneers and FDJ members practiced modern warfare and learned of the evils of West German imperialism.[112]

Ulbricht's reunification policies ultimately failed, Ulbricht himself collided with the Soviet leadership, and he was removed from power in 1972. When his successor Honecker spoke of "revolution," he meant not only the Revolution of 1918, the "antifascist resistance struggle," and the "antifascist-democratic upheaval" in the SBZ and GDR. He also meant the antifascist Honecker's assumption of power along with the political,

---

112. *Geschichte der FDJ*, 433–37.

ideological, and technological innovations that this change of leadership brought about. Beginning in the Honecker period, antifascism gained pre-eminence over all other myths. The spirit of Ernst Thälmann, which the new regime invoked incessantly, really meant the spirit of Erich Honecker. This was expressed in the enormous "Tenth World Youth Festival" held in East Berlin from 28 July to 5 August 1973. Its many events were explicitly dedicated to promoting the antifascist spirit, and it is a fateful coincidence that Walter Ulbricht—discredited and already nearly forgotten—died while it was under way.

The Honecker regime brought with it even greater coordination than had existed under Ulbricht. What little "freedom" may have been left in the Free German Youth gave way to strict bureaucratic supervision and incessant busywork for all members. Throughout the 1970s and the tense 1980s, the FDJ staged more and bigger mass events than ever before. Keeping young people busy in mass events seemed to have become one of the major purposes of the organization. These activities were designed to keep youthful spirits up in an increasingly drab GDR and at the same time demonstrate to the SED and the world that the Party still had the young generation behind it.[113] In 1988 alone, the SED staged some *thirty-six thousand* antifascist events with 1.6 million participants, most of them young people.[114]

While the "Stalinist" style of the mass events remained basically the same to the end, under the Honecker regime the FDJ became much more sophisticated in its propaganda work in the collectives. For example, at a "theoretical-methodological conference" in 1976, a psychologist spoke to FDJ propagandists on "the role of psychological discoveries in work with youth," the "biological and social conditions of personality development [and] the confrontation with bourgeois viewpoints" such as "milieu theory," "age peculiarities," and so on.[115]

The expansion of the antifascist myth in the Honecker era reached a new plateau in 1978–79 with a campaign called "Youth fulfills the legacy of the revolutionary fighters."[116] Its general purpose, as always, was to reinvigorate German youth and to imbue them even more with the spirit of Ernst Thälmann. This campaign "provided the basis [upon which] the

---

113. Cf. Walter Friedrich and Hartmut Griese, eds., *Jugend und Jugendforschung in der DDR. Gesellschaftspolitische Situation, Sozialisation und Mentalitätsentwicklung in den achtziger Jahren* (Opladen, 1991), 32.

114. Siegfried Vietzke, "Antifaschismus prägt unseren Weg, unsere Macht," *Einheit* 44 (1989), no. 9–10: 940.

115. "Inhaltliche Einschätzung über die Durchführung des FDJ-Studienjahres im Monat Februar (1976)," JA IzJ 7.800.

116. *Geschichte*, 608–9.

entire young generation can assume the class struggle of the working class." Furthermore, "it points youth to its historic task: to perfect Socialism and to master the scientific-technical revolution."[117] But the campaign was also timed to coincide with the thirtieth anniversary of the founding of the GDR, and thus it symbolized one of the GDR's periodic self-redefinitions. As important as friendship with the Soviet Union and the acquisition of progressive German *Kultur* remained, the GDR of Honecker and his generation of resistance fighters was to be celebrated above all as a militant antifascist republic sworn to defend itself against the imperialist and warmongering Federal Republic, which was now to be seen as a foreign country. Beyond the usual empty rhetoric and mass demonstrations at antifascist monuments, it emphasized direct personal contact between FDJ members and local resistance fighters, who were invited to come into the plants and schools to describe their experiences in the underground or in the concentration camps and draw comparisons to the struggles of present-day youth. The recalling and discussion of these experiences "is not limited to a passive adoption, a taking consideration of historical dates," an FDJ functionary told a meeting of the GDR's Central Council of Anti-Fascist Resistance Fighters in 1979, "but must be linked with the acquisition of the ideology of the working class, [and] include one's own coming to terms with the multifaceted and contradictory phenomena of our present. That is what we mean by the living preservation of revolutionary traditions."[118]

The campaign also encouraged the study of local history, especially the early years of the GDR and the role of local antifascist youth committees and FDJ groups in its buildup. The principal reading text of the campaign, a book entitled *From the Dead to the Living—Last Words of Executed German Anti-Fascists,*[119] was used to help inspire a new wave of antifascist name-giving competitions for local FDJ groups and plants. But even more than in earlier campaigns, the emphasis was on present-day uses of the antifascist spirit. "For us, tradition doesn't mean preserving ashes, instead for us tradition means keeping a flame alive. Thus it is only natural that today the youth organization, with every step it takes— whether it is a matter of the material economy, a membership meeting, or finally the ideological preparation of the thirtieth anniversary of our

---

117. "Wie nutzen wir die erzieherischen Potenzen der Bewegung zur lebendigen Bewahrung der revolutionären Traditionen der Arbeiterklasse stärker für alle Bereiche in der Arbeit der FDJ und Pionierorganisation?" (1978) JA IzJ A 7.816.

118. Protocol of a meeting of the "Komitee der antifaschistischen Widerstandskämpfer," Leipzig (1979) JA IzJ A 10.522.

119. *Die Toten an die Lebenden—letzte Worte hingerichteter deutscher Antifaschisten* (East Berlin, 1977).

Republic—that with every step it takes it keeps in mind the history of our movement."[120]

The FDJ youth press of the 1970s and 1980s reflects this growing obsession with the antifascist past. Every issue of *Junge Generation,* for example, was filled with "on this date in [antifascist] history" columns, articles on antifascist leaders and events, melodramatic antifascist speeches by Egon Krenz and other leaders, and article after article on how best to cultivate the antifascist tradition among young people. These articles were always accompanied by exciting accounts of the glorious early days of the FDJ and its heroic feats in the construction of Socialism. The articles on the Socialist present and future of the GDR, by contrast, were becoming increasingly dull and helpless. At the same time, the emphasis was shifting to Communist antifascist heroes alone. In the first years, non-communists (such as the White Rose group) had been given recognition, and to some extent the early antifascist myth had been integrative. Now the Communists reigned supreme. One consequence of this new view was the politically motivated suppression of a new filmed version of Hedda Zinner's classic antifascist play *Ravensbrücker Ballade* from GDR television in 1985. The original play, written in 1961, had presented the unity and fundamental equality of both Communists and noncommunist prisoners, who all were fighting for the same ideals. This view was counterproductive in Honecker's GDR.[121]

The permanent monument of the FDJ's antifascist campaign was to be the official *History of the Free German Youth,* which had been prepared by a collective of FDJ scholars under the chairmanship of Karl-Heinz Jahnke of the *Wilhelm-Pieck-Universität* in Rostock. Jahnke had already written several histories of the proletarian youth movements and the KJVD, which were also used in the organization. The *History of the Free German Youth* had been scheduled to appear at the time of the GDR's anniversary. This book is a lavishly illustrated list of the FDJ's triumphs and was designed for indoctrination sessions in local FDJ organizations. Unfortunately, as we have already seen in chapter 1, the project was plagued by censorship and bureaucratic and ideological interference from the beginning. Its publication was delayed until 1982 in order to allow Honecker's memoirs, which had priority and was not to be contradicted by the FDJ book, to appear first.

The final chapter of the book, describing the events of the thirtieth anniversary and summing up the FDJ's contributions, was entitled "The

---

120. Protocol of a meeting of the "Komitee der antifaschistischen Widerstandskämpfer," Leipzig (1979) JA IzJ A 10.522.

121. Jan Herman Brinks, "Political Anti-Fascism in the German Democratic Republic," *Journal of Contemporary History,* vol. 32, no. 2 (April 1997): 207–8.

Bond of the Generations is Untearable." While this slogan expressed a great deal of wishful thinking, it also represented Honecker's most important myth-building strategy. After all, Honecker (who turned 67 in 1979) was going to retire eventually, and in any case it seemed certain he would have retired or been removed from power by 1989 or 1990 for health reasons. Antifascism was now to provide the basis for all activity in the FDJ and the Young Pioneers. Specifically, the strategy would create situations in which young people would prove themselves "in the revolutionary praxis of today, at work, in learning and in the defense of our Socialist fatherland." It would also bring about "the unity of historical and future consciousness" and "the unity of rational and emotional education." In this last regard "the movement connects with the actual interests of the girls and boys and corresponds to their yearning for romanticism." This was tied to the orientation on role models and their character traits designed to make history come alive, and was predicated upon "the unity of education to Socialist patriotism and to proletarian internationalism." The organizers of this campaign hoped in this way to promote "the autonomy of the FDJ and Pioneer collectives through the identification and solving of the revolutionary tasks of today in their concrete areas of responsibility, and thus [to autonomy] in the local organization." Finally, looking to the future the campaign should lead to the "creation and preservation of [local] revolutionary traditions upon the foundation of the fighting and working traditions of the FDJ and the Pioneer Organization 'Ernst Thälmann.'"[122] Thus the revolution and the antifascist resistance struggle would be carried on long after Honecker and his generation had passed on.

But life would have gone on (and has gone on) without Honecker. Leaving the great geopolitical considerations aside for a moment, just what was so revolutionary about his legacy? The revolutionary spirit under Honecker was summed up in a poem by the SED propagandist Max Zimmering.[123]

> Who is a revolutionary in our Republic?
> He who is there when you need him for the good of the community,
> Who at the plant shows the others the way to quality,
> Who always as a good comrade advises his collective.
> Who is a revolutionary? He who serves our country,
> Who selflessly, as a volunteer, defends the borders of our homeland,
>   etc.

---

122. "Wie nutzen wir . . . ?"
123. Max Zimmering, "Wer ist ein Revolutionär?" *Auferstanden,* Deutsche Schallplatten GmbH, 0 03 040, 1990.

This probably sums up the real "spirit of Ernst Thälmann" better than anything else. By using the terms *revolutionary* and *antifascist* to describe a model citizen who never asks questions—especially when ordered to shoot "Republic deserters" trying to cross the "antifascist defensive wall" into the West—the SED had gone full circle back to that alienating, priggish quality that the antifascist myth had been designed to combat. It never found its way out again.

Results

Did the GDR's youth propaganda really cultivate a nation of devoted ex post facto "antifascist resistance fighters"? The FDJ always kept close tabs on its propaganda and mass events, and the records show virtually no serious opposition to the antifascist myth and its uses. During the Ulbricht era young people in the GDR seem to have accepted and even respected Thälmann, Becker, and the others. But that is about as far as it went. The records also reveal widespread apathy and very, very poor homework in the "Socialist circles." The results of the 1970s and 1980s are harder to judge. As we saw earlier, the Honecker regime showed little interest in public opinion polls. FDJ documents for the final frenetic stage of antifascist propaganda in the Honecker era are largely useless. The demands on both functionaries and members were simply too great to be fulfilled, and former members will tell you that many of the optimistic reports on the results of indoctrination evenings and sessions with the Thälmann biography were simply made up to keep the next higher level of bureaucrats happy—and so on, all the way to Honecker's desk.

The FDJ's myth-building efforts only showed results during the mass events. In quieter times the interest slacked off dramatically. Although 1953 had begun very well with the stimulating mass events surrounding the "Karl Marx Year," by the end of the year the FDJ's propaganda campaigns had nevertheless failed "to gain influence over the mass of youth, to persuade them of the rightness of the policy of the New Course, and to tear them out of a certain inactivity. So it is that still not insignificant portions of youth face our struggle apathetically, and we did not succeed in arousing understanding of our struggle within them; indeed, they more or less even have open cars for enemy arguments."[124] The June uprising of that year clearly had a hand in this and set back the FDJ's modest myth-building progress among many non–Party members by several years.

FDJ functionaries complained of youth apathy throughout the entire history of the organization. The cults surrounding Thälmann, Becker, and

---

124. "Einschätzung der Entfaltung der Lektionspropaganda in Auswertung der 6. Zentralratstagung," (1953) IzJ JA A 341.

others seem to have meant nothing whatsoever to most young people outside of the mass events. "In this connection," stated a confidential FDJ status report from the Neustrelitz district in December 1961, "let us examine the thoughts of apprentices on the [collective farms], their role models, their plans for the future."[125]

> So one would have to say that the girls spend most of their time in the dream world of pop songs.
>
> Their role models are male and female singers and to some extent actors as well . . . . The girls love mostly pop music, light films, [they] collect pop magazines, collect postcards of film actors and singers.
>
> Among the girls there are very few plans for the future, they hardly make any plans at all and do not commit themselves. The girls mostly participate in such activity groups as volleyball, embroidery circles, cooking, Red Cross training, and to some extent GST training, especially radio and teletype.

Among the boys too the spirit of Ernst Thälmann also appeared to be limited to antifascist ceremonies. Their future plans were

> first service in the National People's Army and then work in technical professions. They especially like to watch exciting crime films, but also love and comedy films. In regard to TV the apprentices are especially enthusiastic about TV movies and sports broadcasts. The enthusiasm for watching the *Aktuelle Kamera* [the GDR's daily news/propaganda show] is minimal.
>
> Interest in newspaper reading too is still very weak. The sports and technical page in the *Junge Welt* is read very closely. Also such topics in the *Junge Welt* like friendship, what is love?, etc. encounter great interest. Nevertheless, the interest in socio-political events and interest in world events is not very strongly developed.

In 1968, after a year of grinding through the *Communist Manifesto,* Marxist-Leninist theory, antifascism, and the history of the German workers' movement, FDJ propagandists lamented that "There are currently *still many unclear perceptions of the dangerousness of West German imperialism-militarism,* even though according to the opinion of the circle

---

125. "Analyse über einige Probleme, über die Lage in der Berufsausbildung und die Tätigkeit des Verbandes besonders in der Landwirtschaft speziell LPG und VEG," (1961) JA IzJ A 6.624. This report is written in execrable German, a style which unfortunately cannot be carried over in the translation.

directors whom we consulted we had always presented a direct link with all the problems of West Germany" (emphasis in original).[126]

Nearly three decades later, and after eighteen years of Honecker's renewed antifascist myth-building program, the enthusiasm of GDR young people for the practical spirit of Ernst Thälmann had hardly changed at all. In the mid-1980s, when the internal crises of the GDR had become obvious to most young people and the transformations in the Soviet Union had put the very concept of socialism into question, the system began to break down entirely. In March 1989 the Leipzig Institute for Youth Research completed a confidential survey of the historical consciousness of young East Germans, the first and last full-scale survey of this kind to be conducted in the GDR.[127] Even though the sample population contained a higher than average percentage of young SED members, the results were devastating for both the schools and the FDJ's mythbuilders. They indicated that "the vast majority of young people exhibit a too poorly developed interest or even a disinterest in our depiction of the political development of the GDR, its historical roots, its leading Party, and its Socialist youth organization. . . . The acceptance or rejection of the image of the political history of the GDR thus represents one of the fundamental problems in the development of the Socialist historical consciousness of young people." Even worse: "This critical attitude or even rejection of the official view of GDR development can lead to the fact that young people turn away from their fatherland and become increasingly interested in other countries, including their history. Thus on the average, high school students are more interested in the history of the Federal Republic than in that of the GDR!"[128]

Most disturbing for the authors of the study was the examination of young people's feelings about Fascism. Despite years of antifascist education and solemn antifascist mass ceremonies, the young people's knowledge about the Hitler era was poor, their emotional response to its horrors was generally cool, and only 57 percent said yes when asked if they would do

126. "Anlage zum Vorschlag über die Weiterführung der Propaganda der FDJ bis 1975. Ergebnisse, Probleme, Schlussfolgerungen zur Propagandaarbeit der FDJ"; JA IzJ 7357.

127. Wilfried Schubarth, "Zum Geschichtsbewusstsein von Jugendlichen der DDR" (Leipzig, March 1989), JA IzJ B 5858. The survey was based on the responses of 1,909 young people from a fairly representative group made up of high school and university students, apprentices, young workers, and peasants. Despite the ideologically unsatisfactory results of this study, Schubarth states in his introduction that the sample is slightly distorted in a positive sense in regard to ideological questions by the preponderance of SED members questioned (7–8).

128. Ibid., 23.

everything they could "so that something like Fascism does not reoccur." "The insufficiently developed readiness to action on the part of young people is above all an expression of the insufficient ability of our society to bring young people personally in touch with the Fascist era. Since this does not only apply to the Fascist era, it is not surprising that the lessons and experiences of history as action maxims [*Handlungsmaxime*] play such a subordinate role in the thoughts and actions of young people."[129]

These results are not surprising considering the poor quality and poor presentation of much of the propaganda material, its obvious half-truths, and most of the population's ready access to western radio and television. In any case, the goal of GDR mythology was acceptance and compliance, not profound belief subject to "objectivist" contradictions. As long as the regime and its guarantors—the Wall, the *Stasi,* and the Soviet Army— were in place, such mediocre results were not really a worry. The FDJ and the SED contained thousands of loyal members and functionaries who still believed in the rightness of their cause regardless of its presentation to the masses.

The myth was most successful at the highest level of the Party. The sight of hundreds of thousands of FDJ members and Young Pioneers swearing oaths to Ernst Thälmann and Artur Becker, and marching in torchlight parades past the SED leadership—as late as the GDR's fortieth and final anniversary celebration on 7 October 1989—continually reinforced the SED's myth of its historic mission and presented it with a grotesquely distorted image of "its" people and above all "its" youth. Even if some Party members may have been skeptical about the actual extent to which loyal young East Germans really were "prepared to fight for the cause of Ernst Thälmann," the notion that nearly all of them would drop the entire package the first chance they got was inconceivable. This illusion contributed to the surrealist atmosphere within the Party in its last year of power. In the spring of 1989, despite obvious signs of a terminal crisis, Honecker bragged to President Jaruzelski of Poland that the SED's fraudulent election victory of 7 May was proof that Socialism was on the offensive and would one day win over the Federal Republic and West Berlin.[130] As Honecker himself admitted in December 1989, "I deluded myself and let myself be deluded."[131]

The myth was even more successful in making the SED believe that Fascism in eastern Germany really had been eliminated "with its roots." In

---

129. Ibid., 67.

130. Gerd-Rüdiger Stephan, "Die letzten Tagungen des Zentralkomitees der SED 1988/1989. Abläufe und Hintergründe," DA 3/1993, 305.

131. Letter to the Central Party Control Commission of the SED, 1 December 1989, printed in Erich Honecker, *Erich Honecker zu dramatischen Ereignissen,* 80.

fact, right-wing groups had been active in the east since the 1970s and 1980s, and the *Stasi* knew about it. But since industry and agriculture had long since been collectivized, and since the vast majority of young people had been enrolled in militantly antifascist organizations, the actual resurfacing of neo-Nazi activity in the GDR was consistently ascribed to West German influences and individual asocial behavior, and punished accordingly. Internal warnings that neo-Nazism might have causes outside of mere "finance capital," or that the SED and the FDJ with their pseudo-Fascist public events, their growing self-delusions, and their alienating propaganda campaigns actually contributed to its rise, were consistently stifled.[132] The sudden outbreak of neo-Nazi violence in eastern Germany after 1990 was a late consequence of the SED's refusal to take seriously the *Ulenspiegel*'s warning in 1949.

By the end of 1989, some 343,854 East Germans had crossed the "antifascist defensive wall" into the Federal Republic.[133] The Wall itself was opened on 9 November, beginning a process that would bring about the collapse of the GDR and its annexation by the Federal Republic less than a year later.

The date 9 November is an awkward one in German history. It is the date of the German Revolution of 1918, the date of Hitler's Beer Hall Putsch of 1923, the date of the *Kristallnacht* of 1938, and finally the dreaded "Day X" of the SED's nightmares: the date of the fall of the Berlin Wall in 1989. Although the antifascist myth lives on, for many East German Communists, 9 November was also the day Ernst Thälmann finally died.

Conclusion

In spite of these problems, the myth of antifascism served the SED well until 1989. Antifascism commanded respect among most young people even if it aroused little interest. But just how binding was the "Oath of Buchenwald," and how firm was the covenant? The proof of the pie was in the eating. The fatal flaw of the antifascist myth was that the SED could only uphold its legitimacy as long as genuine antifascists were in power or at least on hand for representational purposes. Thus the fortunes of the Party and the state were intertwined with the individual life cycle of Erich

---

132. Especially interesting in this regard is Wolfgang Brück, "Skinheads als Vorboten der Systemkrise. Die Entwicklung des Skinhead-Phänomens bis zum Untergang der DDR," in Karl-Heinz Heinemann and Wilfried Schubarth, eds., *Der antifaschistische Staat entlässt seine Kinder,* 37–46.

133. Hermann Weber, *DDR. Grundriss der Geschichte 1945–1990,* completely revised and expanded new edition (Hannover, 1991), 347.

Honecker, and the GDR almost inevitably fell with him. Honecker was briefly succeeded by Egon Krenz. Krenz was eight years old at the end of the war, joined the FDJ in 1953, attended the CPSU academy in Moscow, rose up through the bureaucracy of the Young Pioneers and the FDJ, and served as First Secretary of the FDJ from 1974 to 1983, when he left the organization to become a full member of the Politburo.[134] Krenz had been groomed to replace Honecker for years. He was the very model of an FDJ/SED careerist and embodied (in Stephan Hermlin's words) the "millionfold second line" of antifascist youth. But without Honecker at his side, Krenz's tired antifascist clichés and class struggle histrionics had become ridiculous. As the East German psychologist Hans-Joachim Maaz writes, "hardly anyone could imagine ever being able to tolerate Egon Krenz as head of state; this 'crown prince' was perceived as the undisguised bastard of a degenerate dynasty." Krenz's brief reign demonstrated that the antifascist covenant had been dissolved by the passing of the antifascist generation, and what little legitimacy the SED might have had before was gone forever. For, Maaz concludes, "Without a critical confrontation with authority, no one is or can become an authority!"[135]

---

134. Hermann Weber, *DDR. Grundriss der Geschichte, 1945–1990*, revised and expanded edition (Hannover, 1991), 269–70.

135. Hans-Joachim Maaz, *Der Gefühlsstau. Ein Psychogramm der DDR* (Munich, 1992), 138–39.

CHAPTER 4

"To Be a German Patriot Means to Be a Friend of the Soviet Union": The Myths of the Great Socialist Soviet Union and of the Socialist Fatherland

Learning from the Soviet Union means learning victory!
—Walter Ulbricht, 1951[1]

And lead us not into temptation, but deliver us from evil: For thine is the kingdom, and the power, and the glory, for ever. Amen.
—Matthew 6:13

Of all the myths we have seen so far, none has such clear religious overtones as the myth of the Great Socialist Soviet Union. We have already remarked on the messianic implications of Marxism and the concept of resurrection underlying the Thälmann cult. The Soviet Union represented the fulfillment of this messianic vision. The Great Socialist October Revolution was a "turning point in human history." Through it History itself had intervened in human affairs and suspended the laws of human society and human behavior. Lenin and Stalin were at once the embodiment of History and its executors on earth. The success of the five-year plans of the 1930s was incontrovertible proof of Marxism's validity. In fact, the Soviet Union meant Socialism, and "constructing Socialism" meant constructing the Soviet model. The defeat of Fascism was a continuation of the miracle

---

1. Cited in Hermann Weber, *DDR. Grundriss der Geschichte,* revised and expanded edition (Hannover, 1991), 66.

of 1917. In Erich Honecker's words, "The victory of the heroic Soviet people and its glorious army . . . was, after the Great Socialist October Revolution, the second world historic act of liberation for mankind."[2] It held out the promise of final victory.

The Soviet Union was also a promised land. It was not to be a state like other states, with cruelty and injustice, but was (or was rapidly and undeniably becoming) a society of an entirely new type. As the fatherland of all workers, the Soviet Union taught how to liberate one's own fatherland and defend it against its enemies.

The KPD first used the expression *German–Soviet friendship* in the 1920s. For the SED, "friendship" was one of the organizing principles of Socialist society. It expressed the allegedly spontaneous and voluntaristic quality of the new society, and implied "enmity" to those outside it. "Friendship!" was the greeting of the FDJ. FDJ members were usually referred to as "youth friends," and Young Pioneer groups were called "friendships." The relationship between the German and Soviet youth organizations was also referred to as a special "friendship" (*druzhba* in Russian), for by eliminating want and exploitation the Soviet Union had made true, disinterested friendship among young people possible.

But *friendship* did not adequately express the GDR's relationship to the Soviet Union. By 1949 it had become a passionate relationship, and was usually symbolized by fire. According to Elias Canetti, fire is one of the most important and variable mass symbols of mankind. It has a fascinating quality. "The image of fire appears to us as a blaze: powerful, inextinguishable, and determined. . . . It is the same everywhere; it spreads rapidly; it is infectious and insatiable; it can arise everywhere, very suddenly; it is multifaceted; it is destructive; it has an enemy; it is extinguished: it appears to be alive and is treated accordingly."[3] It is a profoundly religious symbol, representing illumination, purification, renewal, and fertility.[4] Sacred flames are among the oldest of symbols, appearing in ancient pagan rituals, and can be found in synagogues, in the ceremony of the "Easter fire" in Jerusalem, in the various "eternal flames" of twentieth-century war memorials, or in the fire rituals of the Third Reich, which gave birth to the modern-day Olympic torch in 1936.[5]

The communist movement is rich in fire imagery: The color red is reminiscent of fire and the eastern sky at daybreak. The thousands of red flags carried in mass parades resembled a spreading fire. The "spark" of

---

2. *Die Befreiung und die Befreier* (East Berlin, 1985), 1.

3. Elias Canetti, *Masse und Macht* (Frankfurt am Main, 1980), 82–83.

4. Gerd Heinz-Mohr, "Feuer," *Lexikon der Symbole* (Freiburg im Breisgau, 1991), 111–13.

5. Duff Hart-Davis, *Hitler's Games: The 1936 Olympics* (New York, 1986), 52.

the *Iskra* newspaper that Lenin founded in Leipzig in 1900 is said to have touched off the flame of the Bolshevik Revolution in 1917. A shot fired by the battleship *Aurora* preceded the storming of the Winter Palace. The GDR had "arisen" from the ruins left by the firestorm of World War II. A sacred flame formed part of the insignia of the Young Pioneers. The red "Soviet star" evoked the salvation-bringing star of Bethlehem. The KPD's youth organizations celebrated the summer solstice as a symbol of the new age beginning in the 1920s and carried on the tradition in the GDR. The FDJ was symbolized by a rising sun.

Friendship and fire were logical choices to symbolize the myth of the Great Socialist Soviet Union, but they eventually proved to be poor ones compared to "the drama" and "the oath." A friendship may grow thin and become burdensome if it is cultivated one-sidedly, and it is rare for any friendship to last more than one generation. A passion may die suddenly, or change into hatred, when the adored proves unworthy. A flame will burn only as long as it is provided with sufficient fuel and protected from the wind and the rain, and not a moment longer. Symbolic depictions of sunrises and sunsets are easily confused.

The Friendship Is Forged

The term *friendship* was not, as so often in these cases, descriptive, but pre-scriptive. German–Soviet friendship needed to be constructed. Neverthe-less, its foundation was real. Even if the Soviet government shot thousands of German Communists during the Great Purge of the 1930s and delivered thousands more to the Gestapo during the period of the Hitler-Stalin Pact, there is no denying that the Red Army liberated thousands of other Com-munists and resistance fighters from Nazi prisons and concentration camps. For those whose lives were saved in this way (such as Erich Honecker and Hermann Axen), German–Soviet friendship was very much "a reality lived." Germany's defeat literally meant liberation to them, as symbolized by the antifascist monument at the former Sachsenhausen con-centration camp near Berlin: In a variation on the medieval motif of the Virgin Mary protecting the virtuous beneath her cloak, a Soviet soldier comforts two emaciated inmates and envelops them in his broad cape.[6] The same applies to those surviving Moscow émigrés (such as Ulbricht, Pieck, Johannes R. Becher, and many others) whom the Soviets entrusted with creating a Socialist society on German soil and who thus could go ahead to fulfill their life's work. Devotion and gratitude toward Stalin and

---

6. Volker Frank, *Antifaschistische Mahnmale in der DDR. Ihre künstlerische und architektonische Gestaltung* (Leipzig, 1970), 18–19.

the Red Army were genuine emotions, but whether this dependence can honestly be called friendship is questionable. As Antonia Grunenberg has written, "The surviving anti-Fascists were not high-flyers seeking to 'remake' the world. They were physically and spiritually weak, humble, submissive, and gratefully received the orders of the Soviet occupation force as a gift."[7]

This gratitude applies above all to Communists, who were by definition friends of the Soviet Union from the beginning. It applies less to noncommunist resistance fighters, who were often skeptical of the Soviet Union's intentions, and hardly at all to the general population. Most Germans, raised on Nazi propaganda and fearing retribution for Nazi crimes, viewed the Soviets as barbarians. There is no denying that the Soviet Army treated German civilians harshly. Thousands were interned and executed. Thousands more were deported to Soviet gulags. Literally millions of people were driven from their homes in the eastern provinces, and thousands of women were raped. Thousands of Germans had been arrested after the German capitulation, many of them never to be seen again, and thousands more were being held in Soviet POW camps. Entire factories and rail lines were dismantled and shipped off to the Soviet Union years after the German capitulation, and horrendous reparations had to be paid.[8] But as severe as these actions were, they were much milder than the images created by Nazi horror propaganda about the "Asiatic hordes." When Johannes R. Becher, on a journey through Mecklenburg in 1945, asked a peasant woman what had most surprised her about the Russians, she replied, "That they don't have horns on their heads!"[9] And these actions were as nothing compared to German behavior in the Soviet Union, which ended up costing some twenty million Soviet lives. After the war, Soviet commanders helped organize food shipments to the hungry cities of their zone and quickly restored public order. For some eastern Germans, a combination of relief, shame, and gratitude led to a limited kind of "German–Soviet friendship." This was expressed in the slogan: "Thank-you, you Soviet soldiers," which the Party posted throughout the GDR during "German—Soviet Friendship Week," held every May to mark Germany's capitulation in 1945.

But the sense of liberation did not only apply to those who were actually freed from prisons and concentration camps by the Red Army, or who

---

7. Antonia Grunenberg, *Antifaschismus—ein deutscher Mythos. Essay* (Reinbek, 1993), 120.

8. For a vivid look at the atmosphere of this period, see Norman M. Naimark, *The Russians in Germany. A History of the Soviet Zone of Occupation, 1945–1949* (Cambridge, 1996).

9. Personal interview with Jürgen Kuczynski, Berlin-Weissensee, 20 January 1994.

were fed by Soviet commanders. It was also felt by people who had never seen a Russian in their lives. In fact, the less experience one actually had with the Soviet Union, the easier it was to believe in it. This phenomenon is perhaps best expressed by Ralph Giordano, who, as the son of a German Jewish mother and an Italian father, was persecuted by the Nazis and later served as an FDJ and KPD functionary in West Germany before leaving the Party in 1957.[10]

> Although it was the British 8th Army that marched into Hamburg on 4 May 1945, I had always felt as if I had been liberated by the Soviet Army—through its tremendous exertions, its incomparable loss of blood in the military crushing of Hitler-Germany. This feeling was always confirmed whenever, on photos, in films or in reality, I had seen the Soviet armed forces. Then a great tranquility came over me, a sense of the certainty of victory and of profound security, of an impregnable protection which held its steely hand over me.

The problem for the GDR's leaders lay in transmitting both these genuinely held feelings and the obeisance due to an occupying power to a population that in its majority feared and despised the Soviet Union and Communism. This was necessary in order to acquaint the population with the series of radical changes that were about to be introduced with Soviet help, and to justify what most Germans viewed as shameful collaboration on the part of the Communists. An informational campaign was in order, and beginning in the summer of 1945 the antifascist youth committees and later the FDJ conducted *Heimabende* on the wonders of the Soviet Union and the life of its "happy youth."[11] This went along with liberal doses of classical Russian literature and music, which received almost as much attention as German *Kultur*. Even though serious indoctrination with Marxism-Leninism was not introduced until 1951, in the early stages the FDJ presented anti-anticommunist programs designed to neutralize years of National Socialist propaganda.[12] In all of these efforts the concept of friendship toward the USSR was taken so seriously that soon an East Ger-

---

10. Ralph Giordano, *Die Partei hat immer recht. Ein Erlebnisbericht über den Stalinismus auf deutschem Boden* (Freiburg im Breisgau, 1990), 222.

11. See, for example, the *Heimabend* pamphlet *Glückliche Jugend* (East Berlin, 1946).

12. FDJ historians have examined both topics in detail. See, for example, Monika Ittner and Elke Steinmüller, "Die bewusstseinsbildende Rolle der sowjetischen Kunst und Literatur bei den Mitgliedern der FDJ von 1945–1951" (master's essay, Wilhelm-Pieck-Universität Rostock, 1964); Walter Parson and Eckehard Gunsilius, "Zum Kampf der FDJ bei der Überwindung des Antikommunismus (1946–1949)" (master's essay, Wilhelm-Pieck-Universität Rostock, 1963).

man could not even use the term *the Russians* without being labeled "anti-Soviet." The approved terms were *die Sowjetmenschen* (the Soviet people), *die Sowjetbürger* (the Soviet citizens), and *unsere sowjetischen Freunde* (our Soviet friends). This was often reduced to *die Freunde* (the friends), an expression that gained instant popularity among both USSR fans and, used cynically, by its despisers. Other approved names were *our Soviet brothers* and even *our Big Brother.*[13]

But friendship with the Soviet Union implied distaste and eventually (during the Korean War) "holy hatred" of the FRG and the United States. For whatever the Great Socialist Soviet Union lacked, it had a superabundance of Great Ideals and self-sacrifice. The *Sowjetmenschen* were a race of stoics, and one did not have to be a Communist to appreciate this. In fact, one could loathe the Soviet Union yet still admire the fortitude of the Soviets themselves, and SED propagandists exploited this phenomenon for all it was worth. In the eyes of the SED, the notion of "German–American friendship" cultivated in the FRG was tainted by greed and bad taste, and was depicted as a mere euphemism for exploitation. It could only lead to war. German–Soviet friendship was founded upon comradery and mutual admiration of one another's cultures. But "friendship" and "holy hatred" remained largely rhetorical. Because of the Soviet Army's antifraternization rules and the stilted quality of official German–Soviet encounters, genuine friendship between individual East Germans and Soviets was rare—even more rare than genuine hatred of the West.

In any case, young people had few opportunities to inform themselves objectively on the Soviet Union. They mostly relied on what the schools and the youth organizations served up to them. Beyond these clearly partisan sources, they were regularly confronted with the leftover horror stories of the Nazi propaganda machine about the Stalinist purges and the Katyn Massacre (both of which were, of course, true), reports from their discredited elders about what they had seen during the Nazi invasion or in Soviet POW camps, wild rumors about Soviet atrocities in the SBZ, and the daily "slander" broadcasts by the "poison station" RIAS in West Berlin. None of these sources was particularly credible to disillusioned young people in the eastern sectors of Germany.

One of the most important tasks was to take away East Germans' distrust of the Soviets' sweeping reforms in the SBZ. The good intentions of the Soviet occupation forces needed a historical foundation. In 1949 the German Communist and economic scholar Jürgen Kuczynski published his *Land of Happy Confidence: A History of the Soviet Union for Young*

---

13. East Germans often preferred the phrase "our Soviet brothers" to "our Soviet friends" because, as the saying went, "at least you can choose your friends."

People Which Can Also Be Read by Adults.[14] (We have already met Kuczynski, the GDR's most celebrated and above all *parteilich* intellectual, as one of the promoters of that Bach celebration in 1950.) Professor Kuczynski enthusiastically presented the Bolshevik Revolution as a turning point in history, and the book contained the usual business about The Great Lenin and "his most devoted pupil, Stalin," "the heroes of Socialist labor," and so forth. But what distinguishes this book from all the clearly self-serving pamphlets written by professional propagandists were the impeccable academic credentials of its author and his clear, folksy style. But for a true believer, which Kuczynski was, impeccable academic credentials are no defense against naive self-deception. The book is a textbook example of *Parteilichkeit.* For Kuczynski in 1949, the Soviet Union was quite simply a "wonderland." Its revolution was glorious, its industrial growth and high living standards were a triumph of economic planning. In achieving all of this, according to Kuczynski, no one was hurt—that is, no one worth mentioning. The collectivization of Soviet agriculture, during which at least seven million people were killed, is presented as the spontaneous and unanimous decision of peasants to form collective farms. The Great Purge and the show trials of the later 1930s, which killed uncounted millions more, including almost the entire Bolshevik Old Guard, are mentioned only briefly in connection with a broad campaign of industrial sabotage paid for by foreign capitalists. "Sometimes," Kuczynski told East German youth, the spies "also sat in offices and gave false instructions or held back the correct ones. Or they argued against the resolutions of the Party, tried to carry confusion into the population and to divide the workers and peasants. But the *Sowjetmenschen* always tracked them down. Then they were punished; for example, they were sentenced to special, very useful, but also very hard work, such as canal construction."[15]

For Kuczynski, the consequences that young Germans were to draw from the glorious history of this "wonderland" were obvious.[16]

> This is the secret of our strength:
> When we fight for peace, we stand up for our fatherland and are a friend of the Soviet Union.
> When we stand up for our fatherland, we help peace and are a friend of the Soviet Union.
> When we are a friend of the Soviet Union, we help peace and stand up for our fatherland.

---

14. Jürgen Kuczynski, *Das Land der frohen Zuversicht. Eine Geschichte der Sowjetunion für Jugendliche, die auch Erwachsene lesen können* (East Berlin, 1949).

15. Kuczynski, 77.

16. Kuczynski, 117.

Everything is connected, because everything is good and right. Everything is simple and clear so that every girl and every boy can understand it—for everything good and right is, when it is explained, easy to understand.

Unlike the professional propagandists, Kuczynski wrote this book entirely on his own initiative and based it on his own visits to the Soviet Union in the 1930s. He believed every word he wrote.[17] *The Land of Happy Confidence* provided the model for all pro-Soviet youth propaganda over the next decade.

In 1947 Kuczynski had become the first president of the "Society for the Study of the Culture of the Soviet Union," which in 1949 was renamed "Society for German–Soviet Friendship" (DSF). This organization was founded by the SMAD and the SED on the basis of largely uncoordinated German–Soviet cultural societies scattered throughout the SBZ. It held a near-monopoly on popular information about the USSR. Its main purpose was to counteract anti-Soviet and anticommunist sentiments in the general population and show that the Russians were and *had always been* both profoundly cultured people and friends of Germany. As in the youth committees and FDJ groups, the DSF did this through lectures both in German–Soviet *Kulturhäuser* and on the shop floor, and through cultural programs featuring classical Russian music and readings from Tolstoy, Gorki, and other Russian/Soviet authors. The organization also provided a means of keeping track of and correcting popular attitudes toward the Soviet Union. For this reason the discussions within the DSF were remarkably open in its early years. It agitated together with the FDJ, and

---

17. Personal interview with Jürgen Kuczynski, Berlin-Weissensee, 20 January 1994. Kuczynski symbolizes an entire generation of SED intellectuals who believed the Soviet myth in its entirety. By his own account, Kuczynski was a solid supporter of the Moscow show trials and had no knowledge of any injustice in the Stalin era until Krushchev's "secret speech" in 1956. In fact, he had no knowledge of the Soviet Union's mass terror until the 1970s. None of his Communist friends, even those Germans and Soviets who themselves had done time in NKVD prisons, ever said a word of what they knew. While Kuczynski no longer agreed with the content of his book, neither was he ashamed of it. If anyone was to blame, it was the Soviet propaganda apparatus. For him, the book was evidence of "the skill of the deception" of the Soviet government at that time. Nevertheless, the infectious wishful thinking of those years, combined with the SED's *Parteilichkeit* principle, kept him even from asking questions. Kuczynski also told me that while he viewed Stalin's Soviet Union as "the greatest deception in human history," he quickly noted that as an atheist he also viewed the notion of God as an equally infamous deception extending over thousands of years. Kuczynski's complete response to my written questions, which he simply read aloud to me during the interview and which seems to be so typical of the views of the GDR's "critical intelligentsia," can be found in his *Ein hoffnungsloser Fall von Optimismus? Memoiren 1989–1994* (Berlin, 1994), 318–21.

young people were strongly encouraged to join.[18] But as usual in the GDR, the DSF's early activism gradually became more and more formalized until the DSF became a mass organization like any other in which nominal membership was more or less mandatory for anyone who wanted to rise in society. It is thus nonsense to claim, as Erich Honecker did in 1992, that "A people was literally transformed from enemies of the Soviet Union into friends of the Soviet Union,"[19] unless one goes by DSF membership lists alone, which eventually included half the population fourteen years and older. (In its later years, the organization chiefly maintained contact with its members through its dues collectors.) But in its early years, the DSF worked vigorously to convince East Germans of the Soviet Union's good intentions.

But the warm feelings that many East Germans had toward the Soviet Union, as genuine as they may have been in many cases, were largely restricted to the elite. As a progress report from the FDJ organization in Mecklenburg in 1948 concludes, "The attitude of the labor, regional, and district functionaries towards the S[oviet] U[nion] is a good one, [and] is constantly promoted by the generally very positive cooperation with the [Soviet] district commanders. However, among the group functionaries and the membership the attitude varies widely. From Greifswald we are informed that only very few members are convinced of the friendship of the Soviet Union to Germany. They still view the occupying power as an enemy who has come to suppress and exploit us."[20] Three years later the situation had improved very little. During the sessions of the first "Indoctrination Year of the FDJ" in 1951, a young worker in Löbau stated that "he couldn't join the Society for German–Soviet friendship because the reports on life in the Soviet Union are mostly lies"; in Krauschwitz: "Yes, the Russians have liberated us, but they've liberated us from everything"; in Leipzig: "If the Soviet occupying power has so far consistently carried out the Potsdam Agreement, why doesn't it withdraw its troops?"; in a village near Rostock: "Are the Russians really disarming and aren't Stalin's statements just a trick?"[21] Horror stories about the Soviets still abounded

---

18. See Thomas Schönknecht, "Gesellschaft für Deutsch-Sowjetische Freundschaft (DSF)," in Hermann Weber, ed., *SBZ-Handbuch* (Berlin, 1990), 734–42; Jutta Petersdorf, "Die Rolle der Gesellschaft für Deutsch-Sowjetische Freundschaft bei der Entwicklung der Freundschaft zwischen DDR und UdSSR (1947–1955)" (Diss., Humboldt-Universität Berlin, 1973).

19. Erich Honecker, *Erich Honecker zu dramatischen Ereignissen* (Hamburg, 1992), 22.

20. "Auszüge aus den Berichten der Kreise des Landes Mecklenburg, 12.11.48," JA IzJ A 10.492.

21. "Information Nr. 11. Negative Argumente, die in den Zirkeln des Schuljahres der Freien Deutschen Jugend auftreten" (22 March 1951), JA IzJ A 1.015.

seven years after the end of the war. As a member from the Querfurt district told his collective in 1952: "Near Weissenfels there are once again a great number of Red Army soldiers. These Red Army soldiers have recently raped and kidnapped twenty-six German women. . . . [They] ask the population whether they are members of the German–Soviet Friendship Society, and when the people say they are not, then they are stripped naked by the Red Army soldiers and chased away."[22] If attitudes like this were only rarely expressed later on, this had less to do with any measurable increase in the number of actual German–Soviet friendships than with the strict segregation of the Soviet Army and the general decline of free speech within the youth organization.

"The Most Glorious Thing in the World"

In a status report on the progress of the antifascist youth committees in Leipzig in the summer of 1945, a KPD functionary worried aloud about the inadequate indoctrination of the young people under his supervision. "In the Soviet Union our world-outlook is already taught to children in an appropriate form and with a progressive expansion and deepening. Why can't we adopt the principle of these methods ourselves and teach German youth the most elementary things with easily understandable books before they are given the well-known 'primers'?" The functionary's suggestion was to make available "the youth literature of the Soviet Union and the democratic peoples," above all Nikolai Ostrovsky's autobiographical novel that had been translated as *Wie der Stahl gehärtet wurde* (*How the Steel Was Tempered*).[23]

This classic of *Sowjetliteratur* is a Marxist-Leninist *Bildungsroman* describing the coming of age of Pavel Korchagin, a young Ukrainian Komsomol functionary, during the firestorm of the civil war of the early 1920s and in the turmoil of the early Stalinist period. After a hard proletarian childhood, Korchagin survives prison, various beatings, an array of battles against vulgarly stereotyped White Guards and Poles, assorted Party purges, and a bout with typhus before finally being laid up with a case of progressive paralysis and other ailments caused by an old spinal injury. Bedridden and going blind at age twenty-four, Korchagin is terrified by the prospect of being invalided out of the Communist Party, which is his only home. He finally gathers up all his remaining energy to write a book about his struggle: *Die Sturmgeborenen* (literally: *Those Who*

---

22. "Information Nr. 2/52, Tätigkeit des Gegners" (8 January 1952), SAPMO BArch IV 2/16/84, Bl. 6–7.

23. "Bericht über die Jugendarbeit der KPD-UBL Leipzig (vom 18.5.–1.9.1945)" (3 September 1945), SAPMO BArch, NL 36/726, Bl. 87.

Are Born in the Storm), a clear reference to Ostrovsky's own book. At one point in the novel, standing over a mass grave of his fellow townspeople slaughtered by White Guards, Korchagin ponders the meaning of life itself.[24]

> The most valuable thing which a human being possesses is his life. It is given to him only once, and he should use it in such a way that purposelessly spent years do not weigh upon him, that the shame of a shabby and petty past does not burn him, and that with his dying breath he can say: I have devoted my entire life and all my strength to the most glorious thing in the world—the struggle for the liberation of humanity.

In the first Ukrainian edition of 1934, Ostrovsky had substituted "the liberation of humanity" with "the idea of Communism," which was more to the point.[25] The novel appeared in 1947 as the very first literary publication of the FDJ's *Neues Leben* publishing house. The magazine *Neues Leben* had little to say about it in its review except that "the book is important so that we can learn under what conditions outside of Germany young people grew up who face us as adults today."[26] *How the Steel Was Tempered* eventually sold a million copies in the GDR, a success that owed less to the book's literary merits than to the fact that it was required reading in the schools until 1989. The novel's monotonous exposition of proletarian virtues over the course of 453 crudely illustrated pages (laced with a stiff dose of adolescent eroticism as bait) make it rough reading today. But in the heady years of the "antifascist democratic upheaval" it helped mold the sensibilities of an entire generation of young East German Communists eager to learn the truth about the Soviet Union and Socialism itself. The FDJ skillfully presented Korchagin's struggle and suffering as a model for youth activists during the "construction of Socialism" in the GDR. If Korchagin and his generation were tempered in the fire of the civil war, the youth of the GDR was to be tempered in the solidarity of common labor. As Erich Honecker, who himself had dedicated his young life and strength to his understanding of humanity's cause during ten years in a Nazi prison, wrote in his introduction to the forty-fourth edition in 1986: Korchagin "was greeted by the young builders of the peace dam in Sosa and the boys and girls at the construction site of the Trattendorf youth power plant with the same enthusiasm as the young activists in fac-

---

24. Nikolai Ostrovsky, *Wie der Stahl gehärtet wurde,* 44th ed. (East Berlin, 1986), 285.
25. Raissa Ostrowskaja, *Nikolai Ostrowski. Leben und Kampf eines Unbeugsamen* (East Berlin, 1977), 222.
26. NL, 9/1948, 27.

tories and mine shafts and in the countryside. The Komsomolets Pavel Korchagin fought, laughed, suffered, and triumphed with us."[27] One of these activists, Hans Modrow, an early FDJ functionary and the GDR's last Communist head of state, later pointed to Ostrovsky's book as one of his greatest inspirations.[28]

When the FDJ in 1949 issued its decree on the organization of group libraries, Ostrovsky's book headed the list.[29] The FDJ held up both Korchagin and his author as personal models for each member. To be sure, the book described not only how youth was "tempered," but above all how it was brutalized. Its heroes are noble but merciless. It graphically depicts the classic dichotomy between the extreme cruelty of the Soviet system toward its enemies and the transcendent beauty of "the most glorious thing in the world." It explains a great deal about the attitudes responsible for the tragedy of the Ukrainian people during the Stalinist collectivization, which was under way even as Ostrovsky was writing his book.

To the FDJ, the novel was just as relevant in the Ulbricht and Honecker eras as in the 1920s and 1930s, and Ostrovsky's own life provided a perfect illustration of Marxist-Leninist values. As Lenin had told Young Communist League members in 1920, and as the SED's youth organizations now drummed into their own functionaries and members, "The generation of those who are now fifteen will see a Communist society, and will itself build this society. This generation should know that the entire purpose of their lives is to build a Communist society."[30] Personal considerations must never get in the way of the cause, the FDJ informed its members after their less than heroic performance during the "fascist coup attempt" (a.k.a. workers' uprising) of June 1953. Ostrovsky, the organization proclaimed to its functionaries in *Junge Generation,* "was of the rock-solid conviction that no man has the right to live only for himself, his wife, or his family. 'Only to live for one's family is brutish egotism, to live for a human being—a perfidy, only to live for oneself—a disgrace.'" One of Ostrovsky's most admirable traits was his invitation of criticism. "He said to the members of the writers' association . . . : 'I ask to be treated like a fighter. . . .' He challenged them to aim 'the artillery fire of criticism' at his writings."[31]

27. Erich Honecker, introduction to Ostrovsky, 11.

28. Christoph Dieckmann, "Gewärmt vom ewigroten Licht," *Die Zeit* (30 April 1993), 2.

29. "Entschließung zur Verbesserung der ideologischen Arbeit der Freien Deutschen Jugend, 16.17./ Juli 1949: Plan für den Aufbau der Gruppenbüchereien," DGV 8 (1949): 6.

30. V. I. Lenin, "The Tasks of the Youth Leagues" (1920), in *Collected Works* (Moscow, 1966), vol. 31, 299.

31. Günter Rudolph, "Erzieht das Aktiv der FDJ nach dem Vorbild Nikolai Ostrowskis," JG 23 (1953): 7.

How the Steel Was Tempered and Aleksandr Fadeyev's *The Young Guard*[32] were classics of the new *Sowjetliteratur* and provided the model for a wave of similar agitprop FDJ sagas in the GDR, such as Fritz Hauptmann's *The Mystery of Sosa,* Willi Bredel's *Fifty Days,* Eduard Claudius's *The Hard Beginning,* and so on. A Komsomol pamphlet circulated by the FDJ at this time explained the importance of this literature in the following way.[33]

> While Soviet literature and the progressive literature of all nations serve the great and noble ideas of progress, and depict shining figures of courageous fighters for the happiness of mankind, bourgeois literature plays the miserable role of a lackey of imperialist reaction. . . . The literary hirelings of American imperialism try to make the toilers spineless, to disarm them morally, to corrupt their consciousness with the poison of a dull imagination, and cosmopolitanism—indifference towards the fate of their own country.

Ostrovsky's novel served as an introduction to the Komsomol, which, beyond lectures in the *Heimabende,* was virtually unknown in the youth organizations in 1947. The FDJ youth academy did not teach functionaries about the Komsomol until its third course in the fall of 1946, when a Soviet officer gave a lecture on "The role of Soviet youth in the struggle for the construction of Socialism in the USSR."[34] In the summer of 1947 Erich Honecker led a delegation of FDJ functionaries to the Soviet Union. There they traveled throughout the country, visiting Moscow, Leningrad, Stalingrad, and other cities, witnessed mass events, and conferred with Komsomol leaders. The Soviet Union they saw, and that they described in a series of articles in the *Junge Welt,* was very much in the spirit of Kuczynski's book. The high point of the entire visit, however, was their negotiation with the Komsomol. This, the SED historian Inge Pardon wrote (incongruously echoing Rick in *Casablanca*), was "the beginning of a great friendship."[35] There is little point in presenting the long and predictable history of FDJ–Komsomol relations in this study. GDR historians have already described this relationship with an eye to detail (and *Parteilichkeit*) that would be difficult to

---

32. Aleksandr Fadejew, *Die Junge Garde* (East Berlin, 1949).

33. I. Wostryschew, "Die Auswertung der schönen Literatur in der propagandistischen Arbeit," *Bibliothek des Propagandisten* 3 (1952): 15.

34. "Lehrplan für die zentrale Jugendschule der FDJ im Waldhof am Bogensee," SAPMO BArch IV 2/16/100, Bl. 174.

35. Inge Pardon, "Der Beginn einer großen Freundschaft," *Schriftenreihe der FDJ* 17 (1973).

match.[36] For our purposes it is enough to say that beginning in the early 1950s the FDJ began systematically imitating the Komsomol in its organizational structures and in its Marxist-Leninist indoctrination. The Young Pioneers, which began as a Marxist-Leninist mass organization in the late 1940s, modeled itself after the Lenin Pioneers from the beginning.

The development of this "friendship" included adopting the rich treasury of Lenin Pioneer and Komsomol mythology in the Young Pioneers and FDJ. Beyond reading Ostrovsky, Fadeyev, and other Komsomol authors, this meant learning Komsomol songs and games. Like the Komsomol, the FDJ encouraged its members to work "subbotniks," unpaid Sunday work shifts. The Young Pioneers erected Lenin altars in their clubhouses and genuflected before the Lenin bust on special occasions. They quickly adopted the tradition of the "Timur brigades," in which Lenin Pioneers went about doing good deeds for the elderly. One Lenin Pioneer hero given particular attention was Pavlik Morosov, a thirteen-year-old Ukrainian farm boy who during the collectivization of the 1930s denounced his father to the NKVD and was himself lynched by angry kulaks. Lenin Pioneers treated him as a martyr and a model to be emulated, and beginning in the early 1950s his picture and life story adorned GDR school exercise-books.[37] While FDJ members might become acquainted with Komsomol members at mass events or on organized visits to the Soviet Union, Young Pioneers had no real contact with Lenin Pioneers outside of the official pen-pal campaigns the organization promoted. The Soviet Union remained very much a "wonderland" for them throughout their childhood. Pioneer magazines lovingly described the Soviet Union's wonderful vacation camps for workers' and peasants' children. Young Pioneers who had distinguished themselves in their organization could win expense-paid trips to these special camps and so learn about life in the Soviet Union firsthand. One Lenin Pioneer installation given particularly extensive coverage was a holiday camp on the Crimean Peninsula bearing the simple name "Paradise."

All in all, Young Pioneer publications in the late 1940s and early 1950s devoted on average two-thirds of their content to the happy life and the great accomplishments of Soviet youth. Most of these articles were

36. For a brief introduction to this field, see Karl-Heinz Jahnke and Inge Pardon, "Die Herausbildung freundschaftlicher Beziehungen zwischen der FDJ und dem Leninschen Komsomol 1946–1949," *Beiträge zur Geschichte der FDJ* 2 (1975).

37. Cf. Wolfram Dittrich, "Das Schulheft im Dienste der bolschewistischen Politik," *SBZ-Archiv,* 21/52, 326–28.

taken directly from Lenin Pioneer publications and translated into German. If this slavish imitation of the Soviet Union slowly dropped off in the late 1950s, this had nothing to do with the "de-Stalinization" process of those years, but rather with both youth organizations' successful transformation into German versions of the Lenin Pioneers and Komsomol, a process that was officially completed by 1957.

"The Greatest Friend of the German People"

At the core of the myth of the Great Socialist Soviet Union lay the myth of The Great Stalin. If the SED depicted Thälmann as a Christlike figure who suffered, died, and rose again for Germany's sins and who offered redemption to all who believed in him, it depicted Joseph Stalin as a triumphant savior. We do not need to study all the details of this personality cult. Unlike the other myths presented in this study, the myth of The Great Stalin was a direct Soviet import. But even if the Russian Orthodox imagery that accompanied the myth was purely Russian in origin, this did not keep German Communists from embracing it and spinning it further.

The Stalin cult in the Soviet Zone developed slowly. Much of the early propaganda material aimed at young people did not mention him at all.[38] By 1949 it was clear to the Party that a united Germany was not imminent and that a new confrontation was looming. In this atmosphere, German–Soviet friendship took on a new quality.

The cult began in earnest with preparations for Stalin's seventieth birthday on 21 December. This date conveniently coincided with the winter solstice, that is, the return of the sun from the darkness of winter, a point that the propagandists emphasized. These preparations began already before the GDR's founding in October. The FDJ and the Young Pioneers distributed informational materials to the local organizations on Stalin's youth, his political life, his role in the liberation from Fascism, and his meaning for Germany. FDJ members in schools and factories prepared gifts for Stalin that they exhibited at public demonstrations and ceremoniously delivered to representatives of the Soviet forces for delivery in Moscow. FDJ members in mines and factories organized special work shifts in honor of Stalin's birthday. Meanwhile, the youth press printed scores of articles on the Great Stalin and on the preparations for the great event. On the eve of the birthday, FDJ members and Young Pioneers carried out rallies and torchlight parades. On the next day FDJ cultural

---

38. See, for example, the Young Pioneer manual *Seid bereit!* (East Berlin, 1949), in which Stalin's name is not mentioned even once.

groups danced and sang songs in Stalin's praise. Theatrical groups performed plays based on works of *Sowjetliteratur* in town squares, in schools, in factories, on construction sites.[39]

This vision of an omniscient leader in far-off Moscow was essential to the establishment of socialism in the GDR and the other people's democracies. The transcendent myth of The Great Stalin guaranteed that the tremendous sacrifices that the "Antifascist Democratic Upheaval" and later the "Construction of Socialism" demanded were not only worthwhile, but were certain to succeed. Stalin's own achievements in the Soviet Union were proof of this. His ingenious leadership in the defeat of Fascism held out the promise of the liberation of all humanity. He was the "wise *Führer*" of all workers and peasants. Stalin meant peace, Stalin meant victory. Stalin was a modern Prometheus. He was, true to his pseudonym, a "Man of Steel." His name evoked the fiery blast furnaces of the Soviet five-year plans. Stalin bore the flame of the revolution. He was the greatest friend of the German people. Above all, Stalin meant power. Standing next to him in Potsdam, the transient leaders of the Western powers (especially the "haberdasher" Harry Truman) were a pitiful sight. Stalin showed how to get power and keep it. He offered a model for the personality cults created around Pieck, Ulbricht, and other lesser functionaries. His nomenklatura provided the model for the privilege system within the SED. Stalin never formally visited the GDR, and so young people made do with his portrait, which they decorated and carried before them like an icon. The fact that young Germans had sworn allegiance to a similar role model only a few years before was to the Communists' advantage. As leader of all progressive people in the world, Stalin was in effect a *Führer* whom one could follow with a clean conscience. He was also a father figure for a terribly confused young generation. Historian Dorothee Wierling has discovered through her interviews that many young people in the early years were eager to accept the SED's vision of the Party as a symbolic "mother of the masses" dominated by Stalin, "the father of the peoples."[40]

The thousands of hymns and poems to Stalin generated by this cult all reflect these emotions and are characterized by a religious quality that lingered in all celebrations of Soviet power long after Stalin's passing. Most of them were written for youth and translated from the Russian, like the

---

39. "Plan zur Vorbereitung und Durchführung des 70. Geburtstages J.W. Stalins am 21. Dezember 1949," JA IzJ A 2.391; see also the articles in ND, JW, JG, *Forum, Der Pionierleiter.*

40. Dorothee Wierling, "Is There an East German Identity? Aspects of a Social History of the Soviet Zone/German Democratic Republic," TAJB 19 (1990): 199–201.

song "Sing the Song of Stalin—A Morning Song," suitable for Young Pioneer holiday camps.[41]

Sing the song of Stalin
And greet the day in song!
Sing the song of songs,
And the whole world sings along.

East German contributions to the Stalin cult were in the same style. This FDJ song, "We Salute Stalin," combines in one verse nearly all elements of the myth of the Soviet Union.[42]

Youth, heart of all the land,
Take your destiny into your hand
And fight for and build
Yourself a free fatherland.

Chorus: We salute Stalin, the teacher,
Who sets peace ablaze for us.
We greet Stalin, the best of friends!
German youth, guarding the peace!
German youth, guarding the peace!

The youth organizations carried out countless unpaid "Stalin-shifts" and competed for the consecrated "Stalin-Banner" at the Third World Youth Festival in Berlin in 1951. But youth's greatest contribution to the Stalin cult developed through the construction of a grandiose east–west boulevard through a bombed-out workers' district of East Berlin. This project had been decided on at the Third Congress of the SED in 1950. The chief architect, Hermann Henselmann, incongruously combined Soviet "wedding cake" architecture with elements of Friedrich Schinkel's classicist Berlin building style. The buildings were to be constructed according to efficient "new work methods." Young Pioneers helped collect money and materials for the project, and FDJ brigades did much of the building. The apartments in these buildings were to be large, modern, inexpensive, and reserved for ordinary workers. This utopian ensemble was not an end in itself but the model for the reconstruction of all of Berlin and eventually

41. Kossenko/M. Rilskij, "Stimmt das Lied auf Stalin an (ein Lied zum Tagesbeginn)," in *Stalin unser Lied. Lieder aus der Sowjetunion und der Deutschen Demokratischen Republik* (Weimar, 1952), 46.

42. H. Keller and J. Werzlau, "Wir grüßen Stalin," in *Stalin unser Lied,* 104–5.

all of Germany after reunification. One of the buildings on the *Straus-berger Platz* bore—what else—a Goethe quotation ("Aye! such a throng I fain would see . . ."). This was the way all young people would live in the Communist future. The "first Socialist street in Germany" was also designed for parades and political demonstrations, and it was only appropriate that it should be named after The Great Stalin.[43]

The *Stalinallee* symbolized the SED's ambitious program of "the Construction of Socialism" and was accompanied by an immense propaganda campaign. The murderous pace of construction on this project was a model for the rising work norms to which all workers were now being submitted. Countless poems and songs were written about the project, one of which found its way into the E. H. Mayer/Johannes R. Becher cantata, "The Certainty of Victory."[44]

> Columns and freestones like strides, firmly planted on the earth,
> And a blooming middle, blooming, glorious Today and Now!
>   O glorious Today and Now!
> Glorious Today and Here. A banner glows with the words,
> Flag-wreathed is the gate, flag-wreathed,
> Through which peace, through which peace marches.
> We! In swaying, waving stride, like a triumph, like a triumph
>   without end.
> See the jubilation of the raised hands in the singing of the
>   peoples! . . .
> Name that everyone knows, name, more radiant than ever,
> Name that everyone knows, name! A street as his monument!
> Street! Proud, proud *Stalinallee*!

Stalin's sudden death in March 1953 shocked the SED and the FDJ leadership. Upon hearing the news in his West German prison cell, Ralph Giordano hung a smuggled Stalin picture on the door of his locker and stared at it for hours.[45] The workers' uprising in June of that year was also shocking, especially because it began—of all the embarrassing places!—among the construction workers of the *Stalinallee*. Even if the SED leadership did its best to represent this rebellion to its members as a "Fascist coup attempt," the fact that it could only be suppressed by Soviet tanks once more cast a new light on the meaning of "German–Soviet friendship" for both Party members and non–Party members. Nevertheless, Stalin's personality cult continued in his absence, if with less intensity. But soon

---

43. Tilo Köhler, *Unser die Strasse, unser der Sieg—Die Stalinallee* (Berlin, 1983).
44. E. H. Mayer and J. R. Becher, "Stalinallee," in *Stalin unser Lied,* 121–31.
45. Giordano, 70.

references to Stalin gave way to greater attention to Lenin, who had been in Stalin's shadow for years. As early as 1955 Ulbricht personally ordered the creation of Lenin memorials and commemorative plaques throughout the GDR and did so without mentioning his "best pupil" Stalin even once.[46] This was in keeping with Soviet practice at the same time.[47] A year later, informed Party members were shaken by the revelations of Khrushchev's "secret speech" at the Twentieth Party Congress, which was never published in the GDR. Khrushchev's statements produced a crisis for propagandists, especially since none of Stalin's successors really met the demands of a new personality cult. The Party never admitted that Stalin might have done anything specifically improper, merely that, in Ulbricht's words, by placing himself above the Party "Stalin cannot be counted among the classics of Marxism."[48] But this "de-canonization" had little immediate effect on the propaganda. If Stalin's personality cult was quietly dropped, Ulbricht's continued without interruption. Stalin did not become a public issue again in East German society until after 1989. Some of the most visible manifestations of the Stalin cult were only eliminated in 1961: the *Stalinallee* was renamed *Karl-Marx-Allee,* and its Stalin statue was secretly removed in the middle of the night; *Stalinstadt,* originally *Eisenhüttenkombinat-Ost,* the GDR's first "Socialist city," which had received Stalin's name shortly after his death in 1953, was discreetly renamed *Eisenhüttenstadt.*

The emotional content of the name *Stalin* was now divided up between worship of the Communist Party itself and of an increasingly remote, godlike Lenin. Pro-Soviet propaganda took on a routine and increasingly bureaucratic quality that it would retain until 1989. During the celebration of the fortieth anniversary of the Great Socialist October Revolution in 1957, the FDJ told its members among other things: "All achievements of the Soviet land, its historic victories and successes are founded on the fact that a Marxist-Leninist party, which has at all times remained true to the teachings of Marx, Engels, and Lenin, and has preserved the close bond with the masses, has stood at the top of the Soviet people and has guided its steps."[49] There was nothing especially inspirational in this self-glorification to non-Party members, and it was a happy

46. "Aktennotiz" (Kurt Hager, 12 May 1955), SAPMO BArch IV 2/904/118, Bl. 2; "Beschluss-Entwurf zu Massnahmen über die Einrichtung von Lenin-Gedenkstätten in Deutschland," ibid., Bl. 18–23.

47. Nina Tumarkin, *Lenin Lives* (Cambridge, 1983), 261.

48. "Walter Ulbricht: Stalin ist kein Klassiker des Marxismus, 4 March 1956," Hermann Weber, *DDR. Dokumente,* 226.

49. "Direktive des Sekretariats des Zentralrates der FDJ über die Aufgaben des Verbandes zur Vorbereitung des 40. Jahrestages der Grossen Sozialistischen Oktoberrevolution," JA IzJ A 586.

coincidence for GDR propagandists that Khrushchev's "secret speech" of 1956 was quickly followed by the launch of the first Sputnik spacecraft in 1957.

The success of the Soviet Union's space program meant not just (temporary) superiority over the United States and imperialism, but also a profound symbolic shift from heavy industry to high technology, from the blast furnace to the rocket engine. From now on the Soviet Union's superior technology—not a mortal leader—was going to be the guarantor of victory.

Learning Victory

"Victory" was a key feature of the myth of the Great Socialist Soviet Union. Its appeal becomes obvious when one considers the vastness of Germany's defeat in World War II. As we have seen in the previous chapter, Stalin early on removed the war guilt from eastern Germans. In his congratulatory telegram upon the founding of the GDR in October 1949, he wrote to Pieck and Grotewohl that "the formation of the peace-loving German Democratic Republic is a turning point in the history of Europe." Furthermore, "the experience of the last war has shown that the German and Soviet peoples made the greatest sacrifices in this war, that both peoples possess the greatest strengths in Europe for the realization of great actions of world importance. If both peoples display the decisiveness to fight for peace with the same exertion of strength as that with which they waged the war, then one can view the peace in Europe as guaranteed."[50]

Soon after the foundation of the GDR, the SED began spreading the slogan "Learning from the Soviet Union means learning victory."[51] This became the Party's central propaganda slogan in 1951 and was discussed endlessly in the youth organizations. The slogan was ambiguous; it ostensibly referred to the Soviet economic system, which the Party was imposing upon a skeptical public. "Victory" meant the triumphant success of Stalin's five-year plans of the 1930s, which had been so enthusiastically described in Kuczynski's book. The apocalyptic rhetoric of Communist songs and poems regularly evoked "battle" and "victory," meaning the final victory of the Communist society. But victory also meant the Soviet victory over Fascism, the necessity of which was a regular topic of youth group meetings and *Heimabende*. This victory was symbolized by a spec-

50. "Aus dem Telegramm J.W. Stalins zur Gründung der DDR, 13. Oktober 1949," in Hermann Weber, ed., *DDR. Dokumente zur Geschichte der Deutschen Demokratischen Republik 1945–1985*, 3d ed. (Munich, 1987), 163–64.

51. Cited in Hermann Weber, *DDR. Grundriss der Geschichte*, revised and expanded edition (Hannover, 1991), 66.

tacular (staged) photograph of Red Army soldiers planting the Soviet flag on top of the ruins of the Berlin *Reichstag* on 30 April 1945. It adorned the walls of schools and FDJ clubhouses and quickly became even more familiar than that other document of the GDR's birth, the Soviet soldiers liberating the Goethe–Schiller statue in Weimar. It seemed odd to many visitors that East Germans would celebrate Germany's defeat in such a way. But the photograph did not symbolize defeat, but liberation—a victory that belonged to "the working class and its Marxist-Leninist Party."

The utter renunciation of the Nazi cause and acceptance of the Soviet victory meant that German war victims had no legitimate place in public memory. Until 1989 speaking of the millions of fallen *Wehrmacht* soldiers and the thousands of civilians killed during the forced evacuation from the eastern provinces was largely taboo. The only exception were civilian bombing victims, who were commemorated as victims of the "Anglo-Americans." What few monuments there were to fallen soldiers (and hence to fallen fathers, sons, husbands, friends, etc.) were erected by the churches, which were also in charge of military cemeteries. As we saw above, even the "monument for the victims of fascism and militarism" in East Berlin placed the remains of the unknown soldier next to those of an unknown resistance fighter, but this theme was not developed further. The psychological effects of this suppressed grief have yet to be explored. In any case, the combination of friendship with the Soviet Union and indigenous antifascism made it appear as if the Soviet war dead and the German antifascist martyrs were somehow all the same thing. True to the spirit of the Stalin telegram, by the early 1970s East German school textbooks actually claimed that, alongside the Soviet Union and Poland, the German people had suffered the greatest losses in the war against Fascism.[52]

The Soviet government immortalized its victory by constructing a vast memorial in the East Berlin Treptow Park, the largest and certainly the most fantastic of the thousands of Soviet monuments and cemeteries scattered throughout the GDR. Next to the uncompleted *Stalinallee,* the war memorial was the greatest "Stalinist" monument built in the GDR. The government began making plans for a fitting memorial even before the end of the war. A competition was held in 1946, which was won by the Soviet sculptor E. V. Wuchetich and the architect Y. B. Belopolski. Construction began in 1947, and the dedication took place on 9 May 1949.[53] Because of its striking Christian symbolism it is worth examining in some detail.

---

52. On textbooks, see Wilfried Schubarth and Thomas Schmidt, "'Sieger der Geschichte'. Verordneter Antifaschismus und die Folgen," in Karl-Heinz Heinemann and Wilfried Schubarth, eds., *Der antifaschistische Staat entlässt seine Kinder* (Cologne, 1992), 15.
53. V. Frank, 9–11.

The memorial can be entered by one of two triumphal arches located at its northern and southern ends. Tree-lined paths then lead to an open space, in the midst of which a large figure of "Mother *Rodina*" sits, her head bowed in sorrow. A hundred meters in front of her, two enormous stylized red granite Soviet flags stand to the right and the left, both lowered in mourning and engraved with the words "Eternal glory to the fighters of the Soviet Army, who gave their lives in the struggle for the liberation of humanity from Fascist servitude," in Russian and German. At the base of each kneels a mourning soldier, his helmet in his hands. One is middle-aged, representing the generation of the Revolution; the other is a young man, representing the Stalinist generation that defended Socialism in the Great Fatherland War. This group forms a gateway to the actual "sacred ground" of the memorial. One descends a wide flight of steps into a vast rectangular space suggesting a great open-air cathedral. In the center lie five mass graves, one behind the other, containing the remains of more than five thousand Red Army soldiers who fell in the Battle of Berlin. On each side of this compound stands a row of eight symbolic white marble sarcophagi bearing dramatic relief sculptures in classical style depicting scenes from the Great Fatherland War and engraved with excerpts of Stalin speeches on the war—one row in Russian, the other row in German. The number sixteen refers to the sixteen Soviet Republics, but these sixteen stations of victory are also reminiscent of the fourteen Stations of the Cross in a Catholic church. At the very end of the compound, behind the last of the mass graves, rises a ten-meter-high mound reminiscent of a *kurgan,* an ancient Slavic burial mound. A flight of steps leads up to a round white marble structure in the form of an ancient Roman mausoleum, containing a sacred "hall of honor." On top of this structure stands the actual monument—"the Liberator." It and the entire memorial are placed toward the southeast in such a way that the sun rises directly behind the sculpture.[54] "The Liberator" is not a fierce, sword-wielding "*Rodina*" like the one standing above the Stalingrad monument on the Volga. This figure is a twelve-meter-tall Soviet soldier, in his right hand a huge sword pointing to the ground, his feet trampling a shattered swastika. In his left arm he holds a little girl, who clings to him for comfort. This striking image ostensibly derived from an actual event in the Battle of Berlin, when a Soviet soldier rescued a German child at the risk of his own life. In an interview twenty years later, the sculptor explained: "His figure was supposed to represent victory, but not frozen in pompous triumph; it was supposed to recall the fallen, but also direct its eyes at the future. The child on

---

54. Although this effect is impressive, it is nevertheless coincidental: the monument was built upon an old soccer field dating back to the previous century.

the soldier's arm has survived the disastrous war; the fighter, who liberated mankind from the brown plague, carries it toward peace, toward a new world."[55] But Wuchetich consciously modeled the figure on medieval and Renaissance traditions.[56] In fact, "the Liberator" adapts one of the most familiar images of Christian iconography for the Soviet cult. The soldier is a secular male version of the Virgin Mary in medieval and Renaissance sculpture, standing upon the sickle moon, holding in her left arm the Christ child and in her right hand a scepter. This image illustrates one of the most powerful visions of the Book of Revelation, describing a great cosmic battle between the Archangel Michael and Satan: "And there appeared a great wonder in heaven; a woman clothed with the sun, and the moon under her feet, and upon her head a crown of twelve stars. . . . And she brought forth a man child, who was to rule all nations with a rod of iron."[57] Of course, a proper Marxist-Leninist would not recognize the biblical reference, nor would an atheistic Young Pioneer. But the exact quotation was not necessary, for the symbolism was clear: "the Liberator" represented resurrection from the dead, the transformation of sorrow (as represented by Mother *Rodina*) into triumph. The Liberation was the dawning of a new era of human history. The crushed swastika, like the sickle moon, represented the old order that was overcome by the new, symbolized by the sun in both cases. In contrast to the Virgin's scepter of heaven, the sword symbolizes Soviet military power. The Red Army was the liberator of humanity and the father of a new Socialist generation that would inherit the earth.

The monument is impressive and is one of the most intriguing uses of prerevolutionary forms for a revolutionary message. It is profoundly ironic that the memorial was largely built from marble and granite that the Nazis had been hoarding for their own victory monuments in Berlin following their "*Endsieg*" ("final victory") in World War II.[58] But there is also an eerie quality to the statue, which may arise in part from the way in which the sculptor inverted the salvation-bringing symbolism of the old Christian icon, that is, the transformation of a woman holding a small boy to a man holding a small girl. The inversion of the symbol suggests the inversion of that which is being symbolized. Thus although the Liberator consciously symbolizes liberation, it hardly expresses freedom.

---

55. Arbeitsgemeinschaft "Junge Historiker," *Das Treptower Ehrenmal* (East Berlin, 1987), 21.

56. Ibid.

57. Revelation 12:1, 5. On the iconography, see "Mondsichelmadonna," in Hannelore Sachs et al., *Christliche Ikonographie in Stichworten* (Leipzig, 1980), 261; "Mond," in Gerd Heinz-Mohr, *Lexikon der Symbole. Bilder und Zeichen der christlichen Kunst* (Freiburg im Breisgau, 1991), 230–31.

58. *Das Treptower Ehrenmal,* 107–8.

The memorial was commissioned by the Soviets, but placed under GDR administration from the beginning. Like all Communist monuments of this type (and like any cathedral), the Treptow Park memorial was not intended as a mere tourist attraction but as a center of constant pro-Soviet and antifascist ritual. It was the site of thousands of ceremonies, most notably the annual celebrations of the Soviet victory on 9 May and Revolution Day on 7 November. But in between it was used as the backdrop for youth consecrations, the initiation ceremonies of Young Pioneer and FDJ groups, the oath-taking of soldiers and officers, flag consecrations, antifascist rallies, anti-imperialist demonstrations, countless torchlight ceremonies, FDJ–Komsomol meetings, wreath-laying by newlyweds, and many other events. Virtually every GDR or foreign youth group visiting the capital was bused in to see it. The youth organizations' periodic retracings of the path of the Red Army from the Oder to Berlin usually ended with a march to the memorial. One such action, performed in preparation for a dramatic torch-lit ceremony at the monument on the thirtieth anniversary of the Liberation in May 1975, was a "Pioneer task" under the name "Follow the Path of the Red Star." Young Pioneers tended 2,926 Soviet memorials throughout the GDR and studied the history of both the "Great Fatherland War" and the "antifascist resistance struggle."[59]

Demonstrations at the memorial were always rich in symbolism. For example, on 13 August 1971 a group of one thousand officer candidates, all members of the FDJ, took part in a great "honorary roll call" at the foot of "the Liberator." They swore friendship to the Soviet Union and loyalty to their fatherland, declared their hatred of Fascism and imperialism, and proclaimed their support of the SED's erection of the "Antifascist Defensive Wall" on that day ten years earlier.[60] All of this went on alongside Soviet military ceremonies, which were also attended by NVA (National People's Army) soldiers and delegations from the GDR youth organizations.

Beyond inspiring gratitude toward the Red Army, one intention of this constant pageantry was to make young Germans feel that the Soviet victory was also their own victory. Pioneer friendships explored the history of the liberation of their own hometowns. This aim was served also by a flood of Soviet war movies beginning in the late 1940s. One example was "The Battle of Berlin," which celebrated the destruction and subjugation of the German capital and the raising of the red flag over the *Reichstag*. But throughout most of these films a careful distinction was made between "the Germans," who were victims of the war, and "the Fascists," who were the perpetrators. In their *Heimabende* and in the songs and poems that

---

59. *Geschichte der FDJ. Chronik*, 355.

60. "Ehrenappell der jungen Offiziersbewerber," JW 14/15 August 1971.

they memorized for their roll calls, Pioneers and FDJ members were taught to identify themselves with *all* Russian and Soviet victories. They were to view them as steps toward the great victory in World War II and toward the final victory of Communism, for which they themselves were now fighting. As battles of the class struggle, all of these conflicts were essentially the same battle, only with different combatants. The Russian civil war, already popularized by Ostrovsky's novel, was one example of this. The FDJ adopted several civil war heroes, including Chapayev, a Red Guard officer killed in battle. In a *Heimabend* pamphlet issued in 1952, young East Germans were told: "Chapayev is a hero. A hero of the kind that only a people can bring forth which with all its strength is leading a life and death struggle, a struggle for its freedom. Chapayev, the hero of the Civil War, must be for us today a role model and example in our fight against the general war treaty and for the conclusion of a peace treaty with Germany, in the struggle for our national freedom and independence. We must be prepared boldly and fearlessly to crush all criminal war plans of the American aggressors and their German accomplices with such force that they will forever lose all desire to touch our glorious German homeland, our blossoming, beautiful, proud Republic."[61]

The "victory" myth-building strategy insisted that Communism's victories in the Bolshevik Revolution and World War II were not only irreversible, but that there could be no doubt whatsoever that they would lead to consistent future victories all the way to the ultimate victory of communism the world over. But unlike the downright messianic forecasts of the Khrushchev era, youth in the Brezhnev–Honecker age were to be taught patience. One popular technique used in building this myth was the time capsule. For example, at a mass event at the Soviet memorial on the Seelow Heights (which recalled a particularly bloody battle in the last phase of the war), FDJ members from Frankfurt an der Oder buried a time capsule containing the following letter to the youth of the year 2017.[62]

The banner of Communism shines brightly above us. We, Frankfurt youth of 1977, are living in a time which is characterized by the unstoppable advance of Socialism and of the forces of peace and progress.

A new age is opening up to us, the age of human progress. We are striding along the path toward a radiant future, characterized by happiness for every person, by unimagined possibilities of the use of science and technology for the good and happiness of man.

61. "Volksheld Tschapajew," *Heimabendreihe der FDJ* 5 (1952): 5.
62. "Brief an die Jugend im Jahre 2017," 6 November 1977, JA IzJ A 11.241.

Greetings to you, who are continuing our work and are successfully advancing towards the establishment of the Communist society, towards the establishment of Communism in labor.

In 1970, the one hundredth anniversary of Lenin's birth on 11 April was celebrated in conjunction with the twenty-fifth anniversary of the victory over Fascism on 9 May. The FDJ organized a "Lenin Mobilization" and the Soviet Union sent the historic "Banner of Victory" for the occasion. This was the red banner that the Soviet soldiers had hoisted on the Reichstag in 1945. For months, the banner was carried by a special motorcycle escort from Moscow and traced the advance of Soviet forces in the Great Fatherland War through Poland, Romania, Bulgaria, Hungary, Czechoslovakia, and finally the GDR. As Egon Krenz proclaimed as the banner neared the GDR border: "After twenty-five years the victory banner is returning to Berlin, to a Berlin which is joined with the Soviet Union in unswerving friendship."[63] It was used in victory celebrations and "Lenin Mobilization" events all the way to Berlin. Upon arrival in the capital, the banner was taken to a climactic mass event at the giant new Lenin statue on the *Leninplatz,* where it was greeted by a formation of fifteen thousand FDJ members along with old antifascists and Soviet war veterans. NVA soldiers fired artillery salutes and the crowd shouted "*Druzhba!*—Friendship! *Druzhba!*—Friendship!" as the banner came into view.[64]

The Komsomol repeated this action in 1975. This time, the banner was loaded onto a car and driven along one of the routes of the Soviet campaign from Moscow to Berlin, where it arrived in time for a massive FDJ demonstration at the Treptow memorial on 7 May. The symbolism of these events made it clear that East Germans as a people were not only the victors of history, but were long since victors over Nazi Germany as well. This idea is summed up in a popular anecdote in the former GDR. A young boy on a tour of the Buchenwald memorial is asked, "Who won the war?" His reply: "Why, we did of course!"

"Our Socialist Fatherland"

A reader might leave this description of the Soviet cult with the impression that the GDR itself was nothing more than a self-effacing Soviet puppet state with no national pride whatsoever. Nothing could be further from the truth. The Great Socialist Soviet Union was the model for and sole guarantor of the SED's notion of the "Socialist fatherland." The "Social-

---

63. "Ab 4. Mai haben wir bei uns das Siegesbanner," JW 29 April 1970.
64. "Das Siegesbanner wieder in Berlin!" JW 9/10 May 1970.

ist fatherland" always bewildered visitors to the GDR. In fact, the nationalist rhetoric with which the SED began indoctrinating youth in the late 1940s and especially the early 1950s would have been unimaginable a few decades earlier. As we have already seen in chapter 2, the early Communist children's and youth groups were trained in the spirit of a radical anti-Republicanism and antinationalism. A report given in 1922 on the efforts of K.K.Gr. activists in the public schools of the Weimar Republic showed that the children[65]

> are adherents of direct action, and rip out patriotic songs and reading selections, leave the classroom when patriotic songs are being learned, paint—instead of black-red-gold [Republican] flags—red flags with the Soviet star; [and] write essays—which are supposed to be about the Hohenzollern or about some other such figures—instead about Liebknecht, about Russia, about their [Communist] Children's Group.

But Stalin's Soviet Union had adopted an increasingly nationalist course in the early 1930s, and the KPD immediately followed suit. As Alexander Abusch stated at the Brussels Conference in 1935, it was essential "in the struggle against Fascism and war . . . to unmask the Nazis' historical lies and to confront them with the models of true German national heroes recommendable to youth."[66]

The shift to nationalism showed pragmatic thinking. The KPD had frightened millions in the Weimar era with its militancy and antinationalism. One consequence of this policy was that the Nazis were able to stake their own claim to nationalist rhetoric and symbolism. The middle and upper classes viewed the KPD's internationalism as treasonous, making the *National* Socialists seem like a lesser evil. But the impression of national indifference had also plagued the governing parties of the Weimar Republic, which simply lacked the pomp and self-confidence of the Wilhelmine era. As Peter Gay has written,[67]

> The wholehearted commitment to Weimar required the repudiation of all [nationalist] mythology. By its very existence, the Republic was a calculated affront to the heroes and cliches that every German child knew, many German politicians invoked, and, it turned out, most

---

65. "Bericht über die Kinderkonferenz der K.K.Gr.D. in Suhl/Thüringen am 22. Juli 1922," SAPMO BArch ZPA I 4/1/80, Bl. 3.

66. Cited in Karl Heinz Jahnke, *Jungkommunisten im Widerstandskampf gegen den Hitlerfaschismus* (East Berlin, 1977), 165.

67. Peter Gay, *Weimar Culture: The Outsider as Insider* (New York, 1968), 87.

Germans cherished. In the battle of historical symbols the republicans were at a disadvantage from the start: compared with Bismarck and other charismatic leaders, at once superhuman and picturesque, the models available to Weimar were pallid and uninspiring.

The SED took this lesson to heart early on. To be sure, Ernst Thälmann and Joseph Stalin were inspiring and even picturesque after SED propagandists had built up their respective myths. Nevertheless, they were far too remote from the actual experience of most East Germans to be effective as role models, and for much of the older generation the Party's reliance on such figures seemed to be a sellout of German interests to the Red Army and a confirmation of the SED's reputation as the *Russenpartei.* Such sentiments were even more widespread in the West, which was filled with hundreds of thousands of refugees from the GDR and where SED propaganda had little influence. The problem was exacerbated by the Federal Republic's liberal use of "Great Germans" in its own calls for reunification.

German Communists resented being called "*Russenknechte*" (servants of the Russians) by what they saw as the "American lackeys" of the Federal Republic. Fully in keeping with the concept of the "Socialist fatherland," Communists everywhere usually consider themselves the most patriotic of citizens. The SED propagated this belief among youth by means of a letter Ernst Thälmann wrote from his Nazi prison cell in the 1930s.[68]

I am not a hermit, I am a German with great national, but also international experiences. My people, to which I belong and which I love, is the German people, and my nation, which I honor with great pride, is the German nation, a chivalrous, proud, and hard nation. I am blood of the blood and flesh of the flesh of the German workers and thus, as their revolutionary child, I later became their revolutionary leader. My life and work have known and know only one thing: To devote to the working German people my soul and my knowledge, my experiences and my energy, indeed my whole self, my personality, for the victorious Socialist liberation struggle in the new national rebirth [*Völkerfrühling*] of the German nation.

In this passage, Thälmann is referring to the "working German people." While typical of sectarian KPD terminology, such a formulation

---

68. *Leseheft für die Politischen Grundschulen der SED,* part 2, theme 1 (East Berlin, 1952), 86.

would no longer do for the SED, which was hoping to attract intellectuals and other middle-class people in both the GDR and the FRG. But the SED's understanding of the German people—*das deutsche Volk*—did not mean the sum of native-born German-speaking persons living within the borders of Germany, but rather the sum of *progressive* German-speaking persons. Thus anyone stamped as a "war arsonist," a "pacifist," a "reactionary," a "Zionist," an "American lackey," or a "Trotskyist" was not really a member of the *Volk* but rather an "unpatriotic element" (*volksfeindliches Element*).[69] A Communist's national conscience is clear. Honecker reaffirmed this conviction in 1992: "A journalist recently proclaimed that he was surprised how easily Honecker, the former head of state of the GDR, passes the word 'Germany' over his lips. The man is mistaken. We Communists are and will always remain the truest patriots. He who leads the people into wars and aggressions against other peoples, who fans hatred against other races and nations, has long since abandoned this claim."[70]

Thus the SED declared its patriotism early on, and Johannes R. Becher's text of the GDR's national anthem did not praise the GDR and Socialism as such, but instead "Germany united fatherland." "The concept of fatherland," Party theorists argued, "has class character." Capitalist rulers "identify with the fatherland their existing system of exploitation, which attempts to exclude the oppressed classes from the enjoyment of the riches of the fatherland and the organization of societal conditions." Hence the famous slogan of the *Communist Manifesto,* "the workers have no fatherland." Whereas capitalists are nationalistic, the working class is patriotic. Through the elimination of exploitation and thus the roots of imperialist war, the working class seeks "the transformation of the fatherland of the bourgeoisie into the Socialist fatherland of the entire people. Only now can the national cultural and natural riches, beauties and traditions be made accessible to all toilers."[71] From the start, the Socialist fatherland was linked to the Great Socialist Soviet Union, which had given the German working class back its fatherland and which was protecting it from the American aggressors. In fact, the true German fatherland had been linked to the Russian *Rodina* from the beginning. Germans and Russians/Soviets were friends and had always been friends. As Otto Grotewohl proclaimed in a speech marking Stalin's seventy-first birthday in 1950, "To be a German patriot means to be a friend of the Soviet

---

69. Cf. Wolfgang Bergsdorf, "Die Wiedervereinigung der deutschen Sprache," DA 10/1993, 1187.

70. Honecker, 78.

71. "Vaterland," *Kleines politisches Wörterbuch,* 997–98.

Union."[72] This notion very nearly received a profoundly symbolic physical form in the center of East Berlin. In 1951, Schinckel's *Neue Wache,* a monument of Prussian classicist architecture that was also under consideration as a national Goethe shrine, was suggested as an entrance hall to the "House of the Culture of the Soviet Union" located directly behind it.[73]

Despite the nationalist rhetoric, the SBZ and the early GDR practically declared war on German national symbols. Scores of castles and estate houses were dynamited, the most notorious example being the war-damaged Berlin *Stadtschloss,* which was blasted in 1951 to make way for a giant parade ground and reviewing stand, the *Marx-Engels-Platz.* This was to be East Berlin's answer to Moscow's Red Square.[74] Other castles and manor houses were saved only by being transformed into clinics, schools, *Kulturhäuser,* and the like. In 1951 the FDJ formally requested the demolition of the Kyffhäuser monument, which had been built in the Wilhelmine era to celebrate German unification. The monument was saved only by the Thuringian provincial government's argument that "this profitable source of revenue . . . makes a disregarding of ideological concerns seem thoroughly justified."[75] The Party's attitude was reflected by the SED ideologist Alexander Abusch's characterization of German history as one long *Misere* (calamity). As he wrote in his book *Irrweg einer Nation* (1946): "For half a millennium . . . two tendencies have flowed through German history: the efforts of reactionary power-wielders to maintain their power—and the struggle of the people for a free German nation."[76]

All of this changed in 1952. On 1 June an article appeared in *Neues Deutschland* entitled "On the Necessity of Learning from One's Own History." It called upon German historians to learn from the Soviet model and, "in the Leninist-Stalinist spirit," to reevaluate German patriots of the Napoleonic era as inspiring models for the SED's struggle for reunification.[77]

---

72. Otto Grotewohl, "'Deutscher Patriot sein heisst Freund der Sowjetunion sein.' Aus der Rede zur Feier des 71. Geburtstags Stalins, 21. Dezember 1950," in Grotewhol, *Im Kampf um die einige Deutsche Demokratische Republik. Reden und Aufsätze,* vol. 2, 1950–51 (East Berlin, 1974), 306–19.

73. Birgit Spies, "Aus einem unabgeschlossenen Kapitel," in Daniele Büchten and Anja Frey, *Im Irrgarten der deutschen Geschichte. Die Neue Wache 1818–1993* (Berlin, 1993), 40.

74. Gerd-H. Zuchold, "Der Abriß der Ruinen des Stadtschlosses und der Bauakademie in Ost-Berlin," *Deutschland Archiv,* 2 (1985): 178–207; and Peter Jochen Winters, "Wiederaufbau in Ost-Berlin," *Deutschland Archiv,* 12 (1985): 1304–19.

75. Cited in Lothar von Balluseck, "Kunstbauten und ihr Untergang," *SBZ-Archiv,* 3 (1952): 21.

76. Alexander Abusch, *Irrweg einer Nation,* 2d ed. (East Berlin, 1949), 232.

77. Fritz Lange, "Über die Notwendigkeit, aus der eigenen Geschichte zu lernen," ND, 1 July 1952.

Then at the Second Party Conference of the SED a month later, Ulbricht unveiled a militant strategy to reunify Germany under Socialist auspices, a "struggle for national liberation," as Grotewohl described it. The strategy called for among other things the "systematic construction of Socialism" in the GDR, "the toppling of the Bonn vassal-regime," and the transformation of the KVP into "national armed forces." To achieve these goals, especially the creation of "national armed forces," Ulbricht sought greater control over the German past. "Our scholarly historiography," Ulbricht told the Party, "shall acquaint the German people with the classical heritage, it shall tell of the revolutionary struggles and the liberation struggles. Historic personalities who have earned high honors in the struggle for the unity of Germany, such as Scharnhorst, Fichte, Gneisenau, Jahn, must be represented in their historical importance. . . . Our history professors are silent over the battle of the Teutoburg Forest, where the Teutons . . . beat the Romans because the Teutons were free people, whose personal prowess and bravery was greatly superior to that of the Roman troops. They were fighting for the liberation of their country."[78]

The Party Conference coincided with the opening of a "Museum for German History" in the *Zeughaus* in East Berlin, whose periodically revised exhibits combined dialectical materialism, German–Soviet friendship, and nationalist mythology, and which remained a must for school classes and Pioneer friendships until 1989. Ulbricht's comments led to a flood of books and pamphlets celebrating such German heroes as Martin Luther, Marshall Blücher, *Turnvater* Jahn, Ernst Moritz Arndt, General Scharnhorst, etc. Among young people it led to the introduction of "patriotic education" in the schools and youth organizations in the spirit of the "Socialist fatherland."[79]

This was not only cynical. Like Goethe, Schiller, and the other heroes of *Kultur,* the Prussian reformers and selected other German patriots were all digested into Communist mythology. Many Marxist-Leninists genuinely felt inspired by these figures and saw themselves as their successors. The idealists among them hoped to transmit this mythology to the entire German people.

One of the earliest applications of the myth of the Socialist fatherland was in the realm of sports. If the GDR sports establishment has been thoroughly discredited since 1989 by revelations of widespread doping practices and *Stasi* infiltration, it once enthralled millions of East Germans, even critics of the system. Mass sports were equally important in the Third

---

78. *Protokoll der Verhandlungen der II. Parteikonferenz der Sozialistischen Einheitspartei Deutschlands* (East Berlin, 1952), 122.

79. See Georg Michalewicz, *Zur Methodik der patriotischen Erziehung* (East Berlin, 1956).

Reich and the Soviet Union. Beyond their obvious "bread and circuses" value, they prepared young people for military service and demonstrated to the outside world the superiority of socialism. In the GDR, too, sports lay at the core of GDR political culture.[80]

The SED used sports to awaken feelings of national pride and to appeal for reunification under Socialism. Official histories traced the development of the "democratic" GDR sports tradition from primitive society through feudalism, *Turnvater* Jahn and the Wars of Liberation, down to the Social Democratic and Communist sports clubs of the early twentieth century. Speeches about sports always included an exposé of the imperialist heritage of the West German sports establishment. Historical consciousness, some ideologists claimed, gave both participants and spectators a sense of historic mission.[81] Of course, if many East Germans did shed tears upon hearing the GDR anthem played for Katarina Witt or some other Olympic gold medalist, this had less to do with a sense of historic mission than with a genuine national pride that had scarcely any other honest means of expression.

But as in every case of positive myth-building, love of the Socialist fatherland had its negative flip side. "Can there be such a love of fatherland without a burning hatred towards all enemies of our German Democratic Republic?" an SED editorial asked in 1955. "That is impossible. On the contrary, it is natural that a person who genuinely loves his native hearth [*Heimat*] and his people must hate the enemies of his people. This patriotic hatred of the enemies of our republic, who are also the enemies of all of Germany, is, in contrast to the destructive chauvinistic national hatred, a noble and necessary feeling. J. V. Stalin has taught all patriots the precept 'that one cannot defeat the enemy without having learned to hate him with one's entire soul.'"[82]

As so often in the history of GDR myth-building, the construction of the socialist fatherland was as much a matter of self-deception as decep-

---

80. Cf. Werner Rossade, *Sport und Kultur in der DDR* (Munich, 1987); Gunter Holzweissig, *Diplomatie im Trainingsanzug. Sport als politisches Instrument der DDR* (Munich, 1981), 21–24; David Childs, *The GDR: Moscow's German Ally,* 2d ed. (London, 1988), 183–88; Henry Krisch, *The German Democratic Republic: The Search for Identity* (Boulder, 1985), 165–68.

81. See "Grussadresse an die Gründungskonferenz des Deutschen Turn- und Sportbundes" of 27 April 1957, in *Dokumente der SED,* vol. 6, 234–35. On the history of "progressive sports," see Wolfgang Eichel, gen. ed., *Geschichte der Körperkultur in Deutschland,* 4 vols. (1967–73). On the role of Marxist-Leninist historical consciousness in sport education, see W. Riebel, "Zur Rolle des sportpolitischen und historischen Wissens bei der Erziehung zur sportlichen Einstellung," *Theorie und Praxis der Körperkultur* 3 (1969): 253–64.

82. "Aus dem Artikel: Wer ist ein Patriot?, Dezember 1955," in Hermann Weber, ed., *DDR. Dokumente der Deutschen Demokratischen Republik,* 223.

tion. The myth reached its apogee in 1967, when the SED launched a broad *"Vaterlanddiskussion"* designed to acquaint East Germans with the notion of a "Socialist German nation." During this campaign thousands of East Germans more or less spontaneously pledged themselves to their Socialist fatherland and signed petitions bearing the words "Everything binds us to our Socialist fatherland—nothing with imperialist West Germany." The campaign began with a letter written in this spirit to the *Leipziger Volkszeitung* by three students. In fact, the letter had been worked out in the FDJ's Central Council according to instructions from the SED's Politburo in preparation for the Party's Seventh Congress. It is impossible to know just how many East Germans actually supported the notion of a socialist fatherland at that time. But insiders attest that Ulbricht and other leaders were so taken in by the ostensible success of their own campaign that they themselves came to believe in the actual existence of this "Socialist German nation" and imagined that the population had finally turned its back on the Federal Republic forever.[83]

All of this makes perfect sense in theory. But as with the myth of *Kultur,* even if the intended content of the Socialist fatherland myth was "progressive" and "revolutionary," its public expression was patterned after the nationalist imagery of earlier regimes. For the pragmatists (such as Walter Ulbricht), these myths had more immediate applications. Aside from its obvious function as an alibi for the SED's subordination to the USSR, the main idea behind this new "Schlageter course" was to attract both eastern and western nationalists to the SED's cause. The latter's struggle against Konrad Adenauer's conservative Christian Democratic government is obvious enough. But the SED was also forced to compete with Erich Ollenhauer's Social Democrats. Until its Bad Godesberg Program of 1959, the SPD proclaimed itself to be at once a Marxist and an uncompromisingly anticommunist and anti-Soviet party. Like the CDU, it wrapped itself in the flag and denounced the Ulbricht regime as totalitarian. But, like the SED, it opposed German rearmament and the European Defense Community. Thus, paradox upon paradox, SED ideologists felt compelled to surpass both the CDU and the SPD in their nationalistic rhetoric and symbolism, while at all times anchoring both with Marxist and pro-Soviet arguments.

But there is no evidence that many people in the West were listening. For as passionately as the SED protested France's temporary occupation of the Saarland, it had long since lost what few patriotic credentials it

---

83. Gerhard Naumann and Eckhard Trümpler, *Der Flop mit der DDR-Nation 1971. Zwischen Abschied von der Idee der Konföderation und Illusion von der Herausbildung einer sozialistischen deutschen Nation* (Berlin, 1991), 25–26.

might once have had among West Germans by its acquiescence in the permanent loss of Silesia and East Prussia to Poland and the Soviet Union.[84] Despite the "progressive" notions behind it, the Socialist fatherland quickly degenerated into a domestic militarist slogan and remained that way until 1989. Soon the entire GDR propaganda apparatus was reminding citizens to fulfill their "patriotic duties," especially voluntary military service on the inner German border, which with the exception of Berlin had been sealed off in 1952. The year 1955 was devoted to "patriotic education" and military training in the youth organization. It combined a vigorous enlistment campaign for the KVP with an anti-*Bundeswehr* campaign aimed at West German youth.[85] It coincided with the founding of the Warsaw Pact in that year, as we have already seen in regard to the SED's use of the Schiller myth in chapter 2. In that same year, the newly formed NVA (National People's Army) clad its soldiers in gray *Wehrmacht*-style uniforms, taught them to march the Prussian goose step, and laid claim to an alleged progressive German military tradition running from the Peasant War all the way to the GDR. Even if the NVA named its officers' academy after Friedrich Engels, it named its highest medal after General von Scharnhorst.[86] The FDJ carried through an enlistment campaign called "The fatherland is calling! Defend the Socialist republic!" immediately following the construction of the Berlin Wall in August 1961. The introduction of conscription a year later (which had been impracticable with an open border) was also presented as a patriotic act.

"Das Volk steht auf, der Sturm bricht los"

The most dramatic example of the SED's adoption and adaptation of bourgeois nationalist myths is the cult developed around the 1813 War of Liberation and especially the Leipzig Battle of the Peoples (*Völkerschlacht*), whose 140th anniversary was celebrated in October 1953.[87] Ulbricht gave special emphasis to the War of Liberation in his speech at the Second Party Conference in 1952.[88] Ulbricht's exploitation of the events of 1813 is particularly disturbing when one recalls that Joseph Goebbels had done exactly the same thing only nine years earlier. At the conclusion of his

84. Alan Nothnagle, "Die Oder-Neiße-Grenze und die Politik der SED," in Helga Schultz and Alan Nothnagle, eds., *Grenze der Hoffnung. Geschichte und Perspektiven der Grenzregion an der Oder* (Potsdam, 1996), 22–41.

85. For a detailed review of the relevant publications of this year, Heinz Kersten, "Die 'patriotische Erziehung' der Sowjetzonen-Jugend," *SBZ-Archiv* 6 (1955): 120–26.

86. See Thomas M. Forster, *Die NVA* (Cologne, 1979), 284–96.

87. For an extended propagandistic treatment of the War of Liberation, Fritz Lange, *Die Volkserhebung von 1813* (East Berlin, 1952).

88. *Protokoll der Verhandlungen der II. Parteikonferenz,* 122–23.

"total war speech" at the Berlin *Sportpalast* in February 1943, Goebbels evoked the War of Liberation and Ernst Moritz Arndt's words, "*Volk, steh' auf! Sturm, brich los!*" (People arise! Storm break loose!). The Nazis later organized a popular militia known as the "*Volkssturm*" in the tradition of the War of Liberation and ordered the population to resist the Allies to the end, just as the Prussian city of Kolberg had held out to the end against Napoleon in 1807. Goebbels actually commissioned an elaborate color film depicting Kolberg's heroic resistance and ordered copies of it airdropped into besieged "fortress cities" in early 1945. In the film, the city is shot to bits by Napoleon's armies, but at the end the armed populace floods into the streets to fight the French in 1813, singing a musical version of "*Das Volk steht auf, der Sturm bricht los!*"[89]

Although most older East Germans probably remembered Goebbels's myth-building tactics, the SED's version of "*Volk steh' auf*" derived primarily from Soviet historical propaganda during World War II. As early as 1938, the Eisenstein film *Alexander Nevsky* had dramatically portrayed the Soviet response to a potential Nazi invasion in the guise of Prince Alexander's victory over the Teutonic knights in 1242.[90] In his national radio address following the German invasion in June 1941, Joseph Stalin repeatedly evoked the Napoleonic invasion of 1812 and referred to the new war as the "Great Patriotic War" and a "war of liberation."[91] Soviet propaganda used the memory of that great Russian victory throughout the war. After reaching Silesia and the March of Brandenburg, Red Army propagandists recalled the Seven Years' War as well, during which Russian troops had captured Berlin. In April 1945, the troops surrounding Berlin were air-dropped a large ceremonial key to the city, engraved "1760" on one side, "1945" on the other.[92]

The "National Committee Free Germany" (NKFD) was based upon the myth of the "Great Patriotic War" and the "War of Liberation." It evoked the historic meeting at Tauroggen in December 1812, at which General von Yorck and others went over the head of the Prussian king and signed an alliance with Russia (in fact, a descendant of Yorck later took part in the abortive officers' plot on Hitler's life in July 1944). The founding ceremony in Moscow in July 1943 took place beneath black-white-red Prussian banners, as Pieck, Becher, and other participants evoked the memories of Baron vom Stein, Ernst Moritz Arndt, General

89. Veit Harlan, dir., *Kolberg,* UfA 1945.
90. Sergei Eisenstein, dir. *Alexander Nevsky,* Mosfilm, 1938.
91. Josef Stalin, "Rundfunkrede am 3. Juli 1941," in Stalin, *Über den Grossen Vaterländischen Krieg der Sowjetunion* (East Berlin, 1951), 1–15.
92. Christopher Duffy, *Red Storm on the Reich. The Soviet March on Germany, 1945* (New York, 1991), 291–92.

von Clausewitz, Yorck, and others. "Like them we shall stake all our strength and also our lives to do everything that unleashes the freedom struggle of our people and hurries Hitler's downfall."[93] At the founding of the "League of German Officers" in September the participants made much of the fact that a descendant of Yorck's adjutant von Seydlitz had announced the organization's founding to the world.[94] Writing for the organization's magazine *Freies Deutschland* in April 1944, none other than Jürgen Kuczynski quoted the nationalist writer Ernst Moritz Arndt to contrast the honor of the German soldier fighting for Napoleon (i.e., for Hitler) with the "true soldier's honor," by which the German soldier feels that "he was a German man before he knew of German kings and princes; . . . he felt deeply and intensely: the land and the people should be immortal and eternal, but the lords and princes with their honors and disgraces are transitory."[95]

The SED's new national course after 1952 brought forth a flood of nationalist history books, including a new national history textbook in which the War of Liberation/Great Patriotic War of 1813 and the Prussian/Russian alliance displaced the French Revolution as the turning point of pre-1917 history. The Napoleonic era was depicted as the mirror image of the cold war. That these parallels were more than mere coincidence is proven by the detailed studies and directives that preceded the book. Napoleon was no longer the equivalent of Hitler, but bore a striking similarity to the U.S. government, and the "national traitors" of the Confederation of the Rhine were depicted as forerunners of the Adenauer government of the Federal Republic. The anti-Napoleonic "German Legion" was defined as a forerunner of the NKFD, and the old Prussian *Landsturm* (reserve army) prophetically pointed to "the need for national defense," meaning the KVP, which was rapidly expanding at this time. The text emphasized that the reformers vom Stein, Hardenberg, Gneisenau, and so on "were supported by the masses," strongly implying that they were early-nineteenth-century versions of Ulbricht, Pieck, Grotewohl, and associates. The central theme of this section was that German–Russian friendship was the permanent basis of peace and prosperity. The lesson of history was clear: "Russian patriotism brought about the end of the Napoleonic foreign rule on German soil and opened for the German

---

93. "Das Nationalkommittee Freies Deutschland. Manifest und Protokoll der Gründungstagung," July 1943, SAPMO BArch NL 36/575 Bl. 1 (11).

94. "Die Gründung des Bundes Deutscher Offiziere, Protokoll der Gründungstagung," September 1943, SAPMO BArch NL 36/575, Bl. 2 (63).

95. Jürgen Kuczynski, "Kampf um die deutsche Armee 1812," *Freies Deutschland,* April 1944, 20–21.

people, as for all other peoples, the way to national independence and to peace."[96]

In 1953 the FDJ conducted special *Heimabende* dedicated to the War of Liberation and its cold war applications. The official FDJ agitation materials were accompanied by the texts and music to such traditional patriotic songs as *"Lützows wilde verwegene Jagd"* and *"Der Gott, der Eisen wachsen liess."*[97] One *Heimabend* pamphlet, actually bearing the ominous title *"Das Volk steht auf, der Sturm bricht los,"* concluded with the words:[98]

> How hard it was for the patriots of those days! Back then their ally was tsarist Russia, whose ruling house for reasons of self-preservation was forced to support the policies of the European ruling houses. Today our ally in the struggle for the unity of our fatherland is the great Soviet Union.

The War of Liberation myth-building culminated in 1953 in two mass youth events. The first of these was the traditional *Wartburgfest,* commemorating the anniversary of the meeting of some 500 *Burschenschaft* members and professors drawn from across Germany at the Wartburg Castle on 18 and 19 October 1817. The original *Wartburgfest* had been called to celebrate both the three hundredth anniversary of the Reformation and the fourth anniversary of the Leipzig *Völkerschlacht,* and was marked by speeches calling for the unity and freedom of Germany and denouncing the Metternich restoration. It concluded with the burning of some thirty books, including the works of conservative authors and the *Code Napoleon,* together with a Prussian cavalryman's corset, a pigtail (the symbol of absolutism), and an Austrian whipping cane.[99] This deeply symbolic, if contradictory, event came to stand for German freedom and nationalism, and as such it was repeated annually from the Wilhelmine era through the Third Reich by German fraternity members.

The *Wartburgfest* of 1953 was painstakingly planned by both the University of Jena and the FDJ's Central Council. Some 2,000 students from Jena attended, joined by about 200 West German students and several hundred delegates from other universities and from nearby factories. The

---

96. "Ablage, Lehrbuch Geschichte des deutschen Volkes. Die Geschichte des deutschen Volkes von 1789–1815," SAPMO BArch IV 2/904/106, Bl. 61–67.

97. "Lützows wilde verwegene Jagd," *Heimabendreihe der FDJ* 21 (1951).

98. "Das Volk steht auf, der Sturm bricht los," *Heimabendreihe der FDJ* 23 (1953), 46.

99. "Wartburgfest," in Gerhard Taddey, ed., *Lexikon der deutschen Geschichte,* 2d ed. (Stuttgart, 1983), 1296–97.

event included sporting and cultural activities and speeches demanding a peace treaty, unification, and the pullout of U.S. troops from West Germany. It culminated in a torchlight parade past the *Burschenschaft* monument. The climax of the event was originally to have consisted of "the burning of the whipping cane, the pigtail, the Code of the Prussian *Gendarmerie,* a T-shirt, and an *Ami* necktie."[100] In the end, the participants settled for the burning of an interzonal barrier, symbolizing the division of Germany now inflicted by the new Metternich restoration, namely the Adenauer government. They then lit a giant bonfire ("flames of freedom") that could be seen from West German territory.[101] The next morning the participants boarded buses to travel to Leipzig to take part in the celebration of the 140th anniversary of the *Völkerschlacht.*

The enormous Leipzig *Völkerschlachtdenkmal* was built between 1894 and 1913. It had been designed by Bruno Schmitz, the architect who had also designed the Kyffhäuser monument.[102] Ninety-one meters high, in size and form reminiscent of the Egyptian pyramids, with its giant stone warriors, its sacred crypt, its observation platform overlooking the entire landscape, its giant image of the Archangel Michael beneath the words "God with us," it was by any standards the most elaborate of all German national monuments and a precursor to the similarly apocalyptic Treptow Park memorial. It was unveiled on 18 October 1913 in an elaborate ceremony under the motto "Let us fight, bleed, and die for Germany's unity and power."[103] The vast reflecting pool and landscaped grounds around it were designed to make it into the center of nationalist and militarist ceremonies. While it was indeed used in such ceremonies during the Empire and especially the Third Reich, it is ironic that the monument only became the central national monument of (eastern) Germany under the SED regime.

The Leipzig monument had special significance for the German youth movement as a whole, although it is unlikely that most FDJ members were aware of this. In 1913 several *Wandervogel* groups and other members of the middle-class German youth movement had organized a spectacular youth festival to celebrate the anniversary of the battle and at the same time to protest the hollow nationalism represented by the new monument

---

100. "Zum Protokoll 74/IV/53 Anlage 2," JA IzJ, A. 2.501.

101. "Flammen der Freiheit leuchteten weit ins deutsche Land. Zum Wartburgfest der deutschen Studenten in Eisenach," JW 19 October 1953.

102. On the history and varying uses of the *Völkerschlachtdenkmal,* see Steffen Poser, "Das Leipziger Völkerschlachtdenkmal" (master's thesis, Humboldt-Universität Berlin, 1992). See also George Mosse, *The Nationalization of the Masses. Political Symbolism and Mass Movements in Germany from the Napoleonic Wars through the Third Reich* (New York, 1975), 64–67.

103. Cited in Mosse, 66.

and the official festivities—"that patriotism which we reject," as they put it.[104] Instead of traveling to Leipzig, several thousand young people met on the Hohe Meissner mountain near Kassel on 13 October. After long debates a new united youth movement was formed under the name *Freideutsche Jugend* (Free German Youth). This short-lived organization had no connection to the later FDJ, even though both laid claim to German youth. Amid folk dances and theatrical productions, the participants adopted the so-called Meissner formula, whereby *"Freideutsche Jugend, on their own initiative, under their own responsibility, and with inner sincerity, are determined independently to shape their own lives."*[105] This was a bittersweet moment in the history of the German youth movement, since less than a year later many of the participants lay dead on the battlefields of France and Russia.

Forty years later, thousands of Free German Youth delegates did indeed travel to Leipzig to participate as the main players in the GDR's national *Völkerschlacht* ceremony. To be sure, the Hohe Meissner was in the West, and hence the reunion that took place there in late October included only western youth groups. It is interesting to imagine how the FDJ might have used the Hohe Meissner if it had had the chance.

The FDJ's Central Committee began preparing youth for the "Meeting of Young Patriots" in Leipzig several months in advance with a series of articles in the youth press promoting Socialist patriotism and raising interest in dozens of events taking place throughout the GDR marking individual steps leading to the great battle.[106] The *Völkerschlacht* ceremony itself was sponsored by the district committee of the National Front in association with the Leipzig city council and the Central Council of the FDJ.[107] It coincided with a convention in Leipzig of the "National Democratic Party" (NDPD), an SED block party made up of former Nazis and NKFD members who had pledged themselves to Socialism and to the Soviet Union. The ceremony thus was designed to provide a boost for the NDPD as well as for the SED, which was still recovering from the shocks of Stalin's death in March and the June workers' uprising (which was

104. *Freideutsche Jugend. Zur Jahrhundertfeier auf dem Hohen Meissner 1913* (Jena, 1913), 5.

105. "Die Meissner-Formel," in Werner Kindt, ed., *Dokumentation der Jugendbewegung,* vol. 2: *Die Wandervogelzeit* (Düsseldorf-Cologne, 1968), 495–96.

106. See, for example, "140. Jahrestag der Leipziger Völkerschlacht und was die Leitungen der FDJ dazu tun können," JG 18/1953, 24–25; Jürgen Demloff, "Die Pflege der fortschrittlichen und freiheitlichen Traditionen unseres Volkes—eine Herzenssache der FDJ," JG 19 (1953): 3–4; Heinz Helmert, "Die Völkerschlacht bei Leipzig—Symbol der deutsch-russischen Freundschaft," ibid., 8–9.

107. "Plan zur Vorbereitung und Durchführung der 140-Jahresfeier der nationalen Befreiungskämpfe 1813 in Leipzig," StvVR 4141, Bl. 77.

bloodily suppressed by Soviet troops), the stalemate in Korea, and the shaky beginnings of Ulbricht's conciliatory "New Course" of economic and social development. The celebration was also aimed at western youths and adults, especially at former Nazis and war veterans whom the SED hoped to attract to its cause and whose memories of the Goebbels campaign of 1943 were still fresh.

While there was less talk of "fighting, bleeding, and dying" this time, the motto of the new celebration was no less patriotic than the imperial celebration forty years earlier. It was a quotation from the Prussian reformer Baron vom Stein:[108]

> I have only one fatherland, which is Germany, and since I have always belonged to it and to no particular part of it, I am thus also devoted to it with all my heart and not to any one part of it.
>
> It is my wish that Germany may become great and strong, in order to regain its sovereignty, independence, and nationality. That is in the interest of the nation and of all of Europe.
>
> My confession of faith is unity.

The "Slogan of Leipzig Youth" was much more to the point: "In 1813 our fathers broke the Napoleonic occupation—the German people must topple Adenauer in order to save the nation."[109]

Ideological preparations for the ceremony began many weeks in advance, and a propaganda commission set up by the Leipzig National Front began spreading a *parteilich* view of the *Völkerschlacht* throughout the population, especially young people in the public and vocational schools. "The commission sees its task," its members stated, "in bringing the revolutionary traditions of our city from the days of the national liberation struggle of 1813 closer to the masses of the population with the goal of deepening German–Soviet friendship on the basis of the example of the German–Russian alliance, in highlighting the strength of the people in the Wars of Liberation as a model for the national struggle for the reunification of Germany, and thus in the education of the population to militant patriotism."[110] This was not as easy as the commission had hoped. As an FDJ delegate told the celebration's organizing committee on 9 October, "in the majority of the [propaganda] missions it was not the question of the one hundred fortieth anniversary of the Leipzig *Völkerschlacht* [which concerned young people], but rather day-to-day questions, such as

---

108. Motto of celebration, StvVR 4142 (n.p.).

109. Demloff, 4.

110. "Arbeitsplan der Schulungs- und Aufklärungsgruppe für die 140. Jahresfeier der Völkerschlacht bei Leipzig," 23 September 1953, StvVR 4142, Bl. 69.

the lowering of store prices, the realization of the New Course, etc." Nevertheless, FDJ members generally accepted the event and "aggressively countered the question of why such a celebration should take place now, [since it] had been celebrated already in 1913 by the former imperial government and in 1938 by the Fascists."[111]

The first event was the formation of a "Youth Honor Guard" to accompany the individual ceremonies. On 15 October FDJ members, KVP soldiers, "and the friends from the Soviet Army" met at a KVP installation and carried out joint military exercises.[112] At the same time last-minute preparations were being made for an exhibition on the *Völkerschlacht*. A confidential statement of the Party's ideological directives has been preserved. They are interesting since they reflect the awkwardness of the SED's position at this time and the mixed messages the entire event sent to East German youth. While major emphasis was given to German–Soviet friendship and the commemoration of the German–Russian dead of the Napoleonic era (whereby the Russians, it was made clear, suffered the greatest losses), the exhibition was also to point to the armistice in Korea as an example of peaceful conflict resolution. Thus the actual fighting of the *Völkerschlacht* was not to be emphasized. Moreover, since the beginning of the New Course "a high value is placed on not using texts which address the mind and are read very little. Instead, in the exhibition emotional values should be created which serve the struggle for unity and the patriotic education of youth." These "emotional values" were evoked by, among other things, pictures arousing reverence for the Russian/Soviet dead and, in the room devoted to the Napoleonic invasion of Moscow in 1812, gloomy visual effects meant to remind visitors that "Every military stroll to Moscow ends in a catastrophe."[113]

The exhibition was formally opened in a ceremony on 16 October. This was preceded by a formal meeting in the Leipzig city hall, during which an FDJ official addressed the assembled dignitaries and youth friends on the question of patriotism.[114]

> This spirit of glowing patriotism has at all times inspired the best representatives of our people. In this spirit fought such heroes as Herman

---

111. "Protokoll über die 3. Arbeitsbesprechung des Arbeitsausschusses zur Vorbereitung der 140sten Wiederkehr der Völkerschlacht bei Leipzig," 9 October 1953, StvVR 4141, Bl. 1.

112. "Protokoll über die Sitzung des Komitees zur Vorbereitung der 140-Jahres-Feier des nationalen Befreiungskampfes 1813," 14 October 1953, Bl. 2.

113. "Expose der Ausstellung 'Die Völkerschlacht bei Leipzig 1813–1953,'" StvVR 4141, Bl. 136–37.

114. Speech, no title, 16 October 1953, StvVR 4142 (n.p.).

the German, who defeated the Romans, [and] Thomas Müntzer, the great revolutionary of the Peasant's War. This spirit inspired Lessing, Heine, Schiller, Goethe, Beethoven, Schubert, Mozart, Wagner and many other outstanding personalities in the area of art and science. In this spirit fought the greatest sons of the German people, Karl Marx and Friedrich Engels; the fervid labor leaders and patriots August Bebel, Karl Liebknecht, Rosa Luxemburg, and Ernst Thälmann fought untiringly for the cause of our nation. *Today German youth is following the greatest patriots of our present, Comrades Otto Grotewohl, Walter Ulbricht, and at their head, our beloved President Wilhelm Pieck.* (emphasis added)

What followed was not a new Meissner Formula, but the claim that "the great national traditions are for us a commitment."[115] This commitment entailed nine "pledges of German youth," including the pledge "to spare no effort in the education of the youth of all Germany in the spirit of the great patriots of our people, in the spirit of the national resistance of 1813"; "to be watchful against all enemies and to hate deeply the imperialist warmongers such as Adenauer, Ollenhauer, Krupp, Thyssen and consorts"; "to demonstrate a high work ethic in the fulfillment of our Plans"; "to deepen within youth the friendship toward the Socialist Soviet Union, the bulwark of peace in the entire world," and so forth.[116]

The main ceremonies took place on 17 and 18 October. In the early afternoon of 17 October, the "Youth Honor Guard" assembled at the Stalin monument and marched from there to Leipzig's Russian Church, which is located on the former battlefield. There the honor guard and the spectators conducted a memorial ceremony for the twenty-two thousand Russian soldiers who fell during the battle. Then they marched to the *Völkerschlachtdenkmal* for a brief preliminary ceremony. This was followed by a "great friendship meeting" of seventeen thousand FDJ members, Komsomol delegates, and KVP soldiers, two hundred selected West German students, and the Leipzig population in four halls of the Leipzig fairgrounds. The festivities continued until ten o'clock with a German–Soviet cultural program. At eight o'clock, young people had the option of going into any of five Leipzig movie theaters, all of which were showing the Soviet film "*Kutusov,*" based on the Soviet interpretation of the battle, along with a lecture by the DSF. The first day closed with an enormous fireworks display on the grounds of the *Völkerschlachtdenkmal.*[117]

115. Ibid.
116. Ibid.
117. "Plan zur Vorbereitung und Durchführung," Bl. 78.

The next morning, the official parade assembled itself on the Leipzig *Marx-Engels-Platz* and set off for the *Völkerschlachtdenkmal*. Three hundred thousand people crowded onto the monument's grounds, including seventy thousand young people, most of them in FDJ uniform. The demonstration at the monument began with fanfares and fireworks, followed by the marching in of delegations bearing German, Soviet, and FDJ flags, along with a collection of consecrated FDJ "assault banners." A band played the FDJ march, "Blue flags to Berlin." Then came the triumphal entry of some four hundred costumed young people: mounted Prussian and Russian officers, *Landwehr* soldiers on foot, regular Austrian, Prussian, Swedish, and Saxon soldiers, and scores of cheering costumed common people representing the different nationalities involved. As they entered the monument's grounds, an FDJ "mass chorus" standing on bleachers alternately intoned *"Lützows wilde verwegene Jagd"* and "The Song of German–Soviet Friendship." Thousands of white doves were released.[118]

Thereupon followed a set of patriotic speeches by Erich Mückenberger of the Central Committee of the SED, the historian Ernst Engelberg, and the ideologist Fritz Lange. Finally, FDJ chairman Erich Honecker and Werner Lamberz of the FDJ's Central Council laid a wreath in the monument's crypt in the name of German youth. The event closed with the singing of the old revolutionary song *"Brüder zur Sonne, zur Freiheit!"*[119]

That afternoon the participants withdrew to attend a vast public festival on the *Marx-Engels-Platz* "and in all districts of the city." The celebration closed that evening with "dancing in all the halls of Leipzig."[120]

Tens of thousands of young people (including several hundred West Germans) participated in this, the first of many similar *Völkerschlacht* ceremonies, and hundreds of thousands more heard all about it in FDJ and Pioneer meetings, at school, in the newsreels, and in the youth press. But despite the intense effort and great expense the SED and the National Front lavished on the event, there is no evidence that it had much effect. In fact, according to internal reports, hundreds of FDJ members wandered off from the monument in the middle of the speeches. The organizing committee explained this away in typical fashion by pointing to technical factors such as insufficient loudspeakers, making the speeches inaudible, and

---

118. "Kulturkommission, Arbeitsgruppe zur Durchführung aller Massnahmen und Veranstaltungen zur 140. Wiederkehr der Völkerschlacht bei Leipzig, 16. bis 18. Oktober 1953," StvVR 4141 (n.p.).

119. "Grosskundgebung am Fusse des Völkerschlachtdenkmals," JW 19 October 1953.

120. "Plan zur Vorbereitung und Durchführung," Bl. 78.

the fact that hundreds of FDJ members had arrived by the night train and were simply exhausted after marching around all day.[121]

But another reason might lie in the ambivalence of this event. Was the SED, like Goebbels ten years earlier, really preparing youth for total war? Or was the militant rhetoric only meant to persuade young men to join the KVP, work harder to build socialism, develop a positive attitude toward the Soviet Union, and become more *parteilich* generally? Just what storm, if any, was supposed to break loose? Even for the most *parteilich* young people the symbolism of this event must have seemed a bit hollow. To be sure, thousands of young men did join the KVP and the later NVA, and obediently stood guard against their own people on the inner German border. They did this without benefit of conscription and for a combination of pragmatic and idealistic reasons. But the SED was clearly hedging its bets, and that was an understandable but hardly inspiring thing to do in that turbulent year. Friends of the Soviet Union or not, patriots or not, in 1953 some four hundred thousand East Germans, most of them young people, fled to the West.[122] This mass escape gave a new and ironic twist to the slogan: *"Das Volk steht auf, der Sturm bricht los."*

The *Völkerschlacht* ceremony of 1953 remained the model for patriotic ceremonies until 1989. If the historical costumes were occasionally still brought out for special events, they were soon outnumbered by the Prussian gray uniforms of the NVA, as young soldiers swore their loyalty oaths to the Socialist fatherland.

The myth of the Socialist fatherland changed somewhat with Ulbricht's fall from grace (which came about because of his growing independence toward the CPSU). In the 1970s the Honecker regime abandoned the hope of reunification in the near future and began a policy of "demarcation" from the Federal Republic. This went along with a general policy of peaceful coexistence and near-normal relations between the two states. Exactly thirty years after Ulbricht's nationalistic speech at the Third Party Conference, Honecker formally declared the GDR to be a "Socialist German nation," as opposed to the doomed "bourgeois German nation" in the West. In this way he was building on Ulbricht's notion first floated during the *Vaterlanddiskussion* in 1967. According to Honecker, the German nation had never been incorporated into a nation-state until Bismarck, a tool of the reactionary Junker class and finance capital, brutally created the German empire against the will of the people. After leading their people into two disastrous world wars, those reac-

---

121. Review report, no title, StvVR 4142, Bl. 158.
122. Hermann Weber, *DDR. Grundriss der Geschichte 1945–1990* (Hannover, 1991), 295.

tionary classes had "lost the right to lead the nation." From this Honecker concluded that "the working class alone was called upon to renew the nation on a democratic basis and to guarantee its unity in an anti-Fascist/democratic state." Historians began arguing that "the Socialist German nation that is evolving in the GDR is a product of the entirety of German history. Its origins reach back centuries; it is linked to the traditions of the progressive classes, in particular the working class, and is allied with the progressive traditions of all nations."[123]

The practical consequences of this new line were first the abandonment of all unity rhetoric. In the 1970s the SED actually attempted to introduce a major German spelling reform that would have been valid only within the borders of the GDR. This was prevented only through the intervention of the Soviet government, which did not want to have to deal with two German languages.[124] Much more spectacular was the way in which the SED expanded its historical mythology: in 1980 Frederick the Great's statue was returned to its original location on the Unter den Linden boulevard; an elaborate "Luther Year" was proclaimed in 1983, celebrating Luther's progressive features and contributions to the idea of the German nation; the Great Elector was honored in an exhibition in Potsdam; and even Bismarck, the "tool of the reactionary Junker class," was celebrated as a "progressive figure" in a biography by the SED historian Ernst Engelberg.[125] Party historians had actually begun reprocessing the GDR's "feudal heritage" under the Holy Roman Emperors of the Middle Ages when they suddenly found themselves unemployed in 1989–90, and it is intriguing to imagine just how far this all might have gone had the SED been able to maintain its power a few years longer.[126]

This new historical policy was based on an innovation of Marxist-Leninist theory in the GDR, which separated past figures into "*Erbe*" (heritage) and "*Tradition.*" *Erbe* referred to figures who did not necessarily embody progressive values, but who nonetheless were important historical figures and hence contributed indirectly to the creation of the GDR (e.g., Frederick, Bismarck, etc.). As such they were worthy of official recogni-

---

123. Alfred Loesdau, "German History and National Identity in the GDR," in Margy Gerber, ed., *Studies in GDR Culture and Society* 7 (1987), 213.

124. Wolfgang Thierse, *"Sprich, damit ich dich sehe". Über die Sensibilität beim Sprechen unter den politischen Bedingungen der DDR* (Berlin, 1993), 4.

125. Ernst Engelberg, *Bismarck. Urpreusse und Reichsgründer* (East and West Berlin, 1985).

126. If, indeed, it could have gone any longer at all. According to the Dutch historian Hans Brinks, by delving deeper and deeper into the German past to cover up the GDR's deficits in the present, the historians were in fact preparing the way for German reunification. See Hans Brinks, *Die DDR-Geschichtsschreibung auf dem Weg zur deutschen Einheit* (Frankfurt am Main, 1992).

tion. *Tradition* meant revolutionary and progressive figures like Thomas Müntzer and Ernst Thälmann, who directly contributed to the creation of the GDR and who could be celebrated without restrictions.[127]

Although West Germans have made a lot out of this seemingly schizophrenic view of the past, Honecker's new historical line was merely a new edition of Ulbricht's strategy of 1952 adapted to the times. The attention given to Frederick the Great and Bismarck was, of course, new, but the SED had praised Martin Luther's "progressive" qualities in the early 1950s. The SED under Ulbricht's leadership had also promoted "Prussian virtues" without calling them by name. The goose-stepping honor guard had been installed on Unter den Linden in 1962, and Prussian march music had been part of the NVA's repertoire since the mid-1950s. A big part of Honecker's policies was obviously motivated by tourism revenue (the Luther Year alone attracted hundreds of thousands of Western visitors), but beyond that the difference was mainly one of perspective: if Ulbricht was attempting to awaken German pride in the East and West and to coopt it for the SED in a future united socialist Germany, Honecker hoped to awaken pride in the East alone and coopt it to stabilize his regime at home and win it recognition abroad. Beyond its touristic and militaristic applications, Honecker's embrace of Germany's entire historical pantheon was really just another expression of the *Kultur* myth.

Honecker's version of the Socialist fatherland was farcical in many ways, but it had a deadly serious core that only became visible after 1989. According to Warsaw Pact documents discovered in the GDR's military headquarters in Strausberg, the Soviet Union—despite all its peaceful rhetoric—did indeed have detailed plans for the invasion of Western Europe in the event of an East–West war. After the Soviets had obliterated NATO forces with nuclear and chemical weapons, the NVA was designated to take the lead in securing what was left of the Federal Republic and driving forward through French territory to the Pyrenees. Temporary bridges had been prepared for use in crossing the Rhine and the Danube. Road signs, some of them printed in Flemish, were ready for use. Special occupation commissars had already been selected from the ranks of the SED. Internment camps for thousands of foreign and domestic prisoners were planned to the last detail. The GDR's defense ministry under Heinz Kessler had already printed the sum of 4.9 billion "occupation Marks" with which to pay and supply the army. Shoulder boards for the uniforms of NVA field marshals were waiting in storage, as were thousands of medals minted for the first NVA soldiers to cross the Rhine. A special set

---

127. The standard reference on this topic is Helmut Meier and Walter Schmidt, eds., *Erbe und Tradition in der DDR. Die Diskussion der Historiker* (Cologne, 1989).

of eight thousand "Blücher medals," named after the Prussian hero of the War of Liberation, had been readied for other acts of bravery.[128] Symbolically at least, *"Volk steh' auf, Sturm brich los"* had gone full circle back to the Berlin *Sportpalast.*

To be sure, NATO had been making plans as well. They were, however, based upon a defensive strategy. Thus while the United States was prepared to use nuclear weapons to halt a Soviet offensive in Europe, it had no plans to march to Moscow à la Napoleon. The fact remains, of course, that both sides were prepared to risk utter destruction. This difference is largely one of myth: the Warsaw Pact's revised "Battle of the Peoples" vs. NATO's "Armageddon."

But whether friends of the Soviet Union or not, it is hard to imagine East Germans committing mass suicide in this way. Was all of this perhaps just another facet of GDR myth-building? Was it really just another example of mutual deception—the soldiers deceiving their officers, the officers deceiving the Party hierarchy, the Party hierarchy deceiving the Kremlin, the Kremlin deceiving the West? Maybe, but it is one of the great miracles of the twentieth century that we never had to find out for sure.

Flame of the Revolution

As we have seen, the personality cult around Stalin developed after 1957 into a technology cult based on the impressive Soviet space program and the achievements of modern Soviet weaponry. Young Pioneers and FDJ members followed the progress of Soviet spacecraft and wore badges and patches symbolizing the various missions on their uniforms. This went on alongside the standard Mussorgsky concerts, folklore groups, and Pushkin evenings sponsored by the DSF. But the SED was always at a disadvantage compared to the Federal Republic, whose American allies/ occupiers were rapidly catching up in the "space race" and whose *Kultur-barbarei* was wildly popular among young people. In 1961 the SED began propagating Khrushchev's vision of an imminent socialist victory. According to the speeches at the Twenty-Second Congress of the CPSU, by 1970 the Soviet Union would surpass the United States "in material and consumer goods for the entire population." By 1980 the Soviet Union was

---

128. Among the more thorough depictions of this scenario are Der Bundesminister der Verteidigung, ed., *Militärische Planungen des Warschauer Paktes in Zentraleuroppa. Eine Studie* (Bonn, 1992); Otto Wenzel, "Die geplante Wiedervereinigung unter kommunistischem Vorzeichen," *Politische Studien* No. 324, 1992. For a brief and succinct description of the SED's plans for the Federal Republic and especially West Berlin, see Otto Wenzel, "Der Tag X. Wie West-Berlin erobert wurde," DA 5/1993, 1360–71. For a broader view of the Warsaw Pact's overall strategy, see "The Secret Plan for World War III," *Time* (4 July 1994).

to have "erected the material-technical basis of Communism," by which time there would be a surplus of goods. By 1980 as well, the Soviet Union would be able to provide free mass transit, free restaurant food, free rent, free utilities, free education and medical care, and free school clothing for children. At the same time, the Soviet Union would be the country with the shortest work week, the highest wages, and the longest vacations.[129]

But this vision never seems to have captured the popular imagination, and it did not last long in any case. The comparatively uninspiring quality of Soviet leaders from Khrushchev through Chernenko demanded increasing reliance on emotional symbols: the godlike Lenin, the romanticism of the Great Socialist October Revolution, the transcendence of the Liberation, the tantalizing vision of the victorious Communist society. This vision could not be transmitted in Marxist-Leninist indoctrination sessions alone. Leonid Brezhnev somehow did not quite embody it.

The fiftieth anniversary of the October Revolution in 1967 provided the FDJ with an opportunity to put German–Soviet friendship back on track. The "Torch of Friendship" campaign was an FDJ–Komsomol coproduction linked to Great Socialist October Revolution propaganda campaigns already taking place in both organizations. It was the most elaborate mass event in FDJ history. It was formally announced in a resolution of the secretariat of the Central Council on 22 August 1967. The resolution spelled out the precise meaning of the torch: it was a "*symbol* of the triumph of Marxism-Leninism and of the life force of the friendship between the peoples of the USSR and the GDR" and a "*thought* of the concerted and unshakeable struggle against militarism and imperialism— for peace, democracy and Socialism/Communism." Furthermore, the campaign "*mobilizes* all the forces of the organization, is *linked* to the 'Prove Ourselves Worthy of the Revolutionary Fighters [Campaign],' creates deep *emotional* experiences, and *leads* to new initiatives and results in the economic, political-ideological, cultural, athletic, and military spheres" (all italics in original).[130] The burning torch, the Central Council proclaimed, combined "in concentrated form all aspects of the cultivation of the revolutionary traditions of the working class, the revolutionary idea, the revolutionary model, intellect and feeling . . . romanticism and symbolism."[131]

---

129. Hermann Weber, *Geschichte der DDR,* 3d ed. (Munich, 1989), 335–36.

130. "Beschluß des Sekretariats des Zentralrates der Freien Deutschen Jugend vom 22. August 1967. Weg der 'Fackel der Freundschaft' durch die Deutsche Demokratische Republik," 1. JA IzJ AB 5684.

131. "Abschlussbericht. Der Weg der 'Flamme der Revolution' durch unsere Republik," JA IzJ A 5684.

The torch bore the "Flame of the Revolution," which had been kindled in a smelting furnace of the Kirov steel plant in Leningrad during an All Union Conference of the Komsomol, bearing the programmatic title "On the Paths of Glory of Our Fathers" in June. Four torchbearers then carried the fire to the Leningrad parade grounds and lit the torch on the back of an armored personnel carrier. For some time the Komsomol kept the flame burning at the Leningrad Smolny Institute, the seat of the first revolutionary government in 1917. At the close of the All Union Conference in late August, the flame was loaded aboard the coast guard ship "Latvian Komsomol" and sent off to Rostock.[132] On its journey it was accompanied by an honor delegation including an Old Bolshevik and veteran of the storming of the Winter Palace in 1917, a Soviet Army officer and veteran of the battle of Berlin in 1945, a "Hero of Soviet Labor," a "Stakhanov worker," a deputy of the Supreme Soviet of the Russian Federation, along with selected Komsomol and Lenin Pioneer members.[133] In their typically effusive style, the Central Council's propagandists proclaimed: "For the first time the symbol of the victory of the ideas of Red October—the Flame of the Revolution—has crossed over the borders of the Soviet Union. Such a significant occurrence," the propagandists reasoned, "can only be explained by the great confidence of the Komsomol in the strength of the Free German Youth."[134]

It arrived in Rostock on 5 September, greeted by over 25,000 FDJ members and Young Pioneers, marking the anniversary of the murders of the revolutionary sailors Albin Köbis and Max Reichpietsch in 1917. In a solemn ceremony, the Komsomol delegates placed the torch in the hands of the FDJ and Young Pioneers. Two days later, the torch embarked on a vast journey throughout the GDR, mounted upon a flatbed truck and accompanied at all times by an FDJ honor guard. At each station, the flame's arrival was used to highlight local FDJ and Pioneer events such as ceremonial roll calls, "friendship meetings," the completion of "deeds of friendship" (meaning the fulfillment of export obligations to the Soviet Union), name-conferral ceremonies for clubhouses and work brigades, meetings with labor veterans, the opening ceremonies of the local "Hans Beimler Competitions," and so on. After a stopover in Schwerin, the torch traveled to Potsdam where it was used in several ceremonies, including an NVA air show and in events surrounding the "Day of the Victims of Fas-

132. "Presseinformation des Zentralrats der Freien Deutschen Jugend," Nr. 59, Berlin, 4.10.1967, 1, JA IzJ A 5684.

133. "Abschlussbericht."

134. "Einige Gedanken zur agitatorischen Nutzung der 'Flamme der Revolution,'" IzJ A 7009.

cism" at the Sachsenhausen and Ravensbrück concentration camp memorials. From Potsdam it was carried to Neubrandenburg, Cottbus, and Dresden, where the FDJ was celebrating the seventeenth anniversary of the GDR's admission to the Soviet-dominated Council for Mutual Economic Assistance (COMECON). The flame was on hand to celebrate the eighteenth anniversary of the GDR's founding in Karl-Marx-Stadt. On 11 October the torch arrived in Leipzig in time for a great "Festival of Friendship" marking the 154th anniversary of the *Völkerschlacht* and hence, as we have already seen, the birth of German–Russian friendship. Along with FDJ members and NVA soldiers, a Komsomol delegation participated along with Soviet soldiers and a Soviet cosmonaut.[135] The ceremonies there took place at both the *Völkerschlachtdenkmal* and the *Iskra* memorial, where the flame's first spark was struck in 1900. This celebration was followed by visits to Gera, Suhl, Erfurt, and the Buchenwald memorial. After stops in Halle and Magdeburg, the flame arrived in Berlin on 2 November.[136]

Twelve thousand FDJ members, along with thousands of Young Pioneers, NVA and Soviet soldiers, and Party dignitaries met at a dramatic nighttime ceremony at the Treptow Park memorial to mark the anniversary of the Revolution. Wreaths were laid at the base of the "Liberator," until a fanfare announced the arrival of the torch. As a torchbearer touched the flame to a ceremonial brazier, a speaker recited:[137]

> We greet the Flame of the Revolution, which, coming from the heroic city Leningrad, has gone its way through our Socialist German Democratic Republic. It tells of the shots of the cruiser Aurora, which initiated the victory of the Russian proletariat. From it radiates the glow and the fire of the revolutionary heroes of Red October, which turned over a new page in the history of humanity.
>
> May the flame of the Revolution be an inspiration to us, at all times to honor the ideas and ideals of the champions of the international proletariat and to keep and nurture them in our young hearts.
>
> May they be a commitment to us, in their memory, to fulfill with honor the revolutionary tasks of our time.

The event continued with the recitation of a Soviet propaganda poem ("Hammer and Sickle"), a speech by Egon Krenz from the Central Council, and a speech by a Hero of the Soviet Union. Then two Heroes of the

---

135. *Geschichte der Freien Deutschen Jugend. Chronik,* 243.
136. "Beschluss des Sekretariats" (with amendments).
137. "FDJ-Appell am 3.11.1967 im Sowjetischen Ehrenmal in Berlin-Treptow (Sprechtext)," JA IzJ A 7003.

Soviet Union and selected veterans of the October Revolution consecrated twenty red banners with the names of revolutionary fighters.[138]

The FDJ's internal reports on the "Torch of Friendship" campaign are impressive, even after making allowances for the inevitable hyperbole. The flame spent 62 days in the GDR. It traveled 8,000 kilometers, passing through all 15 *Bezirke* of the GDR and 96 districts. No fewer than 300 newspaper and magazine articles announced its presence. It was greeted by the inhabitants of 627 towns and villages. The flame stood at the center of 290 mass events with a total of some 800,000 youthful participants. All in all, more than a million East Germans directly took part in the campaign. They were joined by thousands of Komsomol members, who either arrived directly from the Soviet Union or who were delegated by local Soviet Army commanders. During the ceremonies, 4,109 new FDJ members were formally presented with their membership book by GDR and Soviet VIPs. Thousands of young people joined the DSF. Throughout their journey, the flame's honor guards were repeatedly stopped by local people and handed flowers and gifts. "One could often observe veterans of labor saluting the Flame of the Revolution with raised fists, or Young Pioneers marching alongside the flame, giving their Pioneer salute." Thousands of FDJ members swore oaths of loyalty and friendship to the Soviet Union, and 6,000 soldiers renewed their oath of allegiance. Best of all, "in Görlitz a young wedding couple briefly left the banquet table to offer a salute to the 'Flame of the Revolution.'"[139]

As with every mass event of this kind, it is difficult to judge the depth of such popular adulation. While the official FDJ records contain the usual complaints about poor organization at a few of the events and apathy among some of the youths, there is no trace of any outright opposition.

Immediately following the ceremony in Berlin, the flame traveled to a farewell ceremony in Frankfurt an der Oder. From there it was sent over the bridge to Poland where it took to the road again, this time to visit Polish youths anxious to demonstrate their friendship with the Great Socialist Soviet Union.

The Torch Is Dropped

If the Stalin cult of the early 1950s and such periodic mass events as the demonstrations at the Treptow Park memorial and the "Flame of the Revolution" inspired genuine emotions among many young people, the pro-

---

138. Ibid., "Junge Herzen schlagen für den Sozialismus. 'Flamme der Revolution' am sowjetischen Ehrenmal in Treptow," BZ 4 November 1967.

139. "Zahlen und Fakten zum Weg der 'Flamme der Revolution' durch unsere Republik," JA IzJ A 7009.

Soviet propaganda of the early 1980s slipped into a crisis. This was the time of the Afghanistan invasion and a general heating-up of the cold war. The economies of the entire Soviet bloc, including the GDR, were failing. In an era of such moribund leaders as Brezhnev, Andropov, and Chernenko—and their physical condition was obvious from every photograph—it was hard for anyone to imagine that the Soviet Union was still a "land of happy confidence."

The mass events surrounding the fortieth anniversary of the Liberation were filled with high-minded rhetoric celebrating German–Soviet friendship and a glorious future together. At the obligatory torchlight ceremony at the Treptow memorial on the evening of 8 May 1985, fifty thousand FDJ members, Young Pioneers, Komsomol members, and Lenin Pioneers swore yet another "Oath of Youth":[140]

> In this solemn hour of tribute and remembrance, we profess:
> Never will we forget the blood which you shed for our life! Your legacy will remain forever burned into our hearts!
> We shall continue that which our mothers, our fathers boldly began when they were given the chance to make a new beginning!
> Like Ernst Thälmann we stand by the land of Lenin, true and firm! This friendship makes us strong, it will remain for us forever inviolable . . .

These were, as always, strong words. But some older people, accustomed to reading between the lines of Party propaganda, may have begun to wonder just how long "forever" was going to be. As one propaganda pamphlet stated in 1985: "Between the help of the Soviet Union for the German people in the May days of 1945 and the grandiose perspective-program, which determines our cooperation until the year 2000, there lies a straight and successful path."[141] The wishful thinking expressed in this text was a caricature of the earlier emotional style, when the flame of the revolution seemed about to set fire to the world and Khrushchev promised that the Soviet Union would overtake the United States by the 1970s. Rhetoric such as this had a stilted, almost desperate quality.

Whether Young Pioneers and FDJ members understood the implications of the Soviet Union's crisis is unclear. It is difficult to gauge the success of the entire Great Socialist Soviet Union myth-building strategy among young people in the post-Stalin era. There is no doubt that many young officer candidates and Party members were moved by the pro-Soviet

---

140. "Dankt euch, ihr Sowjetsoldaten," JW 9 May 1985.
141. *Die Befreiung und die Befreier,* 86–87.

pageantry in which they participated. But those young people who actually visited the Soviet Union and strayed any distance at all from their Crimean vacation camps and training academies were profoundly shocked by the poverty they saw. Of course, such an enormous discrepancy as this had to be seen to be believed. Most young people paid their dues to the DSF and gave lip service to The Great Lenin and the Great Socialist October Revolution. No doubt most young people felt a certain awe of the Soviet space program and felt respect for the sacrifices of the Soviet Army in World War II. Lenin and Stalin were great men even if they were far removed from daily reality. But when asked about their personal experiences with the cult of German–Soviet friendship during their youth, most former East Germans recall an atmosphere of mind-numbing boredom. For all their tremendous technology and colorful folklore, the *"Sowjetmenschen"* usually came across as a dull, priggish people somehow beneath Germany on the scale of world cultures.

This state of affairs changed dramatically in 1985. Mikhail Gorbachev's "Perestroika" suddenly made the Soviet Union interesting again as a model to be emulated, and for a short time it looked as if the GDR might yet "learn victory" from its Soviet friends. Then "Glasnost" opened many young people's eyes to the secrets of the Stalin era. Until the SED banned it in early 1989, the Soviet press digest *Sputnik* revealed that Stalin's Soviet Union had not only been a "land of happy confidence," but also one of terror and mass murder. A new generation of Soviet historians was putting the number of Stalin's victims as high as fifty million. The embarrassing details of the Hitler–Stalin Pact were published, and even the greatness of the Great Socialist October Revolution was put into question. In a survey conducted in early 1989, the Leipzig Institute for Youth Research found that interest in Soviet history had risen dramatically over the preceding four years, most of it directed toward the Stalin era and the Soviet Union's role in establishing the GDR. The study's author explained this development to his superiors as "an expression of solidarity with their fatherland and of *Parteilichkeit,"* since this was only a matter of young people attempting "to understand better the development of Socialism as a societal system and, out of its history, to recognize forces for its further development."[142]

But the researcher was mistaken. In the end, the uncovering of the Soviet past destroyed the myth of the Great Socialist Soviet Union. It was the Soviets themselves and not (as DSF functionaries always feared) the East Germans who dropped the torch. Honecker's refusal to follow Gor-

---

142. Wilfried Schubarth, "Zum Geschichtsbewußtsein von Jugendlichen der DDR" (Zentralinstitut für Jugendforschung), JA IzJ B 5858, Bl. 24.

bachev's example and "restructure" Socialism in the GDR represented a blatant offense against German–Soviet friendship. After the Tienanmen Square massacre in June 1989 the German–Soviet friendship cult began to collapse, to be replaced by the beginnings of a German–Chinese friendship cult. The youth press immediately adopted the Chinese interpretation of the massacre and published gruesome photos of lynched and burned Chinese soldiers.[143] Reports of German–Chinese conferences and youth exchanges filled the press almost daily after the crushing of the "Fascist coup attempt" in Peking. For the fortieth anniversary of the Chinese revolution, the FDJ invited a delegation of the Communist Youth League of China to Bautzen for a "Day of Chinese Youth in the GDR." A Chinese youth functionary assured the FDJ leadership that "in the future as well common ideals and a common cause would link the youth and peoples of both countries." He assured them "of the firm solidarity of the Chinese people against all attacks on the sovereignty of the GDR."[144]

But even though the SED was prepared to use the same "antifascist" methods against its own people during the mass exodus and growing unrest in the summer and fall of 1989, China was clearly much too far away to send in tanks, as the Soviets had in 1953. The hastily improvised myth of German–Chinese friendship only emphasized the frailty of the myth of German–Soviet friendship. Finally, Gorbachev's public refusal during the GDR's fortieth anniversary celebration in October to come to the SED's aid knocked away the very foundation of the Socialist fatherland.

It is only fitting that the GDR's last organized mass event took place at the Treptow memorial. After the opening of the Berlin Wall in November, numerous Soviet cemeteries and war memorials were damaged and smeared with Nazi-like graffiti. One monument desecrated in this way was the Treptow memorial. The SED (now, after the purge of Honecker and some other hardliners, transmogrified into the PDS—"Party of Democratic Socialism"—and claiming to follow a reform-Communist, "perestroika" course) reacted to this desecration with horror in its public rhetoric and called the population to a vast rally at the memorial for the sake of creating a "United Front Against the Right." The appeal was cosponsored by the remains of the FDJ and the DSF, the Committee of Antifascist Resistance Fighters, plus the "block parties" (minus the CDU), other SED mass organizations, and a variety of new leftist splinter groups from both halves of the city. Two hundred fifty thousand people carrying banners and hand-painted signs filled the memorial's grounds on 3 Janu-

---

143. See daily JW articles on China, June 1989.
144. "Gemeinsame Ideale verbinden die Jugend Chinas und der DDR," *Berliner Zeitung,* 2 October 1989.

ary 1990 and listened to a series of impassioned antifascist and "eternal friendship" speeches.[145] The fear and outrage the participants expressed was probably genuine in most cases and reflected the strength of the antifascist and pro-Soviet myths within the ranks of SED. But virtually no one outside Treptow Park was paying attention. Even if the desecration was real and had not been staged by the PDS itself (as the rumor persists), the call for a new antifascist "united front" under Communist leadership only three months after the threat of a "Chinese solution," and three months before the GDR's first free election, sounded like pure opportunism. The PDS lost the election and Gorbachev's Soviet Union dissolved itself in 1991.

Conclusion

There is no doubt whatsoever that the GDR was entirely dependent upon the Soviet Union from start to finish. Once the Soviets refused to come to the SED's aid in the fall of 1989, the GDR promptly fell apart. But the SED and Communist Parties everywhere needed the Soviet Union just as much in mythical terms: as long as the Soviet Union existed and could be depicted without contradiction as the highest achievement of human civilization, socialism was real and attainable. Once the Soviet Union itself disintegrated without leaving a credible substitute, the vision of socialism collapsed and once again became "utopian."

To be sure, few young people shed tears over any of this. Few older people did either, especially after they began learning the details of Soviet history. Most East Germans were relieved by Gorbachev's reform attempts and the end of Soviet domination. As one former Communist, who experienced the full forty years and a Nazi prison too, said: "The Russians have liberated us twice—first from the Nazis, then from the Communists."[146] But many of those East Germans who as young people genuinely believed in the Liberation and felt the heat of the flame were profoundly disappointed that the Soviets did not live up to their myth. From the viewpoint of dedicated Marxist-Leninists, it did not really matter that the Soviet Union had a murderous past and a deplorable present as long as it was going to have a glorious future. An entire generation of activists had chosen to remain in the GDR with all the hardships that decision brought and build the communist society, only to end up in a capitalist state upon reaching retirement. That the flame was—in their view—negligently

---

145. "Unser Land braucht jetzt eine breite Einheitsfront gegen rechts," ND 4 January 1990.

146. I owe this comment to Frau Charlotte Wasser, who helped establish the *Kulturbund* and occupied important functions within it until the 1980s.

snuffed out on Gorbachev's watch was doubly bitter: it not only brought the destruction of the GDR midway in its painful development toward communism, bringing the permanent defamation of both it and its supporters in the eyes of the world. It also meant a profound spiritual crisis: the loss of their hard-fought fatherland and an abrupt end to "the most glorious thing in the world," for which they had compromised their entire lives, their entire strength:

"The struggle for the liberation of humanity."

Afterword

"Why, but he hasn't got anything on!" they all shouted at last. And the emperor winced, for he felt they were right. But he thought to himself: "I must go through with the procession now." And he drew himself up more proudly than ever, while the chamberlains walked behind him, bearing the train that wasn't there.
                                                              —Hans Christian Andersen[1]

Wanted: Eastern psychiatrist to treat deeply depressed comrade. PDS membership necessary as a guarantee of political tolerance.
                    —From the personals section of Neues Deutschland, *1993[2]*

In this study we have seen how the SED sought to develop a specific GDR mythology in order to establish and maintain its hegemony over the East German people. The Young Pioneers and the FDJ inspired young people to assume a historic role in the creation of a new society of and for youth. The myth of *Kultur* was instrumental in winning over the skeptical educated classes, intellectuals, and their children for Marxism-Leninism and preparing working-class youth for their new status in society. It was instrumental in discrediting the Federal Republic and forging a new "Socialist national culture" encompassing all classes. The myth of antifascism was the most powerful myth of all and served both to legitimize the GDR's undemocratic leadership and to mobilize the population to defend the Socialist system from enemies both outside and inside the country. The myth of German–Soviet friendship presented East Germans with a quasi-religious vision of the Socialist future and sought to convince them that this future was only obtainable through a complete subordination of their state to Soviet interests. The Soviets were not only "friends," but the very

---

1. Hans Christian Andersen, "The Emperor's New Clothes," *Fairy Tales* (London, 1960), 109.
2. ND 7 May 1993.

embodiment of the Marxist-Leninist ideal. Finally, the myth of the Socialist fatherland was used to persuade former Nazis, military officers, and,
later, young army recruits and prospective officers that the GDR was a
model for all of Germany and the climax of the progressive tradition in
Germany. This was essential in the creation of the National People's
Army. In the Honecker era, the Socialist fatherland referred to the GDR
as the legitimate heir to all of German history, identifying it as a German
republic in its own right that as such was worthy of the pride and loyalty
of its citizens.

In contrast to Poland or Czechoslovakia, GDR society was remarkably stable, and after the crushing of the 1953 workers' uprising there were
no more serious challenges to the SED's dictatorship. After the construction of the Berlin Wall in 1961, which finally staunched the disastrous flow
of disillusioned East Germans to the Federal Republic, the GDR
embarked on a period of modest but nevertheless remarkable prosperity,
during which the great majority of East Germans appear to have identified
themselves with their state. To be sure, the Marxist-Leninist consciousness
of ordinary citizens regularly fell short of the Party's expectations, but the
mythology forcefully demonstrated what the GDR was and why it was
ideologically (if not economically) superior to the FRG, who was in control and why. Despite personal doubts and regular contradictions from the
Western media, the Party's hegemony was secure. As we have repeatedly
seen, compliance—not conviction—was always the goal of GDR propaganda, and the East Germans were a singularly compliant people.

However, in 1989 all of this ended. What role did the mythology
described in these pages play in the GDR's collapse? Myths, as we have
seen, are essential in the establishment and maintenance of any state, society, or institution. In Western liberal democracies, such as the Federal
Republic, they were indispensable in the creation of a stable and self-
perpetuating social and political order. But within a few years, the Federal
Republic went beyond appeals to Germany's democratic traditions and its
classical *Kulturerbe* to develop other means of legitimation and continuity:
regular democratic elections, personal freedoms, the material lure of the
1950s *Wirtschaftswunder*. Political leaders no longer needed to harangue
citizens on the superiority of their system, but instead benefited from the
rise of a multitude of opinions and initiatives—in short, the development
of a civil society. As painful as it was, the public debate that accompanied
West Germany's examination of the Nazi past did not weaken "the Fascist
FRG's" social contract, but actually strengthened it much more than even
the noblest antifascist propaganda could have done. "German–American
Friendship" has not been damaged by an open examination of American
flaws and close personal contacts between both peoples, but has instead

become a normal feature of German life. In any case, the FRG did not have to rely on U.S. tanks to ensure compliance to its laws. All in all, an open debate on national values benefits a liberal democratic society.

The situation in the GDR was very different. However, it would be mistaken to assume that the GDR had no social contract at all. Contrary to pre-1989 West German clichés about "the poor brothers and sisters in the East," GDR society was not supported by Soviet bayonets alone. For example, no one was forced to join the border troops, and all those Olympic gold medals were not won by steroid injections alone. But before 1989 the SED was never sure enough of its power to allow itself to be legitimized in a multiparty election, or test the loyalty of its citizens by opening its borders to the West. It never dared allow an unsupervised public debate on national ideals. Instead, decades after its seizure of power, the SED still had to rely on its founding myths for much of its legitimation. To a visitor, the SED—with its ubiquitous red propaganda banners calling for antifascist resistance and friendship to the Soviet Union—looked as if it had taken power just the day before. Instead of using the myths as mere stepping-stones toward a modern civil society, the SED continually tossed new stones before it on its journey to an ever-receding shore.

But if this was still true in 1989, it had been largely true from the beginning. The collapse of the SED dictatorship was not the result of a faulty mythology, but instead a product of the overall crisis of Communism and a link in the chain reaction begun by the Solidarity revolution in Poland and Mikhail Gorbachev's *Perestroika* reform program. Considering the disastrous state of the GDR's economy and the massive dissatisfaction among the population, nothing short of massive police terror could have shored up Honecker's government, an option the SED dared not take without Soviet backing. Even the best public relations offensive could have done little in such a situation. But now the entire propaganda apparatus was literally speechless. Marxist-Leninist ideology was based on the principle of progress. It simply had no contingency plan for failure. The GDR was not only politically and economically, but above all morally and ideologically bankrupt.

But much more happened in 1989 and 1990 than the mere collapse of a government. The East German *Wende* brought with it the implosion of an entire civilization and its mythology. When the SED Politburo resigned, it effectively took orthodox Marxism-Leninism with it. Within a few momentous weeks, the painstakingly constructed myths of *Kultur* and humanism, antifascism, German–Soviet friendship, and above all the Socialist fatherland, had disintegrated. Moreover, the very idea of a separate East German identity virtually disappeared, at least for a short time. The result was not just the end of the dictatorship but also the spontaneous disintegration of the state itself, a phenomenon without parallel in modern European history. Eleven months after the opening of the Wall, the GDR had literally vanished from the map. How could such a thing happen?

As we discussed at length in chapter 1, all state-supporting mythologies are conceived within specific parameters without which they cannot function. The most obvious parameters of GDR mythology were the Wall, the *Stasi* security apparatus, and the half-million Soviet soldiers stationed on East German soil. Other significant factors were ideology, the *Parteilichkeit* principle, language, Marxist-Leninist historiography, and other factors. The *Wende* of 1989–90 eliminated all of these. Once the SED no longer held a monopoly on communication, once it had abandoned its control of symbols and metaphors, contradiction and opposition became not only possible but also unstoppable. This phenomenon is most obvious in regard to language. In the December 1989 issue of *Junge Generation,* the first and also last issue to appear after the opening of the Berlin Wall on 9 November, the journal's editor wrote: "It's being talked about again. Every day it presents itself many thousandfold in our country. It was hidden at first, is sometimes awkward, does not always express the heart of the matter, but is nevertheless willing and able to learn." The "it" to which the editor was referring was "the free word." This, she continued, was going to be the key to the renewal of the GDR and of socialism itself.[3]

Of course, "the free word" did not renew the GDR and Socialism, but exploded the pretensions of both. The shock to *parteilich* Party functionaries was overwhelming. Suddenly, real problems could be discussed openly and without Marxist-Leninist euphemisms: "What is the condition of our economy?" "How do the Party and the *Stasi* really operate?" "What happened under Stalin?" "How many people were killed at the Wall and why?" In short, the sudden revelation of forty years of SED prevarication and ill-doing transformed the myths described here from articles of faith to question marks. Equally shocking was the sudden opening of the Berlin Wall and the inner German border in the night of 9 November 1989. Hundreds of thousands of East Germans streamed into the West and were dumbfounded by the sight of a society that, contrary to the daily admonitions of the SED, had achieved vast prosperity without the benefit of youth unity, *Kultur,* friendship to the Soviet Union, and all the rest. For all but the most orthodox, the personal experience of Western wealth and freedom made the GDR's alleged moral superiority seem absurd. While many of these visitors remained critical of what they saw, a return to the tutelage of the SED was no longer conceivable. With the shattering of the

---

3. Marion Thomas, "Die Macht des Wortes," JG 12 (1989): 13.

mythology on 9 November, the old GDR of "Ernst Thälmann Mobilizations" and *Parteilichkeit* ceased to exist. Under these conditions, the mythology lost all meaning, especially among those elites who were supposed to benefit from it the most; as soon as GDR mythology no longer represented a road map to social advancement in a closed system, and instead became a liability in a uniting Germany, its appeal promptly evaporated.

But dazzled by this light, East Germans were presented with a new universe of "realities" that they were poorly equipped to deal with. For one thing, virtually the entire political class of the GDR was compromised by SED membership, corruption, and *Stasi* connections. In a stunning reversal of fortunes, strict *Parteilichkeit* became the greatest liability of an SED functionary. Those Communists who rose to prominence in the first post-*Wende* parliament largely came from the lower echelons of the Party and lacked political experience. Through the collapse of the mythology, the very meaning of "qualifications" had become unclear. What was really more important, practical administrative experience or a solid progressive and antifascist outlook? And what were to be the goals of the new reformed GDR? Come to think of it, why was a GDR necessary at all? The unexpected return of the "free word" destroyed the public rhetoric of the GDR, forcing politicians into open debates on complex issues. The harangues of earlier propaganda campaigns—in fact, the entire "language of power" of the GDR—became utterly meaningless.

But if SED functionaries were made irrelevant by the *Wende,* their competition from the citizens' groups and the Protestant church was often no less disoriented. To be sure, the GDR opposition had been instrumental in bringing the SED dictatorship down. But although most dissidents had long been skeptical of the SED's claims and were accustomed to critical debates among friends, they too were children of the GDR and were likewise confounded by the gap between high ideals and hard social and economic realities. Systematically kept away from any sort of power before 1989, these leaders were often even more inexperienced than their Communist counterparts, and very few managed to establish themselves in German politics. Many GDR dissidents, both inside and outside the SED, genuinely believed that the *Wende* was really a matter of finally implementing GDR ideals and myths without Party interference, even if they had no idea how this was to happen. The new government was left with noble sentiments but no realistic alternatives, and the state's progressive collapse through bankruptcy and the mass exodus of its citizens left no time to develop a social consensus on fundamental issues. Civil rights leader Bärbel Bohley's celebrated lament:

"We fought for justice and ended up with a constitutional state" is symptomatic of this mentality.[4]

This political and spiritual vacuum helped make reunification seem like the only solution, and thus left the East extremely vulnerable to domination by the West. Its myths and values in chaos, its institutions dissolved, its political class neutralized, its collective social structure in ruins, its people utterly demoralized, the GDR was lost. Once its crutches were kicked away, GDR society had nothing to hold on to, least of all its national values. Not since Cortés and his conquistadors entered Mexico City has a society imploded so thoroughly, with the difference that on that fateful "Day X" in 1989 no Cortés and no conquistadors—and certainly no West German soldiers "marching through the Brandenburg Gate with flags flying"—were needed. At midnight on 3 October 1990, accompanied by only sporadic protests and restrained jubilation in the East, the GDR flag was lowered for the last time.

It is clear that GDR mythology played an important role in the rise and fall of the GDR. Why is this topic still worth exploring today? One reason has to do with memory. The songs, marches, and even the newspaper articles and indoctrination sessions described in these pages are part of the shared experience of the GDR. If GDR society collectively lost its nerve in 1989, the vast dislocations brought by reunification have contributed to the formation of a diffuse post-GDR identity, a living "GDR myth" whose foundations we have examined here. Most of this "*Ostalgie*,"[5] as it is ironically called, stems from the loss of such East German benefits as full employment, low rents, inexpensive child day care, the "warmth" of a collective society, and so on. But much of it also hearkens to the loss of such ideal values as social justice, youth unity, *Kultur,* antifascism, and so on. In the memory of thousands of former East German citizens, ex-SED functionaries, and most notably schoolteachers, eastern Germany was and remains morally and ideologically superior to the West. But while the old SED myths were troubled by the thousand contradictions of GDR life, the new GDR myth is contradicted only by easily ignored history books and tabloid articles. It is here to stay. As important as the issue of memory is to the historian, it is also a political problem, for a fundamental East–West disagreement about the past remains a serious hurdle to genuine unification. Thus it is worthwhile examining these claims. So far, there has been no broad introspection on the GDR past. What little there is has been centered around sensationalist topics such as *Stasi* collaboration and the shootings at the Berlin Wall and

---

4. Hans-Dieter Müller, *Stimmen der Wende* (Berlin, 1991), 14.
5. *Ostalgie* is nostalgia for *den Osten,* i.e., the German east.

the inner German border. But a more general examination of the individual's role in the day-to-day repression of the SED and the questions of idealism, opportunism, and self-deception in GDR society is still in its beginning stages. To be sure, it took West German society more than twenty years to begin an open discussion of the Nazi past. An awareness of the existence and omnipresence of GDR mythology *as mythology* could shorten this time considerably.

The question of memory also has direct political repercussions. The principal beneficiary of this remythification of the German east has been the reform-Communist PDS, the "Party of Democratic Socialism," which arose from the ruins of the SED in early 1990 and is likely to remain a significant political force for many years. The PDS has laid claim not only to the considerable financial assets of the SED and a large part of its membership, but also to much of the Party's propaganda apparatus.[6] By the mid-1990s the new Party had achieved remarkable success in eastern elections, usually capturing around 20 percent of the vote (far more in such former SED strongholds as eastern Berlin and Potsdam). The PDS is more than just a therapy group for unreconstructed SED functionaries, a Socialist reform movement, a giant money-laundering operation, an experiment in grass roots democracy, or an outspoken eastern protest party. It is still far too homogeneous to be categorized in such a way. On the local level, it differs little from the mainstream parties, even if its members do have an annoying habit of quoting Goethe and Heine much more often than a Green or Free Democrat would ever consider necessary. It has, however, proven itself to be one of the last great refuges of GDR mythology in post-1989 Germany. The PDS provides its members with both the security of the old Party collective and that heady atmosphere of politics-as-religion that so many Germans, East and West, miss in the mainstream parties. In their speeches and publications, their talkshow appearances and rallies, PDS ideologues appeal to Great Ideals and moral politics in a manner that few people would take seriously coming from the CDU or the SPD. For instance, the PDS issues periodic appeals for a new national constitution in which, for starters, Germany should declare itself to be an "antifascist republic," as if there were any agreement on just what this means, let alone on how such a state should be organized, who should run it, and how it would differ from the current Federal Republic.

Members of the old GDR opposition understandably resent this party's electoral success and lingering influence in the East, but the PDS shows little similarity to the old KPD or other revolutionary proletarian

---

6. Patrick Moreau and Jürgen Lang, *Was will die PDS?* (Frankfurt am Main and Berlin, 1994), 9f.

parties. Instead, its membership overwhelmingly consists of intellectuals, teachers, and government bureaucrats—in short, the foot soldiers of the SED regime and the main targets of the myth-building system. As in the old GDR, it looks as if the PDS's "struggle for the liberation of humanity" will once again be centered around a struggle over the allocation of secure civil service jobs to Party loyalists.

Finally, the GDR past offers important perspectives for the common German future. Throughout this study we have been examining some of the reasons for the success and failure of one of the "losers" of the cold war. But what of the "winners"? One need not join in the gloating of the German left with its warning that "Capitalism didn't win the cold war, it just survived it" to realize that the fall of Communism raises serious questions for the Western democracies on the threshold of the twenty-first century. The GDR's dramatic collapse offers the Western societies an opportunity to reexamine their own myths and values. What really are the myths and values of, say, the new Federal Republic of the year 2000? To what extent are such inherited values as freedom and human rights genuinely felt, especially by young people, and to what extent are they merely held in place by such parameters as high living standards and an efficient welfare state? If, as Jürgen Habermas has suggested, "D-Mark Nationalism"[7] is the glue that has held the Federal Republic together, what happens when the glue runs out in a genuine economic crisis? And what are to be the common values of the new united Europe? In short, can a modern society survive without a consensus on fundamental issues?

The GDR's unparalleled collapse provides us with a dramatic example of what can happen when a political system is forced to rely on an illusory values system. And yet, while the SED may have been hopelessly misguided in many of its actions, it was justifiably concerned with establishing a solid mythological foundation for its rule. This does not mean that the Federal Republic should in turn construct "Pioneer Republics" and print updated FDJ songbooks to inspire its young people. Far from it. But a reexamination of fundamental values is essential, for whatever success the new united Germany and a united Europe will enjoy in the coming decades will be due in large part to their ability to persuade the younger generation that the values on which they are based are no longer just "a story told" but, finally, "a reality lived."

---

7. Jürgen Habermas, "Der D-Mark Nationalismus," *Die Zeit,* 30 March 1990.

Index